A User's Guide
to the
Manpower
Services
Commission

A User's Guide to the Manpower Services Commission

Alastair Thomson and Hilary Rosenberg

Kogan
Page

First published in 1986 by Kogan Page Limited,
120 Pentonville Road, London N1 9JN

British Library Cataloguing in Publication Data
Thomson, Alastair
  A user's guide to the Manpower Services Commission.
  1. Great Britain. *Manpower Services Commission*
  I. Title   II. Rosenberg, Hilary
  313.12′042   HD5915.A6

ISBN 0-85038-948-8

Printed and bound in Great Britain by
Anchor Brendon Ltd, Tiptree, Essex

CONTENTS

LOCAL STRUCTURE

Part 3: Schemes and Services

EMPLOYMENT SERVICES

SPECIAL EMPLOYMENT SCHEMES

TRAINING AND PREPARATION FOR WORK

INTRODUCTION

Not very long ago the letters 'MSC' meant some kind of higher degree to the very people interested in postgraduate education and very little to the rest of the population. Today they are heard and used widely throughout the mass media and in many people's conversations when talking about training and employment. Master of Science (MSc) degrees are still with us but now the initials are far more likely to stand for 'Manpower Services Commission'.

Despite familiarity with the name, however, the MSC is not an easy organisation to understand. It is extremely difficult to get an overall view of the Commission's work and its direction for two linked reasons:

Diversity: the influence and range of MSC activities has mushroomed in the past three years. This means that while many people are knowledgeable about parts of the Commission's operations (for example, in youth or adult training, work with disabled people or employment services), very few people have an overall picture in any depth — and that includes many of the Commission's own front-line staff.

Change: schemes and services are introduced, withdrawn, tested and modified at a sometimes bewildering rate. At times during our research it almost seemed that the MSC operated on a 'flavour of the month' principle, so frequently were we told of fresh changes as initiatives came in and out of favour. This experience made us well aware that a book can only provide a 'snapshot' picture of the MSC and will require regular updating.

In addition, it must be remembered that the MSC's staff are civil servants; they do not determine the policies they carry out and may not be aware of all policy details. On a few occasions, some officials appeared unnecessarily cautious about divulging public information.

9

Because of this, compiling this book has been an unusually difficult task. Although we have made every effort to ensure that our material is up to date and accurate, we would be happy to hear from users who spot any errors, omissions or misinterpretations that have escaped us.

Our aim throughout the guide has been to inform rather than criticise but it must be stressed that the book is not an 'official' publication. We recognise that many elements of the MSC's work are politically contentious and have tried, where possible, to indicate areas of concern to some. Leaving aside individual schemes and services, the two features of the MSC which struck us very clearly during our research were its centralism and its lack of accountability at local level — especially when contrasted to further education. Of course, many projects are locally designed initiatives (YTS schemes, Community Programmes, adult training courses and so on), simply funded by the MSC — but this cannot mask the fact that the ground rules are set elsewhere. Area Manpower Boards may ensure efficient local operations but they do not mean local control or the accountability of MSC staff to local influence. The MSC is often perceived as a monolithic organisation and we believe that there is a pressing need to open up its decision-making processes to greater scrutiny — which in the long run can only make for greater flexibility and effectiveness.

Finally, our thanks must go to the many people working within the MSC itself and those involved in running various schemes and projects, all of whom have gone out of their way to make our task smoother. All interpretations and responsibility for errors are, of course, ours alone.

Alastair Thomson
Hilary Rosenberg

Part 1:

An Introduction to the MSC and Its Work

Chapter 1.1

The Manpower Services Commission — An Overview

Introduction

The Manpower Services Commission is probably Britain's most influential quango (quasi non-governmental organisation). It is responsible for running the public employment and training services. Although separate from government, the MSC is accountable to the Secretary of State for Employment (and in respect of its operations in Scotland and Wales, to their respective Secretaries of State). The work of the Commission does not cover Northern Ireland.

History and Functions

The MSC was set up on 1 January 1974 by the Employment and Training Act 1973, taking over the functions of the earlier Central Training Council. The main objectives of the Commission in 1986 are:

1. To safeguard the provision of skilled manpower for industry's present and future needs. This includes:

    — promoting the development of occupational training, including apprenticeship, in such a way as to enable people entering at different ages and with different educational attainments to acquire agreed standards of skill appropriate to the jobs available and to provide them with a basis for progression through further learning;
    — opening up widespread opportunities for adults to acquire, increase or update their skills and knowledge during the course of their working lives.

2. To move towards a position where all young people under the age of 18 have the opportunity either of continuing in full-

time education or of planned work experience combining work-related training and education.

3. To offer an efficient and cost-effective employment service whose facilities are easily accessible to employers and job seekers.

4. To offer a range of services to help those job seekers who have particular difficulty in obtaining suitable work or training.

The Commissioners and Senior Staff

The MSC consists of ten Commissioners appointed by the Secretary of State for Employment for a period of three years. They comprise:

— Chair
— three members appointed after consultation with the Trades Union Congress
— three members appointed after consultation with the Confederation of British Industry
— two members appointed after consultation with local authority associations
— one member appointed after consultation with professional education associations.

From January 1986, the Commissioners are:

— Bryan Nicholson (Chair, appointed 1984)
— M Bett (CBI)
— M Bury (CBI)
— K Durrand (Education)
— K Graham OBE (TUC)
— R A Grantham (TUC)
— J M Peake (CBI)
— J Pearman (Local authorities)
— B Vaughan (Local authorities).

The Director of the MSC is Geoffrey Holland.

The Chair of the Commission is a salaried appointee; other members serve part time. The Director is the senior permanent civil servant.

The internal organisation of the MSC is outlined in Chapter 2.1.

Arrangements for Scotland and Wales

Since 1977, ministerial responsibility for MSC activities in Scotland
and Wales has rested with their respective Secretaries of State, to
whom the Commission reports. The ministers and the Commission
are advised by Manpower Services Committees for each country.
The chair and nine members of each committee are appointed by
the MSC with the approval of the appropriate Secretary of State.
As with the Commission itself, members are appointed after
consultation with interested parties.

The Committee for Scotland — July 1985

- Sir James Munn (Chair)
- G R Carter
- J Davidson
- R Gould
- W J Hedley
- W Hughes
- J Milne
- J Morrell
- J D Pollock
- B Vaughan.

The Committee for Wales — July 1985

- Sir Melvyn Rosser (Chair)
- J R Bull MBE
- D M Evans
- J A J Harries CBE
- D Jenkins
- I M Kelsall OBE
- Prof G Philips
- P J Summers MBE
- T D Williams
- G J Wright.

Budget and Finance

In 1984–85, the MSC spent £2065.8 million. Some £637.4 million
was on behalf of the Department of Employment. More than 80
per cent of all expenditure was in the form of grants and

allowances to individuals and organisations.

The largest single budget items were for:
— Youth Training Scheme (£849.5 million)
— Community Programme (£534.3 million)
— Adult Training (£215 million)
— Jobcentres and other employment services (£130.6 million).

In addition to funding from the Treasury, the MSC also receives some £225 million (1983) from the European Social Fund, which operates on a calendar year basis.

Staffing

The activities of the MSC are administered by a permanent staff of 20,803 civil servants (as at April 1985). Staff numbers have been falling steadily over recent years, the current figure being about 5 per cent (1126) lower than 1984; in 1979, the figure was over 26,000.

About half of the staff work in Employment Division, the majority of them in Jobcentres and Employment Offices. The next largest division in terms of staffing is Training Division, which accounts for about a quarter of the total. The exact breakdown at April 1985 was:

— Employment Division 10,726
— Training Division 5069
— Skillcentre Training Agency 3805
— Technical and Vocational Education Initiative Unit 34
— Personnel and Central Services Division 910
— Planning and Resources Division 259.

Analysed by Civil Service grade, 254 staff are at Principal Officer level or above, 7319 are in executive grades and 9066 are in clerical grades. The remainder includes industrial staff such as Skillcentre instructors and training officers; there are also stores and canteen staff and a handful of specialist professionals such as economists, statisticians and psychologists.

Chapter 1.2

The New Training Initiative

Introduction

In May 1981, the MSC under its then Chair Sir Richard O'Brien published a consultative document entitled *A New Training Initiative* (*NTI*) which, with some minor changes, became and has since remained the cornerstone of the Commission's training policy.

The rationale for *NTI* was set out clearly in paragraph 1 of the document and is worth quoting in full: 'Training is not given sufficient priority in Britain. It is costly. The pay-off may take a long time and people's perspectives are short. Not enough training is done and some that is done is misdirected and wasted. As a result, many people are less productive and derive less satisfaction and reward from their work than they might. Although there are many examples of excellent training, our performance overall is patchy and our arrangements inflexible.'

The document was intended to stimulate a programme for action to rectify the position.

Objectives

The consultative document set out three major and linked objectives which would carry forward the change. These are:

— To develop skill training including apprenticeship in such a way as to enable people entering at different ages and with different educational attainments to acquire agreed standards of skill, appropriate to the jobs available, and to provide them with a basis for progression through further learning;
— To move towards a position where all young people under the age of 18 have the opportunity either of continuing in full-time education, or of entering training or a period of planned work experience, combining work-related training and education;

— To open up widespread opportunities for adults, whether employed, unemployed or returning to work, that they may acquire, increase or update their skills and knowledge during the course of their working lives.

The first objective (that of developing skill training) was based on a recognition that traditional apprenticeship training is often narrow and inflexible, especially at a time of rapid technological change. Nevertheless, the paper did recognise the continued value of the off-the-job/classroom/work experience learning combination. This objective of *NTI* is based on a belief that people will increasingly need to develop or change their skills more than once in the course of their working lives. The attainment of this first objective requires a shift away from rigidly age-related or time-served training, towards progression based on competence and the achievement of agreed performance standards.

The second objective (preparation for and entry to working life) is based on a belief that Britain lags behind other countries in providing a broad foundation of generic skills for all individuals entering the labour market. The objective does not, however, tackle the question of whether legal obligations should be placed on employers to provide systematic training and education for all young workers (when the document was published, over 45 per cent of young workers received no formal training or further education whatsoever). A further problem lies in the issues of foundation training at a time of high unemployment. Although the document states, rather piously, 'A continuous process is needed, starting, for all young people in school or further education, and leading, for all, to work' it does not consider how that training may be perceived by young people, if insufficient jobs exist for those completing it.

The final objective (creating wider opportunities for adults) recognises that there are growing numbers of adults, both in and out of paid work, who have skills which are:

— too few
— too narrow
— out of date
— too rusty through lack of use.

These adults require a fresh start, either to retain employability (if out of work) or to progress to new and more demanding or responsible work (if in employment). It is based on a belief that the training and learning needs of adults may not be the same as those of young people and that those opportunities which are available are too few and too inflexible.

The White Paper

In December 1981, the Secretaries of State for Employment, Education and Science, Wales and Scotland presented a white paper to Parliament which set out to develop the MSC's New Training Initiative with a series of new measures. Entitled *A New Training Initiative: An Agenda for Action*, the white paper proposed a ten-point plan which has formed the basis of much MSC work since then.

The proposals announced in 1981 were:

1. The establishment of a Youth Training Scheme to replace the Youth Opportunities Programme and Unified Vocational Preparation and provide a full year's foundation training for all those leaving school at the minimum age without jobs.
2. Increased incentives for employers to provide better training for young people in jobs.
3. The establishment of an 'Open Tech' programme to make technical training more accessible to those with the necessary ability.
4. The establishment of a working group, to report by April 1982 (*a four-month period*) on ways of developing the Youth Training Scheme to cover employed as well as unemployed young people, within available resources.
5. Setting a target date of 1985 for recognised standards in all the main craft, technician and professional skills to replace time-serving and age-restricted apprenticeships.
6. Better preparation for working life in initial full-time education.
7. More opportunities for vocationally relevant courses for those staying on in full-time education.
8. Closer co-ordination of training and vocational and education provision nationally and at local level.
9. A £16 million fund for development schemes in particular localities or sectors.
10. Examination of longer-term possibilities for more effective, rational and equitable sharing of the costs of training between

trainees themselves, employers of trained people and the general taxpayer.

A large proportion of the rest of this Guide looks at how those proposals have come to fruition.

Chapter 1.3

The Adult Training Strategy (ATS)

Introduction

The ATS is not a scheme but a set of proposals put forward by the MSC for action by everyone concerned with adult training and retraining, to make such arrangements more flexible and adaptable. The strategy is intended to carry forward work on the third strand of the New Training Initiative; opening up more opportunities for all adults to acquire, increase and update their skills and knowledge during the course of their working lives.

Identification of Changes Needed

The MSC has identified a number of changes to the country's adult training arrangements, which it believes are required if the quality and quantity of work-skills required for future needs are to be met. These changes include:

— creating a new sense among firms, individuals and training providers, of the central importance of adult training and education to economic survival and prosperity;
— improving the systems for providing and accrediting training so that they better meet firms' needs and those of adults. Such improvements might include the further development of open learning and credit transfer, as well as the full exploitation of new technologies;
— better collaboration and co-ordination among and between employers and training providers.

New Initiatives and Changes to MSC Programmes

The thinking behind the ATS was influential in the reshaping of the MSC's own adult training provision, unveiled in July 1985. This saw the ending of the Training Opportunities Scheme (TOPS) and its replacement by the Job Training Scheme (an industry-focused programme of job-related training directed to known employment needs) and the Wider Opportunities Training Courses (specifically for unemployed people and those on the Community Programme). The established TOPS provision was changed because, it was claimed, the balance between newer and traditional skills was wrong and because it was said to be insufficiently adaptable to local requirements.

The ATS was also instrumental in the establishment of Local Collaborative Projects (see Chapter 3.17) and embraces the already established Open Tech Programme.

In November 1984, the MSC also launched a major Adult Training Awareness campaign. The intention of this is to change attitudes as much as sell courses. The campaign seeks to increase awareness of the importance of adult training among employers, employed and unemployed people, unions, trainers and educationalists. By organising conferences, workshops and seminars throughout the country, as well as producing a bi-monthly newsletter *Focus on Adult Training*, the private consultants managing the campaign hope to:

— improve investment in training by employers;
— change individuals' belief that training is a once-and-for-all activity;
— stimulate providers of training to supply new, improved and more flexible opportunities for adults.

Further Information

Contacts for the Adult Training Campaign, based at Training Division regions and the MSC Scottish and Welsh offices (addresses at end of Chapter 2.5), are:

— London region: G Borlace
— Midlands region: U Whitehouse
— Northern region: K Patterson
— North West region: C Gunning
— South East region: T Brazier
— South West region: D Fielding
— Yorkshire and Humberside region: M Lowe
— Scotland: C Lang
— Wales: D Lord.

Chapter 1.4

The MSC and the Education Service

Introduction

The dividing line between 'training' and 'education' has never been very clear and the relationship between the MSC and local education authorities (LEAs) is a complex one. Leaving aside the Technical Vocational and Education Initiative (TVEI), the MSC's only attempt to influence the school curriculum, the area in which there has been most contact has been that of non-advanced further education.

The recent growth of MSC initiatives has been independent of LEAs, the Department of Education and Science and, indeed, *direct* ministerial control. As the number of MSC initiatives has expanded, the autonomy of LEA provision has been eroded as the proportion of work done for the MSC increased. Although this partnership meant a rapid expansion of resources for financially straitened colleges, it has also allowed the MSC to become an increasingly dominant partner. The extent of this dominance has become apparent since the government's decision to transfer financial responsibility for funding some further education to the MSC. The story of this move is described below.

Background

At the end of January 1984, the government published a white paper (*Training for Jobs* — Command 9135). This proposed the extension of MSC responsibility for work-related non-advanced further education (NAFE) by allowing it to take financial control of 25 per cent of work-related courses provided by local education authorities through their further education colleges. Prior to this proposal, MSC funding of further education had largely been limited to off-the-job YTS training and some TOPS provision.

The proposal was announced without any consultation whatsoever and was greeted with dismay by local authorities of all political complexions, by the National Association of Teachers in Further and Higher Education (NATFHE) and by the National Union of Students (NUS). Even the MSC Commissioners themselves had minimal warning of the plan, although it is hard to see how it could have been developed without the tacit acceptance (and silence) of the then chairman Lord Young (now of course a cabinet minister himself).

Local education authorities faced the prospect of a loss of rate support grant because of the transfer of funding. This would more than double MSC spending in the further education sector within three years, in order to fund the sort of courses favoured by the government.

The proposals, which did win support from employers' organisations, were criticised loudly by the educational establishment on the grounds that they represented:

— a unilateral decision taken without consultation with affected parties, and likey to result in increased bureaucracy;
— a move away from one of the fundamental principles of the education system in Britain — local control. The plans were perceived as a significant departure from a curriculum determined largely by elected local authorities, to one dictated by an unelected and relatively unaccountable body acting at the behest of central government;
— a strong criticism of the record of the education service in meeting training needs.

This third point was brought home by the then Employment Secretary, Tom King's, statement that 'previous training for jobs had been handled in a haphazard and inadequate manner'.

It was left to Education Secretary, Sir Keith Joseph, to attempt to smooth the ruffled feathers of LEAs by praising the record of many authorities while supporting the change on the grounds of the MSC's 'unique ability' to judge training priorities at local and national level.

The White Paper

Training for Jobs, published jointly by the Department of Education and Science and the Department of Employment, called for a more responsive approach to demand on the part of college training provision. It advocated:

— doubling the number of adults trained each year;
— developing a system of certification for YTS trainees;
— priority for courses in certain fields, such as electronics and robotics;
— a restructure of the then existing provision of adult training into two areas:

  1. Job-related training focused on the known employment needs of local industry and commerce;
  2. Basic level training for unemployed people (especially the long-term jobless).

MSC funding need not be spent on financing courses in LEA-run colleges and can be used to fund commercial training organisations such as those operating in YTS.

In 1985–86 provision for financing further education rises from £90 million to £155 million, and the following year to £200 million.

Developments

Non-cooperation by the Conservative-controlled Association of County Councils and Labour-led Association of Metropolitan Authorities led to the delay of plans, but heavy pressure from central government led to negotiations over the summer of 1984. In September, the Employment Secretary all but *instructed* the Commission to go ahead with the plan, despite an absence of agreement. Meanwhile the rate support grant for local authorities had been cut accordingly.

The appointment of Bryan Nicholson to succeed Lord Young as MSC chair provided the Commission with an opportunity to offer an olive branch — in the form of a joint review of work-related, non-advanced further education by the MSC, CBI, TUC and education service. This would examine how to avoid the creation of further bureaucracy and rivalry. In addition, during 1985–86, LEAs would receive the funding lost from the rate support grant and have the power to decide how it would be spent. This arrangement was agreed finally in November 1984.

During the next six months, the review group attempted to break the deadlock and, by the summer of 1985, agreement was reached. This blocked the MSC from 'buying-in' individual courses in colleges but proposed the drawing up of development programmes by individual LEAs and local officials of Training Division, allowing colleges to retain control over their curriculum. The deal has been accepted by the MSC, education authorities' associations and by the government.

Throughout the entire period, the Department of Education and Science's defence of the interests of the further education sector was noticeably absent. This was despite the break from a long-established principle of a devolved and locally autonomous system of post-school education and training.

Part 2

Organisation

Chapter 2.1

Introduction

This section examines how the MSC is organised. At national level, the Commission is split into five divisions, comprising three operating divisions (which provide schemes and services to the public and others) and two support divisions which service the Commission's own operation. In addition there exists, on an organisational par with the divisions, the small Technical and Vocational Education Initiative Unit.

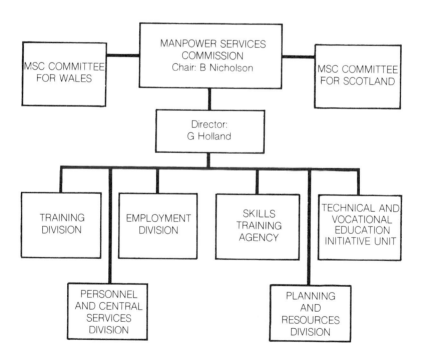

The head office of the MSC and its divisions is Moorfoot, Sheffield S1 4PQ (0742 753275).

Chapters 2.2–2.6 outline the work of these sections and include local addresses for the activities of the three operating divisions. In addition, there is a seventh chapter on the MSC's national network of Area Manpower Boards which have an advisory function for both Employment Division and Training Division.

Chapter 2.2

Employment Division

Introduction

Employment Division (ED) is the largest of the MSC's four operating divisions in size. Its purpose is to oversee all the Commission's employment services and schemes.
It therefore has overall responsibility for:

— the Jobcentre and Employment Office network
— Professional and Executive Recruitment
— Job change (labour mobility) services
— Community Programme
— Community Industry
— Voluntary Projects Programme
— Enterprise Allowance Scheme
— Employment Rehabilitation Centres and other services for the disabled.

History

ED adopted its present title and functions in 1982, before which time it was the Employment Services Division. Its original incarnation was as the Employment Services Agency, set up in October 1974.

Structure and Organisation

ED is based at the MSC's Moorfoot headquarters in Sheffield but the large majority of its 10,729 staff (April 1985) work at local level with under 250 at head office. As might be expected with the biggest division, ED has the most complex structure of any MSC division, comprising five branches, as well as a director responsible for regional and area operations. In addition, there is a parallel Special Measures Directorate which organises schemes for unemployed people. This is best explained diagrammatically:

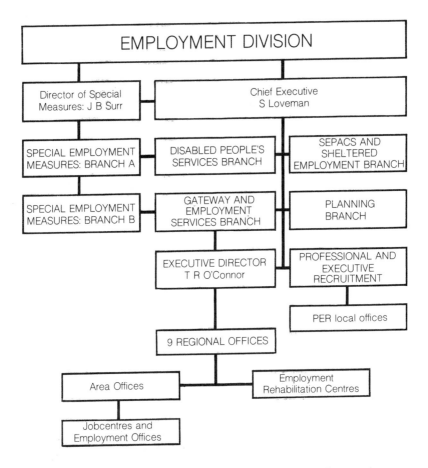

Head Office Branches and Control of Field Operations

Professional and Executive Recruitment

(Head: T Bateman)
This branch is responsible for PER operations, administering its local offices, its publishing and finance.

SEPACS and Sheltered Employment Branch

(Head: D Sullivan)
This branch determines sheltered employment policy and the administration, marketing and product development of the

Sheltered Employment Procurement and Consultancy Service (SEPACS). This service helps sheltered workshops for disabled people to generate more work — particularly from public bodies and government.

Disabled People's Services Branch

(Head: B Swindell)
Jobcentre services for disabled people, Employment Rehabilitation Centres and the division's policy concerning disabled people are the responsibilities of this branch which also administers the Fit for Work award scheme and the Quota system (see Chapter 3.6).

Gateway and Employment Services Branch

(Head: M Weston)
This branch oversees the placing service of Jobcentres as well as their development, marketing and information services. Moreover, the branch operates as a 'gateway' to other schemes and services for training and employment including non-MSC provision.

Planning Branch

(Head: J S Child)
As its name suggests, this branch is concerned with planning and resourcing as well as providing economic and statistical advice for the division, and overseeing labour mobility schemes.

Field Operations Management

(Executive Director: T R O'Connor)
It is through this directorate that the division administers its national network, working through nine Regional Employment Managers, each with one or more Operational Managers. These staff work with Employment Rehabilitation Centres and — through Area Offices — with Jobcentres to deliver the division's services.

Special Measures Directorate

Special Measures Branch A

(Head: A Kidd)
This branch is responsible for policy and operations concerning the Community Programme and other help for long-term unemployed people.

Special Measures Branch B

(Head: B Thomas)
This branch is responsible for the operation of the Enterprise Allowance Scheme, Voluntary Projects Programme and the development of the Community Industry scheme.

Elements of Interest

ED liaises closely with three advisory bodies in carrying out particular aspects of its work. These are:

— Committees for the Employment of Disabled People (working with Jobcentres and Employment Offices);
— Special Employment Measures Advisory Group (advises the Special Employment Measures Branches);
— National Advisory Council on Employment of Disabled People (advises Disabled People's Services Branch).

Committees for the Employment of Disabled People

There are 87 of these committees, established under the Disabled Persons (Employment) Act 1944, to advise the government on matters relating to the employment or self-employment of disabled people in their areas. They work with ED staff on issues such as the Fit for Work campaign, surveys and quota issues (see Chapter 3.6). Membership includes representatives from trade unions and employers' organisations, as well as doctors and others with experience of disablement resettlement. At a very local level, their work is backed up by individuals able to give MSC staff practical assistance and information, known as Recognised Local Contacts. Details of committee members should be available from ED area offices (see below).

Special Employment Measures Advisory Group

This group's remit is to examine and advise upon the
Commission's Special Employment Measures (VPP, CP and the
Enterprise Allowance Scheme). It meets approximately five times
a year and comprises the Chair and Director of the MSC; the
Director of the Special Measures Directorate; three
representatives from the TUC; three from the CBI; three from
local authorities, three from voluntary organisations, and one
person representing professional education and training interests.

National Advisory Council on Employment of Disabled People

Established by the 1944 Disabled Persons Employment Act, this
body has a statutory duty to advise the Secretary of State for
Employment — in practice this is done through the MSC.

Regional and Area Offices

Employment Division regions are geographically the same as
those of Training Division; however, the area structure is not the
same. In addition, there is an extra top tier, composed of an
executive director:
Executive Director (Wales and South), 236 Gray's Inn Road,
London WC1X 8HL (01-278 0363).
Executive Director (Scotland and North), Moorfoot, Sheffield
S1 4PQ (0742 753275).

ENGLAND

London Region
236 Gray's Inn Road, London WC1X 8HL (01-278 0363).

Area Offices

Central London   195–197 Wardour Street, London
                                   W1V 3FA
                                   01-439 4541

East London   714–720 Green Lane,
                                   Dagenham, Essex RM8 1YJ
                                   01-597 2121

North East London
54a High Road, Wood Green, London N22 6BX
01-889 0991

North West London
120 Finchley Road, London NW3 5JB
01-794 0941

South London
92–94 Borough High Street, London SE1 1LJ
01-407 3102

South East London
4-8 Pound Place, Eltham, London SE9 5DS
01-850 0101

South West London
19–21 Fife Road, Kingston-upon-Thames, Surrey KT1 1SX
01-549 5921

West London
Hythe House, 200 Shepherds Bush Road, Hammersmith, London W6 7NR
01-603 3456

South East Region
Telford House, Hamilton Close, Basingstoke, Hampshire RG21 2UL (0256 67111).

Area Offices

Bedfordshire and Cambridgeshire
14–16 Chapel Street, Luton, Bedfordshire LU1 2SU
0582 37551

Berkshire and Oxfordshire
7th Floor, Reading Bridge House, Reading, Berkshire RG1 8PY
0734 586262

East Sussex
13–15 Old Steine, Brighton, East Sussex BN1 1EX
0273 693599

Essex
5 New London Road, Chelmsford, Essex CM2 0LS
0245 84641

Hampshire and Isle of Wight	119 High Street, Southampton, Hampshire SO9 2EF 0703 29900
Hertfordshire and Buckinghamshire	15 Howardsgate, Welwyn Garden City, Hertfordshire AL8 6BU 07073 38191
Medway	37–45 Balmoral Road, Gillingham, Kent ME7 4PQ 0634 576726
Norfolk	1 Theatre Street, Norwich, Norfolk NR2 1TE 0603 611291
South and East Kent	22 High Street, Ashford, Kent TN24 8SL 0233 35151
Suffolk	22 Lloyds Avenue, Ipswich, Suffolk IP1 1HP 0473 217471
West Sussex and South	5 Medwin Walk, Horsham, West Sussex RH12 1QT 0403 55414

South West Region
The Pithay, Bristol, Avon BS1 2NQ (0272 291071),

Area Offices

Avon	PO Box 185, Minster House, 27 Baldwin Street, Bristol BS99 7QZ 0272 291071
Cornwall and Plymouth	Church House, St Clement Street, Truro, Cornwall TR1 1QZ 0872 73186
Devon	25 Guildhall Shopping Centre, Exeter, Devon EX4 3HQ 0392 33851

Organisation

Gloucestershire and Wiltshire   1st Floor, 37–41 Southgate Street,
Gloucester GL1 1TX
0452 414091

Somerset and Dorset   1st Floor, Bracken House,
14–16 Christchurch Road,
Bournemouth, Dorset BH1 3NE
0202 22055

Midlands Region
2 Duchess Place, Hagley Road, Birmingham B16 8NT
(021-455 7122).

Area Offices

Birmingham City 1   92 The Parade, Sutton Coldfield,
West Midlands B72 1PH
021-355 3604

Birmingham City 2   196 High Street, Erdington,
Birmingham B23 6TL
021-382 6090

Coventry and Warwickshire   Bankfield House, 163 New
Union Street, Coventry
CV1 2QQ
0203 555133

Derbyshire   Gower House, Gower Street,
Derby DE1 1JU
0332 362131

Dudley and Sandwell   Jobcentre, 108 High Street,
Smethwick, Warley,
West Midlands B66 1AA
021-565 2771

Leicester   Charles Street, Leicester
LE1 3JD
0533 531221

Lincoln   280–281 High Street, Lincoln
LN2 1JG
0522 40511

Nottingham

4th Floor, Lambert House,
Talbot Street, Nottingham
NG1 5NP
0602 419381

Staffordshire

15 Brickhouse Street, Burslem,
Stoke-on-Trent, Staffordshire
ST6 3AY
0782 89936

Shropshire

Princess House, 17–19 The
Square, Shrewsbury, Shropshire
SY1 1ZR
0743 57321

Wolverhampton and Walsall

55 High Street, Wednesfield,
Wolverhampton, West Midlands
WV11 1ST
0902 733033

Northern Region
Broadacre House, Market Street, Newcastle upon Tyne NE1 6HH
(0632 326181).

Area Offices

Cleveland

Rede House, Corporation Road,
Middlesbrough, Cleveland
TS1 1TN
0642 248191

County Durham

Valley Street North, Darlington,
County Durham DL1 1TG
0325 51166

North Tyne and Wear

Broadacre House, Market Street,
Newcastle upon Tyne, Tyne and
Wear NE1 6HH
0632 326181

South Tyne and Wear

22–24 Walworth Way,
Sunderland, Tyne and Wear
SR1 3DR
0783 44133

Yorkshire and Humberside Region
Jubilee House, 33–41 Park Place, Leeds LS1 2RJ (0532 446299).

Area Offices

Bradford	27 Petergate, Bradford, West Yorkshire BD1 1HB 0274 723711
Humberside	Queens House, 44–46 Paragon Street, Hull, Humberside HU1 3NZ 0482 27065
Leeds	Fairfax House, Merrion Street, Leeds, West Yorkshire LS2 8LH 0532 446181
North Yorkshire	13 Piccadilly, York, North Yorkshire YO1 1PF 0904 59251
Sheffield	Norwich House, 56 Church Street, Sheffield, South Yorkshire S1 2GN 0742 752253
Wakefield	24 Wood Street, Wakefield, West Yorkshire WF1 2ED 0924 371901

North West Region
Washington House, New Bailey Street, Manchester M3 5ER (061-833 0251).

Area Offices

Cheshire	2nd Floor, Rylands House, Rylands Street, Warrington, Cheshire WA1 1DD 0925 58444
Cumbria	1st Floor, Post Office Buildings, 4 Station Street, Cockermouth, Cumbria CA28 7RH 0900 826349

Lancashire — North	Duchy House, 96 Lancaster Road, Preston, Lancashire PR1 1DB 0772 59393
Lancashire — South	12 Lord Street, Blackburn, Lancashire BB2 1LP 0254 678911
Liverpool Central and Wirral	4–6 Milton Pavement, Grange Precinct, Birkenhead, Wirral, Merseyside L41 2YF 051-647 4621
Manchester — City	25 Aytoun Street, Manchester M60 7HS 061-236 4433
Manchester — East	59 Market Street, Hyde, Cheshire SK14 2AJ 061-236 9013
Manchester — North	29–31 Market Street, Westhoughton, Bolton, Lancashire BL5 3AG 0942 816615
Manchester — West	Arndale House, Chester Road, Stretford, Manchester M32 9ED 061-865 7031
Merseyside — Inner	Room 429, Graeme House, Derby Square, Liverpool, Merseyside L2 7SU 051-227 4111
Merseyside — Outer	15 La Grange Arcade, Shopping Precinct, St Helens, Lancashire WA10 1BP 0744 54251

SCOTLAND

Scottish Region
10 Canning Street, Edinburgh EH3 8EX (031-239 9151).

Area Offices

Ayrshire, Dumfries and Galloway	18 Burns Precinct, Kilmarnock, Strathclyde KA1 1LT 0563 33231
Central and Fife	5 Kirkloan, Edinburgh EH12 7HD 031-334 9821
Glasgow — South and Central	1st Floor, Hellenic House, 87–97 Bath Street, Glasgow G2 2EB 041-333 9452
Glasgow — North	1480 Maryhill Road, Glasgow G21 9DJ 041-945 0114
Highlands and Islands	Metropolitan House, 31–33 High Street, Inverness IV1 1JD 0463 239171
Lanarkshire	Brandon Street, Hamilton, Lanarkshire ML3 6BP 0698 283399
Lothian and Borders	11–13 South Andrew Street, Edinburgh EH2 8BT 031-556 9211
Renfrewshire, Dumbarton Argyll and Bute	53 Central Way, Paisley, Strathclyde PA1 1DT 041-887 7801
Tayside and Grampian	City House, 16 Overgate, Dundee, Angus OB1 1VP 00382 23061

WALES

Welsh Region
Companies House, Crown Way, Maindy, Cardiff CF4 3UU
(0222 388588).

Area Offices

Gwent

2nd Floor, Russell House, John Frost Square, Newport, Gwent NP1 1XH
0633 53571

Mid and South Glamorgan

2nd Floor, Golgate House, 101 St Mary Street, Cardiff, South Glamorgan CF1 1LS
0222 399931

North and Mid Wales

2nd Floor, Halkyn House, Rhosddu Road, Wrexham, Clwyd LL11 1NE
0978 354538

West Wales

2nd Floor, Grove House, 2–3 Grove Place, Swansea SA1 5DH
0792 41451

Chapter 2.3

Skills Training Agency (STA)

Introduction

The Skills Training Agency (STA) — known as the Skillcentre Training Agency until February 1986 — manages the MSC's network of Skillcentres offering training services to industry and to the Commission's own Training Division. STA services are available on a full-cost fee basis. This is reflected in the charges made to employers and to any individuals who seek directly to use the services and whose training is not arranged for them by the MSC.

History

The STA was set up in April 1983 as a separate, commercially orientated division of the MSC. Prior to this date, the Commission's Skillcentres had been administered by its Training Division.

The establishment of the STA was designed to separate the functions of commissioning and delivering training, and to improve flexibility of provision and value for money — particularly in the light of the MSC's New Training Initiative and in particular the Adult Training Strategy.

Structure and Organisation

The head office of the STA is based at the MSC's headquarters in Sheffield although the large majority of its staff are based elsewhere — mainly within individual Skillcentres. The Chief Executive is D J Howells.

Branches

The work of STA is divided between four branches at Moorfoot. In addition, there are seven operation managers who oversee the work of individual Skillcentre managers.

Financial and Accounting Services Branch

(Head: T W Kent)
As its name suggests, this branch provides the financial and accounting services required by the STA.

Product Development Branch

(Head: J Mannell)
This branch acts as a link to national bodies (such as City and Guilds, industrial training boards), provides guidance and information on new courses plus general assistance and advice to operations managers and Skillcentre managers. It is also responsible for improving learning methods and it runs the Instructor Training College at Letchworth. Its work is subdivided into three sections:

> PD1 including course development in electronic, and electrical control engineering areas
> PD2 including teaching/learning methods; instructor training
> PD3 including construction/building; office technology; competence testing; wider opportunity courses.

Skillcentre Operations Branch

(Head: S Bishell)
This branch is responsible for the operational efficiency of Skillcentres, the planning of the STA's operations, performance review, Skillcentre policy and stores, supplies and accommodation matters.
  Its work is divided between four sections:

> SO1 operational services
> SO2 policy and planning
> SO3 supplies and accommodation
> SO4 planning and co-ordinating contraction of Skillcentre network.

Operations

In 1983–84 almost 90 per cent of the STA's work was commissioned by the MSC's own Training Division, and its remaining activity was almost wholly devoted to training commissioned by individual employers. This area of work is expanding and includes tailored training conducted both on site at employers' premises through the Mobile Training Service and at Skillcentres, together with various training and development programmes provided at the Instructor Training College. The STA may also be used to provide off-the-job training under the Youth Training Scheme. The STA is also involved in training for overseas employers and agencies both in the UK and overseas.

The sort of training offered by Skillcentres has, in the past, been primarily in craft skills (for example, construction, electronics and engineering) but there is now a growing emphasis towards training for new technology-based occupations. In addition to the Skillcentres listed at the end of this chapter, the STA operates two instructor training colleges and the Merseyside Advisory Training Unit (MATU) described below. (In Northern Ireland, the 13 Skillcentres are the responsibility of the Department of Economic Development, not the MSC.)

New Technology Access Centres (NTACs)

The new Technology Access Centres have been introduced by the Skillcentre Training Agency from April 1984 and, since May 1985, are operated in 17 locations: Birmingham (Handsworth), Durham, Letchworth, London (Deptford), Manchester (Denton), Plymouth, Sheffield, Bellshill (Lanarkshire), Newport (Gwent), Edinburgh, Felling, Leeds, Beeston, Lancing, Southampton, Gloucester and Bristol.

The centres offer training courses reflecting local needs in the main areas of new technology such as office automation, microcomputers, electronic hardware, telecommunications, and computer aided design. Previous experience of relevant equipment is not required prior to entry, as courses are arranged both for those who start with no previous knowledge and for those who wish to develop existing skills. As the Skillcentres wish to attract employers with staff training needs, they offer tailor-made courses to suit the individual; these will vary in content, length and times of delivery.

Employers can also visit the centres to try out equipment before investing in it. Potential clients should contact STA Head Office, Marketing, Room 521, Moorfoot, Sheffield S1 4PQ.

The MSC's Training Division is also commissioning these centres to offer courses under the Access to Information Technology scheme (see Chapter 3.17). See leaflet ATL19 *New Technology Access Centres.*

Merseyside Advisory and Training Unit (MATU)

The Merseyside Advisory and Training Unit (MATU), run by the Skillcentre Training Agency, was designed as a specific response to inner city labour market trends. It is an experimental centre, where ideas which might have national application can be tested. It sets out to train people who wish to improve their chances of getting employment suited to their abilities, in ways different from the usual Skillcentre methods.

MATU offers training in general office work, typing, basic electronics, household electrical appliance servicing, light gauge metal fabrication, basic car maintenance, basic engineering and popular catering.

The courses, which are in modular form, last between 4 and 12 weeks depending on the level of skill trainees wish to achieve. It is possible for a training programme to be made up of modules from different occupational groups; for example, electronics and office work for the trainee suited to and interested in work in an electronics components store or shop.

Recruitment to the Unit has been simplified; potential trainees do not undergo suitability tests before entry, and may apply through the Jobcentre network.

The Unit offers training to adults and young people of both sexes, who are trained side by side with no set distinctions being made.

Normally about 60 per cent of the trainees are adults. Training takes place either on the Unit's site or on the employer's premises. There is an in-built assessment facility which examines individual potential for the various types of training available so that individual training programmes can be drawn up. Social and life skills training is an important element of the training, designed to encourage the trainees' personal development in a working environment.

MATU
105 Boundary Street
Kirkdale
Liverpool L5 9YT
051-207 6031

Performance and Plans

1984–85 saw the end of the STA's first full year of operation on a
full-cost recovery basis. Although the Agency showed a deficit of
£8.57 million, this was a rather better performance than the
budgeted deficit of £24 million. During 1984–85, Skillcentres
provided training for more than 33,000 people at an average cost
of £2700. £70.9 million of STA's business came from within the
MSC, the remaining £3.8 million from services to employers.

During 1985–86, the STA plans to reduce staffing levels from
the present 3871 to 2950. Within that contraction, however, there
will be one area of growth as it is seeking to expand its mobile
instructor force to 300. A further plan is to reduce the deficit still
further although the Agency is not expected to break even until
1987. Over the next two years the STA expects to provide 9.8
million training places in 1985–86 and 10.5 million in 1986–87.

List of Skillcentres

In November 1984, STA unveiled proposals to reduce the
Skillcentre network by about one-third. The plan was approved
by a majority of MSC Commissioners early in 1985.

The Skillcentres closing or closed are: **Midlands** Birmingham;
Long Eaton; Redditch; Kirkby in Ashfield; Dudley Annexe;
Handsworth. **Northern** Doncaster; Killingworth; Middlesbrough.
North West Hindley Annexe; Liverpool; Manchester — Denton.
South East Lambeth; Medway Annexe, Waddon; Waddon
Annexe. **South West** Bristol Annexe; Gloucester Annexe;
Plymouth Annexe; West Sussex Annexe. **Scotland** Bellshill
Annexe; Dumbarton; Edinburgh Annexe; Hillington Annexe;
Queenslie. **Wales** Llanelli; West Gwent.

The list below includes only those centres retained.

Organisation

ENGLAND

Avon

Gill Avenue, Fishponds, Bristol
BS16 2QL
0272 653241

Berkshire

Manor Farm Road, Reading
RG2 0JH
0734 864524

Walpole Road, Off Bath Road,
Slough SL1 6BN
06286 5222

Buckinghamshire

Bleak Hall, Chesney Wold,
Milton Keynes MK6 1LX
0908 670001

Cambridgeshire

Saville Road, Westwood,
Peterborough PE3 6TQ
0733 267242

Cheshire

Castle Rise, Runcorn WA7 5XR
09285 65921/4

Cleveland

Billingham on Tees Industrial
Estate, Leeholme Road,
Billingham on Tees TS23 3TE
0642 506811

Cornwall

Wilson Way, Pool Industrial
Estate, Redruth TR15 3SD
0209 213231

Cumbria

Glasson Industrial Estate,
Maryport CA15 8NY
0900 812771/2

Derbyshire

Chesterfield Training Centre,
Block 2, Dunston Trading
Estate, Foxwood Road,
Sheepbridge, Chesterfield
S41 9RF
0246 450511

Devon

Newnham Industrial Estate,
Strode Road, Plympton St Mary,
Plymouth PL7 4BG
0752 335921

Durham, County

Durham Littleburn Trading
Estate, Langley Moor, Durham
DH7 8HG
0385 780601

Essex

Bentalls, Cranes Farm Road,
Basildon IG11 0HR
0268 3225

Basildon Annexe, Farrow Road,
Rodney Way, Widford Industrial
Estate, Chelmsford CM1 3TF
0245 26533

Gloucestershire

117 Bristol Road, Gloucester
GL1 5SP
0452 27721

Hampshire

Scott Road, off Military Road,
Hilsea, Portsmouth PO3 5LF
0705 668831

West Bay Road, Southampton
SO9 3SH
0703 28281

Southampton Annexe, Auckland
Road, Millbrook, Southampton
SO9 4YN
0703 774503

Hertfordshire

Pixmore Avenue, Letchworth
SG6 1JP
04626 3084

Humberside

Chamberlain Road, Hull
HU8 8HL
0482 20738

Kent

Courtenay Road, Gillingham
ME8 0RY
0634 360404

Lancashire

Eagle Street, Accrington
BB5 1NS
0254 395521

180 Longridge Road, Preston
PR2 5AP
0772 652021

Leicestershire

Humberstone Lane, Leicester
LE4 7JW
0533 769101

London, Greater

Thames Road, Barking
1G11 0HR
01-591 2662

2 Deptford Church Street,
London SE8 4SJ
01-691 5721

Bilton Way, Enfield, Middlesex
EN3 7NZ
01-805 1365

Walmgate Road, Perivale,
Greenford, Middlesex UB6 7NE
01-998 1451

Industrial Estate, Rugby Road,
Twickenham, Middlesex
TW1 1DT
01-892 6285

Manchester, Greater	Guinness Road, Trafford Park M17 1SD 061-872 6042
	Swan Lane, Hindley Green, Hindley, Wigan WN2 4HD 0942 56123
	Chichester Street, Rochdale DL16 2AG 0706 341514
Merseyside	Bedford Street, Park Industrial Estate, St Helens WA9 1PN 0744 34134
Norfolk	Mile Cross Road, Norwich NR2 4LR 0603 49181
Northamptonshire	4 Clayfield Close, Moulton Park, Northampton NN3 1QF 0604 46643
Nottinghamshire	Lilac Grove, Beeston NG9 1QY 0602 221112
Staffordshire	Clough Street, Hanley, Stoke on Trent ST1 4AS 0782 261521
Suffolk	Whitehouse Road, Ipswich IP1 5NX 0473 47464
Sussex, West	Churchill Industrial Estate, Chartwell Road, Lancing BN15 8YB 0903 764331

Organisation

Tyne and Wear

Green Lane, Felling, Gateshead
NE10 0LA
0632 694314

West Midlands

Torrington Avenue, Coventry
CV4 9GR
0203 468141

Craddock Street, Whitmore
Reans, Wolverhampton
WV6 0OJ
0902-27173

Yorkshire, South

Richmond Park Road, Sheffield
S13 8HT
0742 446471

Yorkshire, West

Common Road, Low Moor,
Bradford BD12 0SF
0274 600911

Parkside Lane, Hunslet, Leeds
LS11 5SZ
0532 704661

Doncaster Road, Wakefield
WF1 5EA
0924 375823

Wiltshire

Faraday Road, Dorcan, Swindon
SN3 5HB
0793 641671

SCOTLAND

Fife

Townhill, Dunfermline
KY12 0TB
0383 721148

Lothian

West Granton Road, Edinburgh
EH5 1JB
031-551 1461

Strathclyde

Industrial Estate, Bellshill,
Lanarkshire ML4 3JE
0698 748667

Hillington Industrial Estate,
Queen Elizabeth Avenue,
Glasgow G52 4TL
041-810 3111

Ayr Road, Irvine, Ayrshire
KA12 8ES
0294 78688

Tayside

4 Staffa Place, Dundee
DD2 3SX
0382 816633

WALES

Clwyd

Bersham Road, Wrexham
LL13 7UH
0978 355555

Glamorgan, South

Western Avenue, Cardiff
CF4 3XY
0222 621343

Glamorgan, West

Ceramic Way, Port Talbot
SA13 1RY
0639 884691

Gwent

Corporation Road, Newport
NPT 0YT
0633 271160

Instructor Training Colleges

TD Instructor Training College
Pixmore Instructor Training College
Pixmore Avenue,Letchworth, Hertfordshire SG6 1JP
04626 72872

Organisation

TD Instructor Training College
Hillington Industrial Estate, Queen Elizabeth Avenue, Glasgow
G52 4TL
041-810 3111

Chapter 2.4

Technical and Vocational Education Initiative Unit (TVEI)

Introduction and Description

This unit is organisationally separate from the MSC's four divisions and the Skillcentre Training Agency, although considerably smaller than all of them. It is responsible for co-ordinating TVEI (see Chapter 3.13). Based at 236 Gray's Inn Road, London WC1X 8HL rather than in Sheffield, it comprises just 40 staff (April 1985) headed by Director J G Woolhouse.

TVEI is monitored by advisers on secondment from local education authorities and key decisions are made by the TVEI Steering Group.

Membership of the Steering Group

At April 1985, membership was:

— B Nicholson (Chair, MSC);
— V Glauert (headteacher);
— A Harries (Chair, Welsh Joint Education Committee);
— N Harrison (Chair, Association of Metropolitan Authorities Education Committee);
— J Horrell (Chair, Association of County Councils);
— F Smithies (General Secretary, National Association of Schoolmasters/Union of Women Teachers);
— F Jarvis (General Secretary, National Union of Teachers);
— R Knight (Director of Education, Bradford);
— M McAllister (Principal, Blackpool and Fylde College);
— P Merridale (Chair, Association of County Councils Education Committee);
— B Morris (Education Officer, Association of Metropolitan Authorities);
— Sir James Munn (Chair, MSC Scotland);
— F Pignatelli (Assistant Director of Education, Strathclyde Regional Council);

- P Rogers (Director of Personnel and Europe, Plessy Company plc);
- N Singer (Director, Thames Polytechnic)
- D Stradling (Group Personnel Director, John Laing Ltd);
- H Tomlinson (Head of Education Department, Confederation of British Industry).

The Unit also produces a free journal *TVEI Insight* available from Room E825, Moorfoot, Sheffield.

Chapter 2.5

Training Division (TD)

Introduction

Training Division (TD) is one of the MSC's four operating divisions. Its purpose is to oversee all of the Commission's training services and programmes with the exception of direct training services provided by Skillcentres and the Technical and Vocational Education Initiative.

It therefore has overall responsibility for:

— the Youth Training Scheme (YTS), including ITeCs;
— the Job Training Scheme, Wider Opportunities Training Programme and other adult training activities;
— the Open Tech Programme (OTP);
— Industrial Language Training;
— Industrial Training Boards (ITBs).

Most recently, the division has also been given responsibility for certain areas of work-related non-advanced further education (WRNAFE); namely, those areas for which the MSC has taken over the responsibility of funding from local education authorities. This followed the *Training for Jobs* white paper.

The division's combined operations account for the largest slice of the MSC's budget.

History

TD was set up in September 1982 following the merger of the Commission's Training Services Division and Special Programmes Division. It began as the Training Services Agency, established in 1974 by the 1973 Employment and Training Act.

Structure and Organisation

TD operates from the MSC's Sheffield headquarters but there is also a national network of nine regional offices and 55 area offices. In addition, the Large Companies Unit and Scottish Large Companies Unit (described below) are based in London and Edinburgh. The division's total staffing in April 1985 was over 5000, mostly at area level.

The division's branches are organised into three directorates; overall responsibility is exercised by a chief executive.

Chief Executive: I A Johnson
Director of Adult Training: J Bacon. Responsible for:

the Open Tech Unit (Head: D Tinsley)
Adult Training Programmes Branch (Head: J Robertson)
Adult Training Strategy Branch (Head: D Grover)
Sectors Training Branch (Head: J Wiltshire).

Director of Youth Training: K N Atkinson. Responsible for:

Youth Programmes Branch (Head: J Smith)
Quality and Standards Branch (Head: J Fuller)
Strategy, Evaluation and Research Branch (Head: K Franklin)
Training Development Branch (Head: I Randall).

Director of Field Operations: V J Bayliss. Responsible for:

Field Planning Branch (Head: P Read)
Field Systems Branch (Head: E English)
Labour Market Economics and Statistics Branch (Head: N Davis)
Evaluation and Skills Branch (Head: J Marquand)
Regional Offices
Area Offices.

The Youth Training Directorate works closely with the advisory Youth Training Board (see below) but has no responsibility for it. It is likely that a similar steering group to advise on MSC funding of work-related non-advanced further education will be set up. In addition, regional and area offices liaise closely with the Area Manpower Boards' network to determine actual provision of MSC training.

Elements of Interest

The Youth Training Board

This is an advisory body set up in 1982 to oversee the Youth Training Scheme. Its terms of reference are:

— to advise on the strategy, planning and implementation of the schemes;

— to advise on the policies and standards for its content and operation;

— to advise on measures to ensure equality of opportunity in provision for young people, regardless of sex or ethnic origin;

— to recommend to the MSC appropriate changes to the scheme.

Membership of the board is at present:

— B Nicholson (Chair, MSC);

— P J Daly (CBI) (Company Education and Training Manager, Thorn EMI);

— I Johnston (Chief Executive, MSC Training Division);

— G Hainsworth (education service) (Chief Education Officer, Manchester);

— G Holland (Director, MSC);

— R A Jackson (TUC) (Secretary, TUC Education Department);

— Councillor J F McLean (Convention of Scottish Local Authorities);

— P D Merridale (Association of County Councils) (Chair, Hampshire County Council Education Committee);

— D R Mills (Careers Service) (County Careers Officer, Cheshire);

— J Pardoe (CBI) (Managing Director, Sight and Sound Ltd);

— Councillor J Pearmain (Association of Metropolitan Authorities);

— P Reay (Chair of Advisory Group on Content and Standards) (Group Personnel Director, Cadbury Schweppes Ltd);

— M Ryan (Youth Organisations) (Chair, British Youth Council);

— V Stern (Voluntary Organisations) (Director, NACRO);

— D C Stanley (CBI) (Deputy Director, Education and Training, CBI);
— P Turner (TUC) (National Women's Officer, General, Municipal, Boilermakers and Allied Trades Union);
— L W Wood (TUC) (General Secretary, Union of Construction, Allied Trades and Technicians).

The Advisory Group on Content and Standards

This advisory body reports to the Youth Training Board (above) on the content and standards in YTS. Members are invited to serve in a personal capacity.

Membership at present comprises:

— P Reay (Chair) (Group Personnel Director, Cadbury Schweppes Ltd);
— A G F Chaplin (Head of Group Training and Development, Pilkington plc);
— P J Coldstream (Chair, Southwark Consortium);
— H F Gadd (Chief Education and Training Officer, Engineering Industry Training Board);
— S Green (Group Head of Personnel, Unigate Ltd);
— F C Hayes (Training Policy Consultant, Institute for Manpower Studies);
— J Mansell (Director, Further Education Unit);
— C McCarthy (General Secretary, National Union of Metal Mechanics);
— D McPhail (Principal, Moray College);
— J Rees (Education Secretary, National Association of Teachers in Further and Higher Education);
— M Roberts (Advisor, Education and Training Division, CBI);
— K Walthorpe (Group Personnel Director, Stewart Wrightson Management Services plc);
— A G Watts (Director, National Institute for Careers Education and Counselling).

The Large Companies Unit

The Large Companies Units in London and Edinburgh are responsible for the establishment of those YTS schemes running nationally or those which exist in more than one MSC area (for example, those of Sainsbury's, Marks and Spencer and Pye).

The Youth Training Board (above) is responsible for the approval of such schemes and these are dealt with by a sub-group of the board including a representative from each of the following bodies: the TUC, the CBI, the education service and the careers service. The group ensures that full consultations with appropriate trade unions have been undertaken and their consent obtained before approving national schemes. It also advises the full board where problems may arise.

About 150 organisations have signed contracts with the Unit (plus some 23 with the Scottish Unit) and they provide more than 85,000 YTS places.

Large Companies Unit
236 Gray's Inn Road
London WC1X 8HL

Scottish Large Companies Unit
TD Office for Scotland
OSA3
9 St Andrews Square
Edinburgh EH2 2QX.

Open Tech Steering Group

This group advises the MSC on the overall policy, objectives and criteria for the Open Tech Programme; all aspects of its strategy, requirements and collaborative relationships; allocation of funding and the evaluation of both projects and programme. Its membership comprises (July 1985):

— R J Parker (Chair) (Head of Training, British Telecom);
— M Bennett (Education and Training Manager, Westland Helicopters Ltd);
— P Bowen (Company Training Manager, W H Smith and Sons Ltd);
— J Bridge (National Technical Sub-Committee, AUEW TASS);
— K Carberry (Education Committee, TUC);
— Dr T L Foggo (Training and Development Section, ICI Ltd);
— D Garrard (Business and Technician Education Council);
— D Hemingway (Chief Officer, Scottish Technical Education Council);

Organisation

- G Hubbard (Director, Council for Educational Technology);
- M McAllister (Blackpool and Fylde College of Further and Higher Education);
- M J Morden (Assistant Director of Further Education, Gwent);
- G Platon (Chair, G Platon Ltd);
- J Rees (South West London College);
- J W Sellars (Divisional Education Officer, Lothian Regional Council);
- V S Shirley (F International Ltd);
- Prof R Smith (Pro-Vice Chancellor, Open University);
- L Wells (President, ASTMS);
- W H Wright (Chief Education Officer, Wakefield).

Observers:

- Department of Employment
- Department of Education and Science
- Department of Education, Northern Ireland
- Department of Trade and Industry, Industry and Education Unit
- Further Education Unit
- Her Majesty's Inspectorate
- Ministry of Defence.

Regional and Area Offices

Training Division regions cover the same geographical areas as those of Employment Division. The area pattern is, however, different since there are only 55 TD areas compared with ED's 69.

ENGLAND

London Region
236 Gray's Inn Road, London WC1X 8HL (01-278 0363).

Area Offices

London North 6th Floor, 19–29 Woburn Place, London WC1 0LU
01-837 1288

London North East	3rd Floor, Cityside House, 40 Adler Street, London E1 1EW 01-377 1866
London South and West	Lyric House, 149 Hammersmith Road, Hammersmith, London W14 0QL 01-602 7227
London South East	Skyline House, 200 Union Street, London SE1 0LX 01-928 0800

Midlands Region
Alpha Tower, Suffolk Street, Queensway, Birmingham B1 1UR (021-632 4144).

Area Offices

Birmingham and Solihull	15th and 16th Floors, Metropolitan House, 11 Hagley Road, Birmingham B16 8TG 021-632 4451
Coventry and Warwickshire	5th and 6th Floors, Bankfield House, 163 New Union Street, Coventry CV1 2PE 0203 24100
Derbyshire	4th Floor, St Peter's House, Gower Street, Derby DE1 1SB 0332 360550
Dudley and Sandwell	Falcon House, The Minories, Dudley DY2 8PG 0384 238391
Leicestershire and Northamptonshire	1st Floor, Rutland Centre, Halford Street, Leicester LE1 1TQ 0533 538616
Lincolnshire	Wigford House, Brayford Wharf, Lincoln LN5 7AY 0522 32266

65

Nottinghamshire

4th Floor, Lambert House, Talbot Street, Nottingham NG1 7FF
0602 413313

Shropshire, Herefordshire and Worcestershire

Hazeldene House, Town Centre, Telford, Shropshire TF3 4JJ
0952 507474

Staffordshire

Moorlands House, 24 Trinity Street, Hanley, Stoke-on-Trent ST1 5LN
0782 260505

Wolverhampton and Walsall

2nd Floor, Burdett House, 29–30 Cleveland Street, Wolverhampton WV1 3HA
0902 711111

Northern Region
Broadacre House, Market Street, Newcastle upon Tyne NE1 6HH
(0632 326181).

Area Offices

Cleveland

Corporation House, 73 Albert Road, Middlesbrough, Cleveland TS1 2RU
0642 241144

County Durham

William Press Building, Valley Street North, Darlington, County Durham DL1 1TJ
0325 51166

Northumberland, North Tyneside and Newcastle

1st Floor, Broadacre House, Market Street, Newcastle upon Tyne NE1 6HH
0632 326181

Sunderland, South Tyneside and Gateshead

Derwent House, Washington New Town, Tyne and Wear NE38 7ST
091-416 6161

North West Region
Washington House, The Capital Centre, New Bailey Street,
Manchester M3 5ER (061-833 0251).

Area Offices

Bolton, Bury, Rochdale and Wigan	3rd Floor, Provincial House, Nelson Square, Bolton BL1 1PN 0204 397350
Cheshire	1st Floor, Spencer House, Dewhurst Road, Birchwood Centre, Warrington WA3 7PP 0925 826515
Cumbria	1st and 2nd Floors, Thirlmere Block, Mobet Estate, Workington, Cumbria CA14 3YB 0900 66991
Lancashire	3rd Floor, Duchy House, 96 Lancaster Road, Preston PR1 1DB 0772 59393
Liverpool, Inner	4th Floor, Sefton House, Exchange Street East, Liverpool L2 3XR 051-236 0026
Liverpool, Outer	7th Floor, Sefton House, Exchange Street East, Liverpool L2 3SD 051-236 0026
Manchester, Salford and Trafford	4th and 5th Floors, Boulton House, 17–21 Chorlton Street, Manchester M1 3HY 061-236 7222
Oldham, Tameside and Stockport	1st Floor, 1 St Peters Square, Stockport SK1 1NN 061-477 8830

Organisation

South East Region
Telford House, Hamilton Close, Basingstoke RG21 2UZ
(0256 29266).

Area Offices

Bedfordshire and Cambridgeshire	6th and 7th Floors, King House, George Street West, Luton LU1 2DD 0582 412828
Berkshire and Oxfordshire	8th Floor, Reading Bridge House, Reading Bridge Road, Reading, Berkshire RG1 8PY 0734 586262
Buckinghamshire and Hertfordshire	2nd Floor, 31 Octagon Parade, High Wycombe, Buckinghamshire HP11 2LD 0494 33473
Essex	Globe House, New Street, Chelmsford, Essex CM1 1UG 0245 358548
Hampshire and Isle of Wight	25 Thackeray Mall, Fareham Shopping Centre, Fareham, Hampshire PO15 0PQ 0329 285921
Kent	6th Floor, Victory House, Meeting House Lane, Chatham, Kent ME4 4PS 0634 44411
Norfolk and Suffolk	Crown House, Crown Street, Ipswich, Suffolk IP1 3HS 0473 218951
Surrey, East and West Sussex	Exchange House, Worthing Road, Horsham, West Sussex RH12 1SQ 0403 50244

South West Region
4th Floor, The Pithay, Bristol BS1 2NQ (0272 291071).

Area Offices

Avon	PO Box 144, 4th Floor, Minster House, Baldwin Street, Bristol BS99 7HR 0272 277116
Cornwall and Devon	7th Floor, Tower Block, BR Station, North Road, Plymouth PL4 6AA 0752 671671
Dorset and Somerset	Ground Floor, Michael Paul House, Corporation Street, Taunton, Somerset TA1 4BE 0823 85177
Gloucestershire and Wiltshire	33–35 Worcester Street, Gloucester GL1 3AJ 0452 24488

Yorkshire and Humberside Region
Jubilee House, 33–41 Park Place, Leeds LS1 2RL (0532 446299).

Area Offices

Bradford, Calderdale and Kirklees	Jubilee House, 33–41 Park Place, Leeds LS1 2RL 0532 446299
Humberside	4th Floor, Essex House, Manor Street, Hull HU1 1YA 0482 226491
North Yorkshire and Leeds	Fairfax House, Merrion Street, Leeds LS2 8LH 0532 446181
Sheffield and Rotherham	8th Floor, Sheaf House, The Pennine Centre, Hawley Street, Sheffield S1 3GA 0742 701911

Wakefield, Barnsley and Doncaster

York House, 31–36 York Place, Leeds LS1 2EB
0532 450502

SCOTLAND

9 St Andrew Square, Edinburgh EH2 2QX (031-225 8500).

Area Offices

Ayrshire, Dumfries and Galloway

25 Bank Street, Kilmarnock KA1 1ER
0563 44044

Central and Fife

5 Kirk Loan, Corstophine, Edinburgh EH12 7HD
031-334 9821

Dumbarton, Argyll and Renfrewshire

5 Elm Bank Gardens, Charing Cross, Glasgow G2 4PN
041-226 5544

Glasgow City

4th Floor, George House, 36 North Hanover Street, Glasgow G2 4AD
041-552 3411

Grampian and Tayside

Argyll House, Marketgait, Dundee DD1 1UD
0382 29971

Highlands and Islands

3rd Floor, Metropolitan House, 31–33 High Street, Inverness IV1 1TX
0463 220555

Lanarkshire

Scomagg House, Crosshill Street, Motherwell ML1 1RU
0698 51411

Lothian and Borders

2-3 Queen Street, Edinburgh EH2 1JS
031-225 1377

WALES

4th Floor, Companies House, Crown Way, Maindy, Cardiff
CF4 3UF (0222 388588).

Area Offices

**Dyfed and West
Glamorgan**

3rd Floor, Orchard House,
Orchard Street, Swansea
SA1 5AP
0792 460355

Glamorgan, Mid and South

5th Floor, Phase One Building,
Ty Glas Llanishen, Cardiff
CF4 5PJ
0222 755744

Gwent

Government Building, Cardiff
Road, Newport, Gwent NP1 1YE
0633 56161

Gwynedd, Clwyd and Powys

Block 28, Wynnstay Block,
Hightown Barracks, Kingsmills
Road, Wrexham LL13 8BH
0978 365550

Chapter 2.6

Support Divisions

Introduction

In addition to its operating divisions which provide or fund services to the public and professionals, the MSC has two other divisions. Their functions are largely concerned with administering the Commission's internal administration and operation and it is not necessary to describe them in any great detail as the public are unlikely to have any contact with them. Both divisions were established following a reorganisation of support services in April 1984, when the functions of what were the Corporate Services Division and Manpower Intelligence and Planning Divisions were redistributed.

Personnel and Central Services Division

This division, directed by D B Price, employs 910 staff (April 1985) based largely at the Commission's Sheffield headquarters. Its work is divided between five branches. It also works closely with the MSC's central secretariat (a largely autonomous section), though having no direct responsibility for it. The branches are:

— Personnel and Support Services branch (Head: A T Wisbey)
— Computer branch (Head: I E Turl)
— Staff Training branch (Head: A E Le Sage)
— Psychological Services branch and research section (Head: Dr M C Killcross)
— Marketing and Information branch (Head: B Sutlieff).

Of these, only Marketing and Information branch is likely to be of any great interest to outsiders since it includes the MSC Press Offices in London and Sheffield. It also has responsibility for the Careers and Occupational Information Centre (see Chapter 3.24).

MSC Press Offices
236 Gray's Inn Road, London WC1X 8HL (01-278 3222).

Moorfoot, Sheffield S1 4PQ (0742 703408).

Planning and Resources Division

This division, headed by Director J Wild, employs 259 staff (April 1985). Based at MSC headquarters in Sheffield, the work of the division is done by the following four branches:

— Accounts branch (Head: N Gregory)
— Finance Policy branch (Head: M Horsman)
— Manpower and Efficiency branch (Head: G Kendall)
— Central Planning branch (Head: N Schofield).

Chapter 2.7

Area Manpower Boards

Established in January 1983, Area Manpower Boards (AMBs) form the local advisory machinery of the MSC. They are under review at the time of writing prior to reconstitution in July 1986. The present network of 55 AMBs replaced District Manpower Committees and Special Programmes Area Boards. They are based largely (but not entirely) on the Training Division (TD) Area network.

The work of AMBs includes:

— advising on the planning and delivery of the MSC schemes and services within their area;
— promoting schemes and attracting sponsors to start projects (especially under YTS and the Community Programme);
— developing links between the Commission and local groups influential in manpower decisions;
— advising on allocation of resources (within national guidelines);
— approving training places (within national guidelines);
— responsibility for approving budgets and local policy;
— monitoring opportunities and projects within their area;
— responding to requests for advice from the Commission at regional and national level.

The composition of AMBs is:

— an independent chair;
— five employer representatives;
— five employee representatives;
— one education service representative;
— one professional education representative;
— one voluntary organisation representative;
— one chair of a Committee for the Employment of Disabled People;
— two or three education authority representatives;
— up to four co-opted, non-voting members.

Principal careers officers have the right of attendance when YTS is discussed and representatives of other interests such as Her Majesty's Inspectorate, community industry or young people may attend if invited.

Since their inception, the main work of AMBs has been the scrutiny of scheme proposals under YTS and the Community Programme. Now that these programmes are becoming established, it is likely that the role of AMBs (and possibly their distribution and composition) will change. Details of AMB chairs and members should be obtainable from TD Area Offices.

Part 3

Schemes and Services

Chapter 3.1

Introduction

This, the largest section of the book, examines the various schemes and services run or funded by the MSC. There is also a short chapter explaining recent changes in adult training arrangements.

Chapters are grouped within the following subsections:

Employment services

— Jobcentres and Employment Offices
— Professional and Executive Recruitment
— Job Change Schemes
— Employment Rehabilitation Centres
— Other help for people with disabilities.

Special employment schemes

— Community Programme
— Enterprise Allowance Scheme
— Voluntary Projects Programme.

Training and preparation for work

— Youth Training Scheme
— Information Technology Centres
— Community Industry
— Technical and Vocational Education Initiative.

Adult training

— Adult Training — the 1985 Changes
— Job Training Scheme
— Training for Enterprise
— Access to Information Technology Courses
— Local Consultancy Grants and Local Training Grants
— Wider Opportunities Training Programme

— Open Tech Programme
— Local Collaborative Projects
— Industrial Training
— Industrial Language Training Service.

Careers publications

— Careers and Occupational Information Centre.

Training for trainers

— Accredited Centres.

Chapter 3.2

Jobcentres and Employment Offices

Introduction

The network of Jobcentres and Employment Offices throughout Britain is the most public aspect of the MSC. Their primary function is to offer a public employment service, by providing employers with a means of filling job vacancies, and jobseekers with information about work. In addition, they act as the gateway to many of the Commission's other schemes and services.

History

The Jobcentres and Employment Offices of today are the direct descendants of the first government-funded Labour Exchanges introduced in 1911. Centres today differ from their predecessors in many ways, following radical reorganisation of the service in 1973 when the first Jobcentre opened. Most Jobcentres are located in local high streets with shop-front premises rather than hidden away in back streets. A further difference is that they operate on self-service principles.

Services to Employers

A most important element of the Jobcentre service is the helping of employers to fill their vacancies. When details of a post are notified to the Jobcentre, the staff will help employers word their job description in the most effective form. Details are put on to a card which is then displayed free of charge in the centre itself and in others within the local 'travel to work' area. Hard-to-fill vacancies may be notified over a wider area. The name of the company or employing organisation is not shown and jobseekers who are interested are put in touch with the employer through the Jobcentre. Since Jobcentres and Employment Offices carry details of many people looking for work in their area, they may be able to suggest potential candidates for interview for vacancies notified. Many Jobcentres also have a room available for interviewing if required.

In addition to this work, Jobcentres and Employment Offices can advise employers about the local employment market, rates of pay and provide basic information on many employment matters such as contracts, new legislation or redundancy procedures.

Special help and advice is also available to employers of disabled people — either those considering taking on a disabled worker or organisations where existing staff become disabled.

Jobcentres can put employers in touch with other services run by the MSC including Skillcentre training, Professional and Executive Recruitment and Youth Training Schemes.

Services to Jobseekers

Jobcentre and Employment Offices provide both unemployed and employed people looking for work with details of jobs or training opportunities in their area. Jobseekers can call in without appointment and examine details of notified vacancies on display. Employment advisory staff are available to give further details and to arrange interviews.

Registering with a Jobcentre or Employment Office is no longer necessary in order to claim unemployment benefit, but jobseekers may still leave details with the centre (particularly if they have skills or experience which is in demand or unusual) so they can be notified if suitable work comes up.

Through the computerised National Vacancy Circulation System (NATVACS), Jobcentres and Employment Offices will know of hard-to-fill vacancies in other areas of the country and may be prepared to contact them on behalf of jobseekers. The MSC is currently experimenting with methods of allowing the public direct access to vacancy information through computer terminals in a few Jobcentres.

Performance

The MSC estimates that about a quarter of a million people visit centres every working day. During the year 1984–85 almost 2.4 million vacancies were notified to Jobcentres and Employment Offices — representing about one-third of the total vacancies in the economy. From these notifications, about 1.8 million placings were made (more than 75 per cent of the total).

In addition to job-filling, Jobcentres and Employment Offices placed 113,000 people on the Community Programme in 1983–84, 15,500 people on the Youth Training Scheme and accepted more than 96,000 people for adult training. About 18,000 were helped through labour mobility schemes administered by the centre.

The overall cost per placing at 1983–84 pricing was £70.

Staffing

There are about 8750 staff (April 1985) based in almost 1000 Jobcentres in England, Scotland and Wales.

Organisation

Each centre or office has a manager responsible, through area and regional offices, to the Executive Director of Employment Division (see Chapter 2.2).

Issues and Future Developments

In April 1984, the Commission considered a controversial plan from Employment Division (ED) to restructure the Jobcentre network into a three-tier basis, cutting 800 jobs. Widespread fears that the plan would also mean a significant deterioration in service led the Commissioners to ask ED to make further consultations. Following these, a revised plan was put to the Commissioners in November 1984. It envisaged:

— opening 82 new small Jobcentres to make a total of 1065;
— large-scale investment in new technology to develop the accessibility and quality of information about jobs and MSC and other government programmes;
— a commitment to maintain services to long-term unemployed and disabled people at least at present levels.

The new network would comprise 530 main Jobcentres, a further 453 existing Jobcentres and the additional 82 centres, based in libraries and other local authority premises. In eight towns having two Jobcentres, offices would be merged but no other centres will be closed. Services in the new centres would be less comprehensive than existing centres and while 662 existing centres would maintain services at current levels, in the remaining 329, the level of service would be reduced, because of greater centralisation.

The revised proposals envisaged the loss of 530 staff over three years, with no redundancies and a saving of £8 million by the third year.

The proposals were accepted by a majority of the Commissioners (those from the TUC dissenting over staff cuts and the pace of the change) in November and endorsed by the government soon after. Changes are now under way and it remains to be seen what the consequences for users will be.

Further Information

In addition to services to employers and job seekers, Jobcentres can provide information and leaflets on a wide range of MSC schemes and services such as:

— adult training (information about course availability, allowances and application forms from Training Advisers);
— the Community Programme;
— the Employment Transfer Scheme;
— the Enterprise Allowance Scheme;
— labour mobility schemes (general information and application forms);
— services for disabled people (details of how to register as disabled, special schemes, aids and services);
— the Voluntary Projects Programme (general information, in addition to details of many local opportunities);
— the Youth Training Scheme (in some areas enquiries are passed on to local education authority careers service);
— Department of Employment schemes.

Full details of services can be obtained from Jobcentre and Employment Office managers at the addresses listed in Appendix A.

Chapter 3.3

Professional and Executive Recruitment (PER)

Introduction

PER is a self-financing section of the Employment Division of the MSC. It provides a specialist recruitment and jobs information service for jobseekers in the managerial, professional, executive, scientific and technical groups, using publications, seminars and short courses. In addition PER offers a recruitment service to employers, billing itself as 'Britain's largest executive recruitment consultancy'.

History

PER began its operations in 1974 as one of the main sections of the Commission's Employment Division. Since April 1983 it has operated on a full-cost recovery basis, charging fees to employers, though not to jobseekers. Prior to that date it was not expected to break even. In the year 1984–85 it generated a surplus of about £160,000 and increased substantially its volume of placings, although many of these were to MSC schemes.

Organisation and Staffing

The majority of PER staff are based in its 35 local offices which are listed at the end of this chapter. There is also a London-based section which deals with overseas appointments. Staffing levels have fallen over the past four years from almost 500 in 1981 to about 300 in 1984–85.

Eligibility

People in paid employment may register with PER in addition to those who are out of work. All applicants must either have experience of the type and level of jobs handled by PER or, if immediately out of full-time education, specific qualifications. New graduates can register without previous work experience.

Services

Services to employers

PER offers client employers a service of advertising vacancies, both in its own publications and in other selected papers. In addition it can process applications for clients and undertake initial interviewing of candidates.

PER also produces a monthly magazine *Candidate Focus*, sent free of charge to employers on its mailing list. The publication, as its title implies, focuses on the register of people held by PER and the kinds of jobs they are seeking.

PER's largest single field of recruitment is for staff for MSC-sponsored schemes such as the Community Programme and managerial/supervisory posts in youth training schemes.

Services to jobseekers

The PER service with which people are likely to be most familiar is the publications; a jobhunting handbook is sent to each person enrolling and a free weekly newspaper (*Executive Post*) is also sent for a maximum of two years. *Executive Post*, launched in 1980, carries news and information about employment, self-employment and training but it is mostly devoted to advertisements for job vacancies nationwide. It has a circulation of 130,000 copies. New graduates do not receive *Executive Post*, but copies of it are available for consultation in Jobcentres and Employment Offices and are also available on subscription to individuals or institutions not receiving them free.

All those enrolling with PER are invited to a free half-day jobhunting seminar. These give advice on the jobmarket, self-presentation and jobhunting, details of self-help groups and MSC courses available locally. They are held throughout Great Britain.

PER also offers assistance in recruitment for the Bridge Programme — a part-time course run in some areas and held over a maximum of four months. The programme offers access to expert advice, workshops and a jobsearch base with telephone and secretarial facilities to help unemployed managers and professional staff find work.

PER places suitable applicants in MSC schemes such as Community Programme and in YTS staff posts and administers the application procedure. It also has details of the Job Search and Employment Transfer Schemes.

Overseas division

The overseas division of PER which has been operating since 1974 specialises in recruiting staff for overseas posts. This area of PER's business has grown. During 1983–84 it handled vacancies in 30 countries worldwide, including the Middle East, Africa and Europe with recruitment on behalf of American companies showing a significant increase.

Performance

In the year 1984–85, some 144,000 people were enrolled with PER, which made 10,700 placings from 19,600 vacancies notified (a success rate of 55 per cent of orders filled). This was a considerable fall compared to the previous year, when from 165,000 enrolments the service placed 13,900 individuals. This fall of placing figures is largely due to the tailing off of the Community Programme's expansion rate.

Future Developments and Issues

Although the MSC itself is nominally committed to maintain the PER service, PER has many political enemies who would like to see its work performed by private executive recruitment agencies.

While it is true that PER achieved a modest trading surplus in its first two years of full-cost recovery operations, the methods by which this was done are less encouraging. PER only broke even by virtue of transfer payments from Training Division, for placings on the Community Programme. This business was projected to represent about 45 per cent of PER's operations during 1984–85. Nevertheless PER represents the government's only employment agency which specialises in recruitment and job information for a significant number of jobseekers who are currently not catered for by Jobcentres or Employment Offices.

List of PER Offices

ENGLAND

Avon
Minster House, PO Box 185, Baldwin Street, Bristol BS99 7QZ
0272 277217

Bedfordshire
56–62 Park Street, Luton LU1 3JB
0582 417562

Berkshire
20 The Butts Centre, Reading RG1 7QB
0734 595666

Cambridgeshire
Block A, Brooklands Avenue, Cambridge CB2 2HL
0223 354447

Cheshire
75 Sankey Street, Warrington WA1 1SL
0925 52153

Cleveland
1st Floor, Rede House, Corporation Road, Middlesbrough,
Cleveland TS1 1TN
0642 248191

Devon
1st Floor, Cobourg House, Mayflower Street, Plymouth PL1 1SG
0752 669561

Essex
1 High Street, Chelmsford, Essex CM1 1YN
0245 260234

Gloucestershire
Grosvenor House, Station Road, Gloucester GL1 1TA
0452 35525

Hampshire
62–64 High Street, Southampton SO9 2EG
0703 38211

Humberside
Brook Chambers, Ferensway, Hull HU2 8LU
0482 223671

Kent
London House, 5 London Road, Maidstone ME16 8HR
0622 677966

Lancashire
Victoria House, Ormskirk Road, Preston PR1 2DX
0772 59743

Leicestershire
Northampton House, 177 Charles Street, Leicester LE1 1LA
0533 551418

London, Greater

Chislehurst
Suite 5b, 71–75 High Street, Chislehurst, Kent BR7 5AG
01-467 2662

Chiswick
319–327 Chiswick High Road, London W4
01-995 2424

Leytonstone
616–618 High Road, Leytonstone, London E11
01-556 9714

London North, Central and Overseas
4th Floor, Rex House, 4–12 Regent Street, London SW1Y 4PP
Candidate services & enquiries: 01-930 3484
PER Overseas: 01-930 6573/4/5/6/7
London Recruitment Unit: 01-930 3484
London North Recruitment Unit: 01-930 3484

Manchester, Greater
Lowry House, 21 Marble Street, Manchester M2 3AW
061-832 3366

Merseyside
3rd Floor, Graeme House, Derby Square, Liverpool L2 7SP
051-236 2444

Norfolk
Norfolk Tower, Surrey Street, Norwich NR1 3PA
0603 617426

Nottinghamshire
Lambert House East, Clarendon Street, Nottingham NG1 5NS
0602 419781

Surrey
12a Commercial Way, Woking, Surrey GU21 1HG
04862 20003

Sussex, East
53 West Street, Brighton BN1 2RL
0273 23431

Tyne and Wear
1st Floor, Centro House, Cloth Market, Newcastle upon Tyne
NE1 3EE
0632 618418

West Midlands
Fountain Court, Steelhouse Lane, Birmingham B4 6DS
021-236 6971

3rd Floor, Bankfield House, 163 New Union Street, Coventry
CV1 2PE
0203 23265

Yorkshire, South
Chesham House, Charter Row, Sheffield S1 3EB
0742 77556

Yorkshire, West
1st Floor, Pennine House, 6 Russell Street, Leeds LS1 5UF
0532 445131

SCOTLAND

Grampian
3rd Floor, St Martins House, 181 Union Street, Aberdeen
AB9 1BH
0224 574393

Lothian
2–3 Queen Street, Edinburgh EH2 1JS
031-225 2736

Strathclyde
Hellenic House, 87–89 Bath Street, Glasgow G2 2EB
041-333 9655

WALES

Clwyd
Halkyn House, Rhosddu Road, Wrexham LL11 1NE
0978 356575

Glamorgan, South
4th Floor, Pearl Assurance House, Greyfriars, Cardiff CF1 3AG
0222 383286

Glamorgan, West
Grove House, Grove Place, Swansea SA1 5DH
0792 43481

Chapter 3.4

Job Change Schemes

Introduction

Employment Division, through its Jobcentres and Employment Offices, provides three schemes to promote labour mobility; the Employment Transfer Scheme, Job Search Scheme and Free Forward Fares. These provide financial help to encourage jobseekers to look for and take up work in areas where particular vacancies are hard to fill locally.

The Employment Transfer Scheme (ETS)

The aim of the Employment Transfer Scheme (ETS) is to help fill vacancies which cannot be filled locally, by encouraging people with particular and needed skills to move home permanently and fill such vacancies. The encouragement takes the form of financial help and is more likely to be offered to people who have skills which are in demand.

Eligibility and rules

To qualify for financial assistance under this scheme people must be:

— unemployed at the time they are offered a new job;
— residents of Great Britain;
— not able to find a job in their home area;
— intending to settle permanently in the new area.

They must complete part one of the application form *before* they start the job away from home or move to the new area.
  The job they move to must be:

— in Great Britain;
— more than 21 hours per week;
— sufficiently further away from their present home to make daily travelling impossible;

— expected to last for more than one year.

People will *not* be eligible for ETS assistance if they are:

— moving to self-employment;
— moving to employment funded by one of the MSC's special programmes;
— not appointed to a specific job in a specific place when first offered the appointment (for example, civil servants or bank employees who are recruited beforehand and allocated a job later are not eligible);
— offered a gross salary above the limit in force when the application is made.

The future employers also have to show that they could not fill the vacancy locally. (This rule does not apply in the case of registered disabled people.)

ETS assistance is not given to people who have successfully completed a course of higher education (other than as a mature student) in the six months before the date of offer of the new job. During that period they must not have exhausted a period of entitlement for a previous transfer within the previous six months. They or their spouse must not own or be committed to buying or renting a property in the new area, nor must the spouse have a job or the offer of a job in the new area.

These rules and eligibility requirements are complicated and need to be checked carefully from the *Transfer Schemes Handbook* (*TSH*) which can be seen at any Jobcentre, Employment Office or office of PER. The staff at these offices should be happy to explain any of the rules.

Grants and allowances

The maximum period for receiving grants or allowances is one year from the date when the job in the new area starts.

Grants and allowances *may* be paid to cover:

— travel expenses for the claimant to take up the new job;
— travel expenses for dependants to move to the new area;
— a transfer grant to help with incidental expenses of working away from home and moving to a new area;
— legal and estate agents' fees up to a specified limit;
— removal expenses.

Job Search Scheme (JSS)

This scheme gives financial help towards the costs of attending a pre-arranged employment interview away from home to those people who meet all the conditions listed below. Like the ETS, this scheme attempts to fill vacancies which are difficult to fill locally, by encouraging people to look for such vacancies outside their own area. People with skills in a shortage area are more likely to receive assistance. Although the two schemes, JSS and ETS, are related, there are differences; eligibility for JSS assistance does not necessarily mean eligibility for ETS assistance.

Eligibility

Part A of the application form TS1 (INT) must be filled out and received by an MSC office *before* travelling to the interview.
To receive the allowance applicants must:

— be unemployed at the time the interview was offered;
— be residents of Great Britain;
— be unable to find work locally;
— have an offer of an interview for a job too far away for daily travel.

In addition the prospective employer must confirm that there is a good chance that the applicant will get the job. The job and the interview must be in Great Britain and the job should be longer than 21 hours a week and expected to last longer than a year. There are embargoes on the JSS similar to those on the ETS (see above).

Assistance available

If applicants satisfy *all* the basic conditions they could receive the actual cost of a return journey to the interview by public transport and overnight accommodation if necessary.

Free Forward Fares

This scheme provides help for those people who are not eligible for the ETS, to travel to take up work.

Take Up and Cost of Schemes

During 1983–85 4356 people took advantage of the JSS, 3299 of the ETS and 9352 of FFF. The cost to the MSC for all three schemes in 1983–85 was £4.5 million — a reduction of £500,000 on the previous year.

Issues

These schemes are not widely known or understood among the general public. Many jobseekers who attempt to take advantage of them find the requirement that forms must be submitted before the interview or job start impractical and the whole procedure over-complicated.

Further Information

Full details of the rules and how the Transfer Schemes operate are available in the *Transfer Scheme Handbook* (*TSH*) which can be seen at any Jobcentre, Employment office or office of PER. Also look at leaflets EPL 104, EPL 103 and EPL 136.

Chapter 3.5

Employment Rehabilitation Centres (ERCs)

Introduction

The MSC has 27 Employment Rehabilitation Centres (ERCs) and also funds rehabilitation courses run by voluntary bodies and local authorities for particular groups of disabled people. The ERCs are designed to help disabled people think about suitable work or training, because they have either been out of work for some time or have lost their job because of illness or injury. Clients do not have to be registered disabled to attend an ERC. With the increase in unemployment, ERCs are being used more frequently to assess people who have been unemployed for a long period of time. An ERC does not teach a trade but provides an assessment of a client's ability to perform certain tasks, by offering a variety of work experience under similar conditions to those in a factory or office. The assessment concentrates on the manipulative and practical skills of a job and on the ability to follow instructions. It is geared less towards testing qualities, such as organising ability, managerial skills and initiative, which are harder to define and test.

During 1984–85 nearly 17,000 people attended the centres and about 29 per cent were resettled into jobs after their course, an increase of almost 5 per cent on the previous year.

Courses

Courses are arranged according to each person's needs and the choice of work they can sample includes: commercial or clerical, bench engineering, machine operating, light work such as assembly, packing, electrical, woodwork, and outdoor work. A course normally lasts for six to eight weeks but it can last up to 26 weeks. It is possible to take an adult training course at a Skillcentre or college of further education after finishing at an ERC.

Allowances

There is a weekly allowance similar to that of the Job Training Scheme (Chapter 3.15) for people attending ERCs and help with travel and allowances for dependants. Two of the centres offer residential accommodation.

How to Get on a Course

Clients are referred to a centre, usually by the Disablement Resettlement Officer. They will spend one or two days initially at the centre before being accepted on to a course. If they are accepted they can start as soon as a place is free.

Funding

The total cost of employment rehabilitation in 1984–85 was to be £19.6 million. For 1984, the European Social Fund allocated over £6 million to this programme.

Numbers

In 1983–85, 16,486 people (including 15,030 young people) attended rehabilitation courses and about 29 per cent were resettled into jobs, Community Programme places or Youth Training Schemes after their course. In April 1984, 593 staff were employed in this programme.

Future Developments

The 1985–89 Corporate Plan indicates the MSC's intention to increase the number of disabled people attending the ERCs and to place an increased emphasis on resettlement into employment and further training. A further improvement to the rehabilitation service has been the recent introduction of ASSET (Assistance Towards Employment) teams. These provide a specialist vocational assessment and rehabilitation service to areas not directly served by an ERC.

Issues

A very small proportion of ERC trainees are women, and it is felt by some outside the MSC that ERCs could better meet the needs of women. For example, they do not have child care facilities and courses are generally full time, often from 8am until 4.45pm.

Further Information

Ask at the Jobcentre or Employment Office for leaflets EPL 107 and EPL 86.

List of Employment Rehabilitation Centres

The following list includes all ERCs operational in Great Britain at the start of 1985.

ENGLAND

Avon
Gill Avenue, Fishponds, Bristol BS16 2QG
0272 653241

Cleveland
Leeholme Road, Billingham on Tees TS23 3TE
0642 560811

Devon
Strode Road, Plympton, Plymouth PL7 4BG
0752 335921

Hampshire
Scott Road, Hilsea, Portsmouth PO3 5LF
0703 68831

Hertfordshire
High Elms Lane, near Watford, Hertfordshire WD2 7JX
09273 73388

Humberside
Chamberlain Road, Hull HU8 8HL
0482 20738

Lancashire
Dovedale Avenue, Ingol, Preston PR2 3WN
0772 728211

Schemes and Services

Leicestershire	Humberstone Lane, Leicester LE4 7JW 0533 769101
London, Greater	Stafford Road, Waddon, Croydon CR9 4DE 01-688 6191
	Walmgate Road, Perivale, Greenford, Middlesex UB6 7NE 01-991 1941/1988
Manchester, Greater	Windmill Lane, Denton, Manchester M34 3GS 061-336 5451
Merseyside	Stopgate Lane, Liverpool L9 6AN 051-525 9331
Nottinghamshire	Wilsthorpe Road, Long Eaton, Nottingham NG10 3HH 06076 61311
Staffordshire	Clough Street, Hanley, Stoke-on-Trent ST1 4AS 0782 261521
Surrey	'Woodlee', London Road, Egham PW20 0HH 0784 34393
Tyne and Wear	Green Lane, Felling on Tyne, Gateshead NE10 0LA 0632 694314
	Harvey Combe, Station Road, Killingworth, Newcastle upon Tyne NE12 0QQ 0632 68272
West Midlands	Vincent Drive, Edgbaston, Birmingham B15 2TH 021-472 7151

	Torrington Avenue, Tile Hill, Coventry CV4 9GR 0203 468141
Yorkshire, South	Richmond Park Road, Sheffield S13 8HT 0742 446471
Yorkshire, West	Parkside Lane, Hunslet, Leeds LE11 5SZ 0532 704661

SCOTLAND

Lothian	West Granton Road, Edinburgh EH5 1JB 031-551 1461
Strathclyde	Industrial Estate, Queen Elizabeth Avenue, Hillington, Glasgow G52 4TL 041-810 3111
	Bellshill Industrial Estate, Bellshill, Lanarkshire NL4 3GE 0698 748667
Tayside	Staffa Place, Dundee DD2 3XB 0382 816633

WALES

Glamorgan, South	Western Avenue, Cardiff CF4 2XY 0222 371311
Glamorgan, West	Cramic Way, Port Talbot SA13 1RY 0639 64691

Chapter 3.6

Other Help for People with Disabilities

Introduction

All the schemes and services offered by the MSC are open to disabled people but, in addition, there are certain special schemes and services which are specifically designed to meet the needs of this particular group of people; for example schemes to help people cope with rehabilitation, retraining and resettlement. Some are available only to people who are registered disabled under the 1944 and 1958 Employment Acts. Many of the schemes also provide financial assistance to employers.

In 1982 the MSC published a *Review of Assistance for Disabled People*, the proposals of which have now been implemented. This has meant a reorganisation of facilities at a local level, so that people with disabilities are encouraged to use the Jobcentre services in the same way as other clientele, and are referred to a Disablement Resettlement Officer (DRO) only if they require specialist help. It has also led to the setting up of the Disablement Advisory Service (DAS — described below).

This chapter outlines the many schemes and services provided for disabled people by the MSC whether provided by Employment Division or Training Division.

Definition of 'disability'

'A person who, on account of injury, disease or congenital deformity is substantially handicapped in obtaining or keeping employment or in undertaking work on his own account, of a kind which apart from that injury, disease or deformity would be suited to his age, experience or qualifications.'
(Disabled Persons (Employment) Act 1944)

Registration

This is known colloquially as 'having a green card'. When someone registers as a disabled person they are registering under section 1 or 2 of the Employment Act 1944. Section 1 refers to people who are capable of open employment; section 2 refers to people who are capable of sheltered employment.

Registration is purely voluntary and takes place via the DRO. This is not the same as registering with the Local Authority Social Services in order to receive their special services, although many people think it is.

Specialist Staff

Work of the Disablement Advisory Service (DAS)

First established in April 1983, the Disablement Advisory Service now consists of 62 small, specialist, area-based teams. Each team consists of two or more people who work mainly with employers, and who may have special responsibilities for blind or partially sighted people.

The Service's main aim is to encourage employers to adopt a more progressive approach to the employment of disabled people. It offers practical advice to employers, including information on the MSC's special schemes and services for disabled people at work, and on employers' obligations under the Quota scheme. The service also provides advice and guidance to disabled people at work. The cost of the service in 1983–84 was £2.4 million.

The Disablement Resettlement Officer (DRO)

Since the implementation of the MSC's Review, the DRO's work has become more specialised. As disabled people can receive help from the Jobcentre services in the normal way, DROs can now spend more time with individuals when required. Most of their time is spent dealing with people who are likely to find and keep employment. They provide access to a range of services for people with disabilities and for those who employ or intend to employ them. Their responsibilities include:

— registration;
— admissions to sheltered employment;
— advice and guidance on training and employment opportunities;
— administration of the special schemes for disabled people and employers.

There are approximately 450 DROs and senior DROs based at Jobcentres throughout the country.

The Blind Persons' Resettlement Officer (BPRO)

The BPRO has a similar function to the DRO but works with blind and partially sighted people, and is often part of a DAS team.

Blind Persons' Training Officer (BPTO)

There are 11 Blind Persons' Training Officers (BPTO) who are skilled engineers with wide industrial experience. They carry out initial training on the job and advise on technical matters and aids for blind people in employment. They can visit employers' premises to identify suitable work for blind and partially sighted people and make follow-up visits to ensure that the visually handicapped person is able to do his/her work safely. Further training is given where necessary.

Sheltered Employment

Sheltered employment is provided under the Disabled Persons (Employment) Acts, 1944 and 1958, for severely disabled people who are unlikely to obtain or keep employment except under special sheltered conditions. In July 1976 the MSC took over the administrative and co-ordinating functions from the Secretary of State for Employment.

There are 226 workshops and factories run by REMPLOY, local authorities and voluntary organisations which provide sheltered employment for over 14,000 severely disabled people.

The MSC's role is to subsidise places of sheltered work by contributing towards the difference in costs between real costs and what is received from the sale of goods and services.

Sheltered employment is provided by two broad groups:

— REMPLOY, a limited company funded solely by the government. It is centrally managed and pays its workers a full wage out of which the normal taxes and deductions are made;
— independent workshops, operated under the control of local authorities or voluntary bodies, employing people with severe disabilities.

The Commission funds a major proportion of the sheltered employment available. 1983–84 total funding amounted to £72.7 million (£51.9 million to REMPLOY, £15.3 million to local authorities, £4.1 million to independent voluntary bodies). This is reimbursed in full by the Department of Employment.

REMPLOY is the largest provider of sheltered employment for severely disabled people. It was formed in 1945 and now has 95 factories and employs over 8850 severely disabled people. It organises its work into three different product groups:

— leather and textile products
— furniture and medical equipment
— packaging and assembly

and sells a wide range of goods and services at prices based on fit labour costs.

There are 131 independent sheltered workshops which together employ approximately 5600 severely disabled people.

Sheltered Industrial Group (SIG) Scheme

A Sheltered Industrial Group is an individual or group of people with disabilities, working in an ordinary industrial or commercial setting. Although SIGs are part of the services offered under the umbrella term of 'sheltered employment' they are less well known and understood than the other aspects of 'sheltered employment'. The first Sheltered Industrial Group was set up in Leeds in 1960. There are now over 1000 people employed in SIGs.

The SIG scheme is a way for severely disabled workers — whose disability means they cannot achieve the output of a fully fit worker — to work at an ordinary industrial or commercial job, while having a measure of protection from some of its demands. It is a scheme for people whose disability would make it difficult for them to do a job in a normal working environment.

A host company provides the work and pays for the value of work done, a sponsoring organisation — a local authority, a voluntary body or REMPLOY — is the legal employer and pays the full rate for the job irrespective of output achieved.

The Sheltered Employment Branch of MSC pays grants to the sponsor to offset any loss.

Workers within the SIG receive the rate for the job including locally agreed weightings, after consultation with trade union representatives from all three parties concerned.

Sheltered Employment Procurement and Consultancy Service (SEPACS)

SEPACS is part of the MSC's Employment Division and its aim is to help sheltered workshops operate more efficiently. It is organised into four regional teams served by a central administration section. It has the following main functions:

— to provide a brokerage service to encourage buyers to purchase from workshops;
— to provide a consultancy service to help workshops operate more efficiently;
— to consider and process applications from workshops for grants for capital equipment.

Residential Colleges

The MSC supports four residential colleges run by voluntary bodies for people with disabilities. The colleges offer a range of courses including business studies, secretarial studies, bench carpentry, horticulture, computer programming, basic work skills, literacy and numeracy courses.

Each course varies in length and may be extended to meet individual needs, but most are about 26 weeks long. Some offer the opportunity to gain qualifications, others do not. Trainees receive a training allowance at the same rate as at Skillcentres. Disabled people from any part of the country can apply for a place through their local DRO or careers officer.

Finchale Training College
Durham DH1 5RX
0385 62634

Portland Training College
Harlow Wood
Nottingham Road
Mansfield
Nottingham NG18 4TJ
062 34 2141/2

Queen Elizabeth's Training College
Leatherhead
Surrey KT22 0BN
037 284 2204

St Loyes College for the training of the disabled for commerce
and industry
Fairfield House
Topsham Road
Exeter
Devon EX2 6EP
0392 55428

Schemes Offering Financial Help to Employers

There are several different schemes to help employers, some of
which are only offered to those employing people who are
registered under the Employment Acts of 1944 and 1958.

Grants of up to £6000 are available to employers to make
essential adaptations to premises and equipment to enable them
to recruit or retain in employment a specific person with
disabilities. Financial assistance and advice in altering premises
and equipment is available through the Disablement Advisory
Service. During 1983–84, 180 adaptations were approved under
this scheme.

Special tools or equipment needed by a disabled person to
overcome a particular handicap in order to keep or obtain a job,
can also be issued on free permanent loan to that individual.
1400 such aids were loaned in 1983–84.

Job Introduction Scheme (JIS)

This scheme allows for grants to be given to employers who offer
a job trial to certain disabled people. As an inducement to those
employers who have reservations about employing a disabled
person, the MSC will pay a contribution (£45 per week) to the
employer's wages bill for a period of six weeks; 1900 disabled
people were placed under this scheme during 1983–84.

Individual training throughout with an employer

This scheme offers financial assistance to employers who can
give skilled or semi-skilled training to a disabled person to whom
they are able to offer at least six months' paid employment after
the training is completed.

Release for Training Scheme

Financial assistance may be available under this scheme to enable employers to train or retrain an employee who is disabled and experiencing problems at work. Special arrangements can be made to provide the training.

Special Help for People with Visual Disabilities

Personal reader service

This service can give financial assistance to enable blind and partially sighted people to engage a part-time reader in order to overcome particular difficulties at work. The scheme is administered by the Royal National Institute for the Blind and during 1983–84 about 125 people were helped under this service.

Training for blind people

The Royal National Institute for the Blind's Commercial College in London offers courses in computer programming, shorthand and typing, audio typing and telephone switchboard operating.

Courses in piano tuning lasting two years or more are available at the London College of Furniture, the Royal National College for the Blind, Hereford, and Stevenson College in Edinburgh.

The Letchworth Skillcentre provides introductory courses in light engineering occupations.

Sheltered employment

There are 127 local authority and voluntary body workshops which provide employment for over 5000 blind and severely disabled sighted people. Some voluntary bodies provide sheltered employment on an agency basis for local authorities. The MSC provides capital grants towards expenditure on buildings, plant machinery and capitation grants to meet revenue losses in running workshops.

Fares to Work

This scheme offers financial assistance to certain people with severe disabilities who are unable to use public transport to get to work. Grants of up to 75 per cent of the cost of fares to and from work are paid by the MSC, up to a maximum of £57 per week. The scheme is administered by the DAS teams although DROs handle individual applications.

To meet the conditions of the scheme, applicants must:

— be registered disabled;
— be unable to use public transport because of their disabilities;
— incur extra costs in travelling to work because of disability.

This scheme is very under-used. In 1983, in South London about 30 people claimed assistance.

Professional Training Scheme for Disabled People

Disabled people with the necessary educational qualifications may train for a professional career and obtain a LEA grant in the usual way. If grants are not available, the MSC's Professional Training Scheme for Disabled People may provide financial help for an approved course likely to lead to professional work. Students who take advantage of this scheme have to follow the normal methods of training for the profession concerned. The exception to this is the Royal National Institute for the Blind's School of Physiotherapy in London.

Financial help includes:

— maintenance grant for trainee and any dependants;
— payment of tuition and examination fees.

Entitlement to a grant and its amount would depend on the individual's circumstances.

'Fit for Work' Campaign

A large-scale ongoing campaign was introduced by the MSC in 1979 to encourage employers to look at new ways of providing equal opportunities for people with disabilities; the Fit for Work Award Scheme gives public recognition to firms and organisations which excel in carrying out constructive policies.

The Awards are presented annually to employers who have done most to help disabled people show what they can do, given a reasonable chance to prove themselves. In its first three years, over 300 Award winners were selected from over 11,500 applications.

For further information contact:
MSC (ESG3)
Fit for Work Central Awards Unit (Room W1030)
Moorfoot
Sheffield S1 4PQ

Quota

The Quota system was set up as a result of the 1944 and 1958
Employment Acts and is administered and enforced by the
Manpower Services Commission.

The legislation places a duty and not an obligation on
employers of 20 or more workers to employ a quota of registered
disabled people. The standard quota is presently 3 per cent of the
total staff and applies to all commercial and industrial firms,
local authorities and nationalised industries. It is not an offence
to be below quota, but in this situation an employer has a further
duty to engage suitable registered disabled people if any are
available when vacancies arise.

The Quota system is much criticised and often ignored, and
less than half of employers covered by the system employ their
quota of people with disabilities. Because so many people with
disabilities fail to register under the Acts, it would be impossible
for all employers to fulfil their duty.

Further Information

The MSC has produced numerous leaflets explaining the various
practical and financial schemes available. Many can be obtained
from Jobcentres or Employment Offices. Employers seeking
information and advice should contact their local DAS team via
the Jobcentre.

List of leaflets

The following leaflets have been produced by the MSC.

EPL 30   *Employment Rehabilitation Centres*
EPL 37   *Rehabilitation, Retraining, Resettlement*
              Employment Services for Disabled People
EPL 38   *Employing Someone who is Deaf or Hard of Hearing*

EPL 39 *Helping Your Patient Back to Work*
          (medical profession leaflet)
EPL 40 *Employing Someone with Epilepsy*
EPL 41 *Into Work*
EPL 44 *Employing Someone who is Mentally Handicapped*
EPL 57 *Employment Rehabilitation Allowances*
EPL 63 *Employing Someone who is Blind or Partially Sighted*
EPL 64 *Helping Your Clients Back to Work*
          (social worker leaflet)
EPL 71 *Aids and Adaptations for Disabled Employees*
EPL 86 *Employment Rehabilitation Centres*
EPL 93 *Employing People who have had a Mental Illness*
EPL 95 *Sheltered Industrial Groups*
EPL 97 *Employment Rehabilitation Centres (Helping Young People)*
EPL 98 *Employing Someone with Haemophilia*
EPL 99 *Sheltered Employment and You*
EPL 100 *Fit for Work Award Scheme*
EPL 107 *Employment Rehabilitation Centres*
DPL   1 *The Disabled Persons Register*
          (medical profession leaflet)
DPL 13 *Assistance with Fares to Work Scheme for Severely Disabled People*
TSDN 127 *Training Opportunities for Disabled People*
TSDN 278 *Residential Training for Disabled People*

New Outlook. A quarterly newspaper aimed at employers. It deals with issues relating to the employment of disabled people and gives information about various forms of help.

Code of Good Practice on the Employment of Disabled People. This is a handbook for employers setting out specific and realistic objectives and listing schemes and services available from MSC and other organisations. Launched in November 1984, it also lists many further sources of help and is obtainable from the MSC headquarters in Moorfoot, Sheffield.

Chapter 3.7

Community Programme (CP)

Introduction

The Community Programme (CP) is the latest major initiative in a series of MSC responses to long-term unemployment amongst adults. It provides certain unemployed people over 18 with up to a year's temporary full- or part-time work on projects of benefit to the community. Its stated aim is to help improve employability for this group of people by providing work experience, in some cases training, and a recent work reference from an employer. The Programme is administered by the Commission, on behalf of the Department of Employment, through its Employment Division. The cost to the MSC in 1984–85 was £534 million, although the net cost to the Exchequer is about one-fifth of the gross cost to the MSC. The total budget for 1985–86 is £720 million and for 1986–87, £1.18 billion.

History

The programme was launched in October 1982 as a development from and replacement for the Community Enterprise Programme (CEP), which in turn had replaced the Special Temporary Employment Programme (STEP) and Job Creation Programme (JCP). After a slow start, CP expanded at a faster rate than had been budgeted for and at the end of 1983 many applications were frozen. In January 1984, however, the Commission switched £15 million from the underspent YTS budget to the Community Programme.

The total gross cost of the Programme in 1983–84 which was fully reimbursed by the Department of Employment was around £400 million. By November 1985, the Programme offered 160,000 places throughout Great Britain. Additional funds were made available in the March 1985 budget to increase the number of available places to 230,000 by May 1986.

Eligibility Criteria

Participants within the Programme must be long-term unemployed adults. For the 18–24 age group, participants must have been registered out of work for six of the previous nine months. Participants over 25 must have been registered unemployed for 12 out of the previous 15 months. For all ages, the participants must have been unemployed continuously for the previous two months. People employed on CP projects should not be within a year of normal retirement age on the day the job is due to start. There are occasional exceptions to these rules, particularly for managerial and supervisory staff and there are special eligibility conditions for disabled people.

Since October 1984, only people in receipt of benefit, and fulfilling certain other criteria have been eligible for CP places, a criterion ruling out many married women not claiming benefit.

Projects

The MSC criteria state that projects should involve work that

— is of benefit to the local community;
— would not otherwise have been done;
— can be done by, and is suited to, the local people who have been unemployed for some time;
— will last longer than three months and up to one year initially;
— will not substitute paid employment for work which would normally be done by volunteers;
— will pay the normal 'rate for the job' to workers on the projects.

Projects have included work for the British Trust for Conservation Volunteers, work with archaeologists, genealogical work transcribing parish records, word and data processing work. Examples of sponsoring agencies include polytechnics, borough and county councils and voluntary bodies. The size of individual projects varies but on average they tend to involve about 20 people.

The MSC will pay for:

— wages, within certain limits. Since October 1984 the maximum average wage for participant workers has been

£63 per week. A survey in January 1984 revealed that the average gross weekly wage of managers and supervisors was £117.41 and of other participant workers £58.46;
— employers' National Insurance and superannuation contributions;
— operating costs up to £440 per approved place, over 52 weeks, not including managers and supervisors' places;
— training, which may be funded out of the operating costs element and from the wages element up to a maximum of £10 per head per week.

Full-time CP workers (plus part-time CP participants working at least an average of 15 hours per week) who are eligible for supplementary benefit may claim payments for working clothing when they start work on the programme.

Training within CP

CP is not a training scheme and many projects lack any formal training element. Despite this, the programme can be used to train participants (both on or off the job and by day or block release) if it relates to the work of the project or improves the workers' prospects of permanent paid employment. Training costs can be funded from: the project's operating costs, up to £10 per employee of weekly wage allowance, the agent's fee, or any outside source. CP participants may also take part in training linked to the Wider Opportunities Training Programme (see Chapter 3.19).

Sponsors

Any organisation or group of individuals (but not single individuals) can sponsor a project; for example, local authorities, voluntary bodies, trade unions, charities or local community groups. In practice, about half of all CP schemes were sponsored by voluntary organisations and a further 47 per cent by local authorities in 1984.

Sponsors are responsible for managing and administering their own projects. In practice, large managing agents (such as local authorities) have tended to provide such a service for smaller initiatives wishing to offer CP places.

Participants

About 30 per cent of the 160,000 participants in the Community Programme are women. About 4 per cent of participants are disabled people. By May 1986, the programme plans to provide 230,000 places and is funded at least until 1987.

Issues

In the autumn of 1984, changes in eligibility for the Community Programme restricted the numbers of married women eligible to join the scheme since new entrants had to be registered ie in receipt of benefit. It is expected that this will lead to a substantial fall in the number of women in the programme, closing off an opportunity for employment for a significant number of people.

New Developments

In March 1985, expansion plans for the programme were announced and the MSC earmarked £10 million for experimental initiatives. These involved:

— exploring new ways of encouraging greater involvement by commercial and industrial employers in the programme — for example, by sponsoring projects;
— new schemes for charities and voluntary agencies which, although they may be unable to sponsor 'traditional' CP projects, may be able to provide employment opportunities for unemployed people;
— expansion of the Voluntary Projects Programme (see Chapter 3.9).

The second development, the so-called Charities Initiative, was launched nationally in November 1985 with a budget of £3 million and the intention to help charities create up to 1000 new jobs. Under the new initiative, charities are able to 'graft on' additional posts to their organisations and recruit long-term unemployed people to fill them rather than having to establish specific projects.

Under the initiative, the MSC pays a grant of £75 per week for each week up to a year that a person, eligible under CP is employed for a minimum of 16 hours, in an approved post. Contracts under the initiative are for up to two years, subject to a

12 month review. The posts created under this initiative bypasses Area Manpower Board approval procedures.

Further Information

How to apply

Prospective sponsors should contact their local Jobcentre or the link team in the area. The link team office keeps and processes the application forms.

Adults wishing to work on a project should apply to their local Jobcentre.

Community Programme News

This is a free quarterly magazine, obtainable from MSC headquarters at Moorfoot (Room E824, dept CPN).

Leaflets EPL 113, EPL 114 and EPL 122 can be obtained from Employment Offices or Jobcentres.

List of Community Programme Link Team Addresses

Below follows a list of area link teams which provide information for existing and potential schemes, current at June 1985.

ENGLAND

London

Bexley, Bromley, Lewisham, Greenwich and Dartford

Jobcentre, 4–8 Pound Place, SE9 5DS
01-859 5717

City of London, Enfield, Haringey, Islington and Hackney

Jobcentre, 54a High Road, Wood Green, N22 6BX
01-889 0991

Hammersmith, Fulham, Kensington, Chelsea, Ealing, Hounslow, Hillingdon

Jobcentre, 319–327 Chiswick High Road, Chiswick, W4 4HH
01-995 4071

North West London, Westminster, North London, North East London

Jobcentre, 120 Finchley Road, Swiss Cottage, London NW3 5JB
01-794 8168

South London	Jobcentre, 92 Borough High Street, Southwark, London SE1 1LT 01-403 2055
South West London and North West Surrey	Jobcentre, Woburn House, 155 Falcon Road, SW11 2PD 01-350 1011
Waltham Forest, Tower Hamlets, Newham, Redbridge, Barking and Havering	Jobcentre, 714–720 Green Lane, Dagenham, Essex RM8 1YJ 01-598 8712

Midlands

Birmingham, Aston and Sutton Coldfield	Jobcentre, Acorn House, 196 High Street, Erdington, Birmingham B23 6TL 021-382 7766
Derbyshire	Jobcentre, Gower House, Gower Street, Derby DE1 1JU 0332 372631
Dudley and Sandwell	Jobcentre, 108 High Street, Smethwick, Warley, West Midlands B66 1AA 021-565 2771
Leicestershire	Jobcentre, Charles Street, Leicester LE1 3JD 0533 531221
Lincolnshire	Jobcentre, 280–281 High Street, Lincoln LN2 1LL 0522 40511
Northamptonshire	Jobcentre, Dryland Centre, Kettering, Northamptonshire NN16 0BE 0536 524673
Nottinghamshire	Lambert House, Clarendon Street, Nottingham NG1 5NS 0602 586633

Shropshire	Jobcentre, Priness House, 17–19 The Square, Shrewsbury, Shropshire SY1 1YA 0743 57321
Staffordshire	Jobcentre, 15 Brickhouse Street, Burslem, Staffordshire ST6 3AY 0782 813421
Warwickshire	Jobcentre, Bankfield House, 163 New Union Street, Coventry CV1 2QQ 0203 555133
Wolverhampton and Walsall	Jobcentre, 55 High Street, Wednesfield, Wolverhampton WV11 1ST 0902 736053
Worcestershire and Herefordshire	Jobcentre, Haswell House, St Nicholas Street, Worcester WR1 1UW 0905 26486

Northern

County Durham	Valley Street North, Darlington, County Durham DL1 1TJ 0325 51166
Newcastle, Northumberland, Haltwhistle, Prudhoe and Hexham	Jobcentre, Broadacre House, Market Street, Newcastle upon Tyne NE1 6HH 0632 326181
Teesside and Hartlepool	Jobcentre, Rede House, Corporation Road, Middlesbrough, Cleveland TS1 1TN 0642 248191
Wearside, Felling, Gateshead, Jarrow, South Shields and Blaydon	Jobcentre, 22–24 Walworth Way, Sunderland, Tyne and Wear SR1 3DR 0783 44133

North West

Blackpool, Fylde, Lancaster, Preston, Ribble, and Wyre	Jobcentre, Duchy House, 96 Lancaster Road, Preston, Lancashire PR1 1SQ 0772 59393
Bolton, Wigan, and Ashton in Makerfield	Jobcentre, 29–31 Market Street, Westhoughton, Bolton, Lancashire BL5 3AG 0942 816615
Bury and Rochdale	Jobcentre, 71–75 Long Street, Middleton, Manchester M24 3TT 061-653 2800
City of Manchester	Employment Office, Aytoun Street, Manchester M60 7HS 061-236 4433
Cheshire	Rylands House, Ryland Street, Warrington WA1 1DD 0925 58444
Cumbria	Employment Office, 1st Floor, Post Office Buildings, 4 Station Street, Cockermouth CA13 9QL 0900 826349
Knowsley, St Helens and Sefton	Jobcentre, 15 La Grange Arcade, Shopping Precinct, St Helens, Merseyside WA10 1BP 0744 54251
Liverpool	Jobcentre, 1st Floor, Stanley Road, Bootle, Merseyside L20 3PN 051-933 7077
Salford and Trafford	Jobcentre, Arndale House, Chester Road, Stretford, Manchester M32 9ED 061-865 3373

South Lancashire

Jobcentre, 12 Lord Street,
Blackburn, Lancashire BB2 1LP
0254 678911

Stockport, Tameside, High
Peak and Oldham

Jobcentre, 59 Market Street,
Hyde, Cheshire SK14 2AJ
061-366 0318

Wirral

Jobcentre, 4–6 Milton Pavement,
Grange Precinct, Birkenhead,
Merseyside L41 2YF
051-647 4621

South East

Bedfordshire and
Cambridgeshire

Jobcentre, 14–16 Chapel Street,
Luton, Bedfordshire LU1 2SU
0582 37551

Berkshire

7th Floor, Bridge House,
Reading RG1 8PY
0734 586262

Buckinghamshire, Hertfordshire
and Oxfordshire

Jobcentre, 44–45 Oxford Street,
High Wycombe, Buckingham-
shire HP11 2EY
0494 450351

Essex

Jobcentre, 5 New London Road,
Chelmsford, Essex CM2 0LZ
0245 359044

Hampshire and Isle of Wight

Jobcentre, 91–92 High Street,
Winchester, Hampshire
SO23 9AP
0962 55487

Kent

Area Office, Kingsley House,
37–45 Balmoral Road,
Gillingham, Kent
0634 578121

Norfolk

Jobcentre, 1 Theatre Street,
Norwich NR2 1TE
0603 611291

Suffolk

Jobcentre, 22 Lloyds Avenue,
Ipswich IP1 3HP
0473 217471

Sussex, East

Jobcentre, 13–15 Old Steine,
Brighton, East Sussex BN1 1EX
0273 693599

West Sussex and South Surrey

Jobcentre, 88 High Street,
Littlehampton, West Sussex
BN17 5DX
0273 693559

South West

Avon

PO Box 185, Minster House,
27 Baldwin Street, Bristol
BS99 7QZ
0272 273710

Cornwall

Jobcentre, Circuit House, St
Clements Street, Truro TR1 1DZ
0872 3186/9

Devon

Jobcentre, 25 Guildhall
Shopping Centre, Exeter
EX4 3HQ
0392 33851

Dorset and Somerset

1st Floor, Bracken House,
14–16 Christchurch Road,
Bournemouth BH1 3NE
0202 22055

Gloucestershire and Wiltshire

Spur 5, Block B, Elmbridge
Court, Gloucester GL3 1AG
0452 21421

Yorkshire and Humberside

Barnsley and Doncaster

Jobcentre, 12–16 Midland Street,
Barnsley, South Yorkshire
S70 1SE
0226 243111

Bradford, Huddersfield, Spen Valley, Batley and Dewsbury	27 Petergate, Bradford, West Yorkshire BD1 1HB 0274 723711
Sheffield and Rotherham	7th Floor, Chesham House, Charter Row, Sheffield S1 3EB 0742 752253
Leeds	Jobcentre, Fairfax House, Merrion Street, Leeds LS2 8LH 0532 446181
North Humberside (excluding Goole)	Jobcentre, Queens House, 44–46 Paragon Street, Hull HU1 3NZ 0482 27065
North Yorkshire	Jobcentre, 13 Piccadilly, York, YO1 1PF 0904 59251/7
South Humberside and Goole	Jobcentre, 43 Freeman Street, Grimsby DN32 7AE 0472 55293
Wakefield	Jobcentre, 24 Wood Street, Wakefield, West Yorkshire WF1 2ED 0924 371901

SCOTLAND

Ayrshire, Dumfries and Galloway	Jobcentre, 8–14 Arthur Street, Ayr KA7 1NH 0292 68721
Central Region and Fife	5 Kirk Loan, Corstophine, Edinburgh EH12 7HQ 031-334 9821
Glasgow (Local Authority Projects)	Jobcentre, Hellenic House, 87–97 Bath Street, Glasgow G2 2EB 041-332 9452
Glasgow	Jobcentre, 1480 Maryhill Road, Glasgow G20 9DJ 041-945 0114

Grampian and Tayside Regions	Jobcentre, City House, 16 Overgate, Dundee, Angus DD1 1UP 0382 23061
Highland Region, Western, Orkney and Shetland Isles	Jobcentre, Metropolitan House, 31-33 High Street, Inverness IV1 1JD 0463 39171
Lanarkshire	Jobcentre, Brandon Street, Hamilton ML3 6AB 0698 283399
Lothian and Borders Regions	Jobcentre, 11-13 South St Andrews Street, Edinburgh EH2 2BT 031-556 9211
Renfrewshire, Dumbartonshire, Argyll and Bute	Jobcentre, 53 Central Way, Paisley, Renfrewshire PA1 1EN 041-887 7801

WALES

Clwyd, Powys and Gwynedd	Jobcentre, 2 King Street, Wrexham, Clwyd LL11 1NS 0978 56001
Glamorgan, Mid	9 High Street, Pontypridd CF37 1QJ 0443 403532
Glamorgan, South	Jobcentre, 101 St Mary Street, Cardiff, South Glamorgan CF1 1LS 0222 399931
Gwent	Jobcentre, John Frost Square, Newport, Gwent NP1 1XH 0633 53571
West Wales	Jobcentre, Grove House, 2-3 Grove Place, Swansea, West Glamorgan SA1 5DH 0792 41451

Enterprise Allowance Scheme

Introduction

The Enterprise Allowance Scheme (EAS) provides funding for up to a year to certain unemployed adults who wish to start their own businesses. The belief that an immediate loss of supplementary or unemployment benefit deters unemployed people from setting up their own business was a key reason for the introduction of this scheme. By providing a flat rate allowance to previously unemployed entrepreneurs, the scheme aims to reduce this disincentive.

History

The scheme was first established, on an experimental basis, in five pilot areas from February 1982. It was launched by the MSC on a nationwide basis in August 1983.

Administration

The scheme is administered by specialist teams working from about 70 Jobcentres, with the assistance of the Department of Industry's Small Firms Service and, in Scotland and Wales, the appropriate Development Agency.

It offers a taxable allowance (presently £40 per week) to successful applicants for up to one year, to compensate for loss of benefit and to tide them over while they build up their business. Potential entrepreneurs attend a compulsory two-hour group counselling session with a representative from the Small Firms Service, and the Service also offers three further free sessions on a one-to-one basis.

Eligibility Criteria

The scheme is open to people over 18 in England, Scotland and

Wales who have been out of work for a minimum of 13 weeks and been in receipt of unemployment or supplementary benefit. In order to qualify, applicants must have an acceptable business idea and show that they have or can borrow at least £1000 to invest in the business.

To join the scheme applicants must satisfy all the following conditions, without exception. They must:

— be receiving unemployment or supplementary benefit at the time of application;
— have been unemployed for at least 13 weeks before application (under certain conditions, a period spent under formal notice of redundancy may be counted);
— show that they have available at least £1000 to invest in the business;
— be 18 or over and under pensionable age;
— agree to work full time in the business.

In addition, the proposed business venture must be approved by the MSC as suitable for public support.

No one may enter the scheme more than once.

Approved businesses

The proposed business venture must be:

— *New:* people who propose to take over an existing business will not be accepted on to the scheme;
— *Independent:* the business must not be a subsidiary or be financially supported by another business; nor should it have a relationship with another company which provides essential operating services. People acting as agents will not be accepted on to the scheme;
— *Small:* applications will not be accepted from people who intend to employ more than 20 workers during the first three months of operation.

Application Procedure

People wishing to apply to the scheme should ask their local Jobcentre to be included in an Enterprise Allowance Scheme information session, which provides details about how the scheme operates. Places on this information session are limited and only people who fulfil the eligibility conditions will be given a place. Forms of application to the scheme will only be given to those who have attended an information session. The date when the form is received at the Jobcentre is taken as the date of application for the purpose of satisfying most of the eligibility conditions. The Jobcentre decides from the details on the application form who is eligible to proceed to the next stage, which is an appointment with a member of staff at the Jobcentre administering the Enterprise Allowance Scheme. At this stage evidence of the £1000 to invest in the business is necessary. The signing of an agreement between the applicant and someone at the Jobcentre marks entry on to the scheme.

There are periodic checks to ensure that people continue to remain eligible to receive the allowance which is paid directly into the business bank account once a fortnight after the agreement has been signed. The allowance is taxable.

Evaluation of the Scheme

The Enterprise Allowance Scheme has proved a popular initiative. Between its national launch and October 1985, more than 100,000 people had entered the scheme which, in 1985, was attracting more than 1200 new people each week. More than 50 per cent of entrants to April 1985 were under the age of 35 — and 20 per cent were under 25.

While the scheme does allow up to ten people to join together, most (86 per cent) go it alone or take a single partner. Only some 4 per cent of businesses are registered as limited companies. Overall, about 28 per cent of people joining the scheme had been unemployed for twelve months or more.

Businesses range from agriculture and hairdressing to cleaning and musical instrument making; most successful proposals, however, have been for the service sector of the economy (65 per cent) with only 13 per cent in manufacturing. The three most popular areas are:

— building and maintenance related activities — 15 per cent
— retail distribution — 13 per cent
— restaurants and cafes — 10 per cent.

In terms of business survival the scheme's results are encouraging; only some 15 per cent of applicants drop out or close during receipt of the allowance and 86 per cent of those who survive the year are still in business three months after the allowance has ended. The MSC estimates that about 60 per cent of all scheme participants are still trading at least a year after the allowance has ended.

Even when those EAS participants who have displaced existing jobs are set aside along with those who would have become self-employed without the scheme's help, there remains a net 'new job' creation effect. In addition the MSC believes that EAS businesses create jobs both by taking on additional staff (even if only part-time) as well as by stimulating demand.

Funding and cost effectiveness

The cost of the EAS in 1984–85 was £76.75 million (excluding administrative costs) towards which the European Social Fund allocated £11.9 million in 1984. For 1985–86, £111 million was budgeted.

According to the MSC's calculations, it costs £2690 per year in total to keep each person off the unemployment register; in the second year it costs £650 but by the third year there is no cost to the exchequer.

Issues

Although the EAS has attracted relatively little criticism, there are still areas for concern. The first of these lies in the potential for improvement: although the scheme has a satisfactory success rate it has been suggested that this could be improved through counselling, support and training. If the scheme included better promotion of support agencies and incentives to encourage their use by participants (training vouchers for example) the effectiveness of the allowance might be considerably improved.

The second issue concerns the proportion of women on the scheme. Although the percentage has been rising, only 22 per cent of entrants to the EAS have been women — and disproportionately few have been over 30 years old. This is almost certainly due to the eligibility rules which might be seen as placing many women at a disadvantage.

Future developments

Graduate Enterprise Scheme

In December 1984, the MSC announced an experimental scheme for 40 students graduating in 1984 or 1985 from an English university, polytechnic or college. Carefully selected applicants will be offered a package consisting of:

— funding for market research (up to £1200);
— £40 per week allowance for four months;
— £40 per week Enterprise Allowance for up to one year;
— professional and technical advice from BP, Arthur Andersen and Co, the National Westminster Bank and Cranfield School of Management (all sponsors of the scheme).

If successful, the scheme will be expanded.

Further information can be obtained from Cranfield School of Management, Bedfordshire, or careers services in higher education institutes.

Further Information

General information can be obtained from Jobcentres, the Small Firms Service and Enterprise Agencies. Detailed information can only be obtained from the specialist teams working from approximately 70 Jobcentres. Ask at local Jobcentres for the nearest address.

See MSC leaflets EPL 124 and EPL 127.

Chapter 3.9

Voluntary Projects Programme (VPP)

Introduction

Originally established to involve unemployed people in a broad range of voluntary work, VPP now focuses on the provision of voluntary opportunities which give the unemployed participants job-related skills and enhance their employability. There are no set hours required of volunteers or any enforced attendance. The entitlement of participants to welfare benefits is not affected.

History

VPP was started in August 1982 and until April 1984, all projects were approved centrally by the MSC's Employment Division in Sheffield. Since that time it has been administered by Community Programme Link Teams (see Chapter 3.7). In its early days, VPP funded a wide variety of projects, such as advice and activity centres and volunteer bureaux/skill exchange initiatives. Since then, the criteria have been narrowed and projects must aim to improve the future employment prospects of participants, rather than promote community development work. In the year 1984–85, 279 projects were in operation and some 63,000 volunteers took part during the year.

Sponsors

Like most other programmes run by the MSC, VPP works through organisations sponsoring individual projects. Any individual or organisation such as a trade union, private firm, voluntary body, local authority, charity or religious group can act as a sponsor. To date, more than three-quarters of the projects have been initiated by the voluntary sector, with most of the remainder originating from local statutory bodies.

Sponsors are responsible for the recruitment of project staff and volunteers and for funding supplied by the MSC, and must have suitable management and financial resources to administer the project, for which they may not receive direct material gain.

Project Criteria

For projects to be considered for funding, they must:

- be designed to give unemployed people opportunities to undertake, on a voluntary basis, activities which will be of benefit to them in relation to training for or obtaining work;
- provide opportunities which would not be available without MSC funding;
- provide worthwhile temporary employment for any staff appointed to organise or run them;
- not put any jobs in normal employment at risk through their activity;
- where possible, have the support of relevant trade unions, employers' organisations and local authorities;
- normally recruit any project workers from among unemployed people;
- not employ their sponsors or their relatives;
- account for any income the project receives and use it either to offset MSC costs or, with prior agreement, enhance the project.

Projects should be planned to last at least six months and should allow for the possibility that they will end after a year (although successful projects may be given further support). In addition, sponsors must accept MSC monitoring and evaluation.

Within the criteria laid down by the MSC, there is considerable flexibility concerning the exact nature of projects, which include:

- *Community work projects:* Volunteers help the community while learning and practising skills in fields such as land clearance for community use (gardens, play areas) or furniture repair and renovation linked to distribution to needy families;
- *Education and training projects:* Providing literacy and numeracy classes (often using other volunteer tutors), producing community newsletters, offering computer familiarisation. Education or training leading to formal qualifications is not funded.

Project Funding

The funding for each project varies considerably. Potential sponsors are encouraged to make use of existing resources wherever possible. The MSC will meet all approved costs up to a maximum of £75,000 for any one project. The Commission's 1984–85 budget for VPP was £7.2 million and for 1985–86 is £12 million.

Approved costs may include:

— *Staffing:* The payment of wages and employers' National Insurance contributions at the normal rate for the job (subject to an MSC determined maximum) for any paid employee engaged wholly on a given project and recruited from among unemployed people. Part-time tutors or instructors are paid pro rata on the appropriate Burnham scale subject, over a 12-month period, to a maximum equivalent of a full-time employee. Payment to part-timers is only made if they have been unemployed immediately before joining the project or would not otherwise be paid for any other days on the project. Incidental staff travelling costs may also be reimbursed.

— *Premises:* Where necessary, the MSC will meet rent, rates, heating, lighting, maintenance and telephone costs. Where sponsors already have premises, the MSC will pay for additional expenditure necessarily incurred for the VPP project. Premises costs must not exceed 60 per cent of total MSC support for the project.

— *Materials and equipment:* Contributions up to a maximum of £7500 (£15,000 for community work projects) may be paid towards such items as tools and materials.

— *Volunteer expenses:* Volunteers who have to travel to carry out projects of benefit to the community may have their travel costs reimbursed up to a maximum of £5 a week. This will not normally be available to participants travelling to attend classes or other facilities provided by the project. In addition, sponsors may be reimbursed for up to 50 per cent of approved costs of providing meals for participants on community work projects, up to 50p per meal.

— *Other operating costs:* This may include publicity, stationery, insurance, vehicle maintenance and audit fees, subject to approval.

Recruitment and Volunteers

Project staff must normally be recruited from among unemployed people. Recruitment must be organised through Jobcentres, which will give priority to long-term unemployed people although the final selection of any employees rests with the sponsor. Part-time tutors/instructors may also be recruited but the MSC expects that, wherever possible, unemployed people with the necessary skills will be encouraged to use them to teach others on a voluntary basis.

Jobcentres may carry details of projects operating under VPP but projects may attract volunteers in any number of ways. An evaluation of VPP, commissioned by the MSC from the Policy Studies Institute, found that volunteers are usually aged under 25, semi-skilled or unskilled and had been unemployed for some time. Most of them were reported to be satisfied with the scheme, the greatest benefits of which were said to be psychological and social. Their involvement varies widely with projects ranging from a few hours a week to over 30 hours. On average, there are between 30 and 40 volunteers associated with a project at any time.

VPP Development Officers

In order to raise the quality of VPP projects, the MSC has funded three VPP Development Officers, based in national agencies. Though not covering the whole of the country, they aim to visit projects, offering advice, information and support to staff as well as developing regional networks. The Development Officers can be contacted at these addresses:

National Council for Voluntary Organisations
26 Bedford Square
London WC1B 3HU
01-634 4066
Officer: J Connor

National Federation of Community Organisations
162 Bedminster Down Road
Bristol BS13 3AG
0272 668780
Officer: L Turner

The Volunteer Centre
29 Lower Kings Road
Berkhamsted
Hertfordshire HP4 2AB
04427 73311
Officer: E Willis

Future Developments

The programme's funding is secure until 1987–88 with a budget of £12 million for 1985–86 and the following two years.

In the spring of 1985, along with news of the expansion of the Community Programme, it was announced that funds were to be made available to explore new developments in VPP — for example, by encouraging volunteers to spend longer on projects and perhaps paying an allowance.

Further Information

In addition to the Development Officers (above), Community Programme Link Teams (listed at the end of Chapter 3.7) provide information about VPP. Information about new developments to the Programme and experimental initiatives may be obtained from the Voluntary Projects Unit, MSC Employment Division, Room W808, Moorfoot, Sheffield. See also leaflets ESP 116 and 116A.

Chapter 3.10

The Youth Training Scheme

Introduction

The Youth Training Scheme (YTS) is a comprehensive programme of vocational training, education and work experience designed to prepare young people for working life. Operating throughout Great Britain, YTS was first introduced as a one-year programme in 1983, but from April 1986 it is offering up to two years of full-time training. Unlike special employment measures for adults and former provision for young people, YTS is intended to be a permanent feature of foundation training in Britain.

History

YTS started on a national basis in September 1983, although a number of pilot projects were established before this. It replaced previous MSC schemes for young people, such as the Youth Opportunities Programme (including Work Experience on Employers' Premises [WEEP] schemes and Unified Vocational Preparation [UVP] projects).

YTS was the first element of the MSC's overall New Training Initiative to be established. This was due, in part, to widespread criticism of the earlier Youth Opportunities Programme (YOP). Started in 1978, YOP had some initial success in helping young school leavers into employment. By the early 1980s, however, the proportion of young people leaving the scheme for paid employment had fallen considerably. There was also considerable scepticism about the quality of work experience provided — particularly after the MSC itself estimated that about one in three people on the programme were substituting for paid employees; that is, functioning merely as cheap labour.

Following the introduction of the Government's white paper *A New Training Initiative: An Agenda for Action* in December 1981, the MSC established a Youth Task Group, whose report, published in May 1982, recommended the establishment of YTS. The following month the recommendation was accepted by government.

The scheme had been in operation for less than two years before wholesale changes were announced. In the 1985 budget, the Chancellor of the Exchequer announced the availability of extra funding for a two-year YTS and the Department of Employment asked the MSC to develop proposals for such a scheme.

By June 1985, the Commission had rushed through plans which, in the words of Chairman Bryan Nicholson, were 'far from a "bolt-on" or rerun of the one-year YTS'. Accepted by government in July 1985, the plans proposed extensive changes in the organisation, structure and content of YTS, to come into effect from April 1986.

These moves, made before the original YTS had been fully proven or tested, might be seen as conveniently allowing the MSC to shift the focus of independent attention away from evaluation and possible criticism of the scheme's effectiveness. Instead, debate moved to the mechanics of designing and implementing an extended scheme.

Organisation of Schemes

The way in which Youth Training Schemes are organised is presently in a state of transition as the arrangements for the two-year YTS come on stream.

From 1988, only Approved Training Organisations, satisfying specific criteria (listed below) will be able to provide YTS places. The Commission hopes that the majority of these places will be with industrial or commercial companies — either individually or in consortia — and intends that the number of places provided by colleges, the youth service and voluntary organisations will decline.

Training organisations with contracts to provide two-year courses may apply for Approved status from April 1986. The decision whether or not to approve applications will be made by Regional Directors of Training Division on the basis of recommendations from Area Manpower Boards (see Chapter 2.7), Area Office staff and the applicant's own comments. Organisations failing to secure Approved Training Organisation status may not qualify for further YTS contracts, although there is provision for appeal, and MSC staff will actively help organisations to meet approval criteria. Once approved, training organisations will be granted three-year contracts with the MSC, subject to an annual review.

During the transition period, the MSC intends to decide whether or not to grant Approved Training Organisation status by April 1987 to those schemes currently operating. For the year 1986–87, two-year contracts will be offered to all managing agents offering first-year places.

Criteria for approval

The competence and effectiveness of organisations wishing to take part in YTS will be judged using ten main criteria:

— the ability to arrange and deliver a two-year training programme;
— a satisfactory previous record in training;
— sufficient resources, particularly of staff, to deliver a high quality training programme;
— staff that have been selected, briefed and trained according to the *MSC Code of Practice on the Competence of Adult Staff in YTS* (published with the proposals);
— premises and equipment that are suitable, safe, well maintained and accessible;
— effective methods for assessing and recording trainees' performance and achievements;
— organisations must effectively monitor and review their programmes in accordance with the *MSC Code of Practice*;
— financial viability;
— demonstration of a positive commitment to equal opportunity for all trainees regardless of sex, race or disability, not only in their recruitment procedures, but also in allocation of trainees to the various component parts of a programme;
— demonstration of a positive commitment to health and safety.

Funding

Funding arrangements for the two-year scheme simplified the

earlier complex regime which differentiated between mode A and mode B provision (see above). Under the new procedures, training organisations receive a managing agent's fee of £110 per year per contracted place, plus a basic grant of £160 per month for each filled place on the scheme.

In addition, there is provision for 'premium' payments of an extra £110 per calendar month for each place in certain cases. This is because the MSC realises that, despite its wish to make YTS an employer-led programme, some areas will not be able to supply sufficient training places with employers and will require places provided at greater cost by non-profit-making agencies (such as voluntary organisations). Similarly there is recognition that some young people, particularly those who are disadvantaged in some way, may require initial training away from the pressures of a commercial environment. The nature and number of 'premium places' is however, a contentious matter and is discussed below under 'Issues'.

The MSC has also made special funding provision for up to 4000 first year and 3000 second year places (1986–87) for schemes offering specialist provision for trainees with mental or physical disabilities. This funding of £75 per filled place per month is additional to the basic and premium grants.

Funding arrangements for ITeCs are somewhat different although they are fully involved in YTS; they are detailed in Chapter 3.11.

The total cost of YTS in 1984–85 was nearly £800 million. Once the two-year scheme becomes fully operational in 1987, the scheme will cost £1.1 billion per year. YTS is supported by the European Social Fund (in 1984, by £137.9 million); the cost of one trainee in three is met by the ESF in the following regions: Midlands (part); Northern; North West; Scotland; South West (part); Yorkshire and Humberside; Wales.

Administration

In 1986–87, two-year contracts will be offered to all managing agents, rolled forward annually. Subject to the scheme's quality maintenance and financial viability, the contract provides in its first year for the financing of all first-year places and single-year places at the new rates, plus a number of second-year contin-uation places for 1985–86 entrants progressing to a second

year. In year two of the contract, places will be financed for all
trainees who have completed their first year of YTS and who
wish to continue on the scheme. In addition, the scheme is to be
guaranteed at least a further 75 per cent of the first-year and
single-year places it provided in year one.

Numbers

The MSC's corporate plan for 1985–89 sets a target of 385,000
YTS places for 1985–86, although the introduction of a two-year
scheme will add approximately 200,000 more training places.

When originally planned, it was anticipated that 460,000 young
people would participate in YTS during its first year of operation.
In practice considerably fewer joined — only 60 per cent of
places were filled half way through the first year. On the basis of
that experience, planned numbers for the second year (1984–85)
were reduced to just over 400,000 but even so, the MSC Annual
Report for 1985 showed that only 389,000 entrants took up places,
about 10 per cent of whom were joining schemes for a second
time.

Trainees

Eligibility and entry

Under the two-year YTS, young people's eligibility for training
depends upon when they leave full-time education rather than on
their dates of birth. All those who leave full-time education before
having started a third term of post-compulsory education are
entitled to two years' training. Those who stay on at school or
college longer than this but who leave before the third term of the
following academic year are entitled to one year of training.
Young people who have completed at least seven terms of post-
compulsory education are not usually eligible for YTS.
Exceptions exist, however, for:

— disabled young people who leave full-time education up to
  and including the age of 21 who will continue to be eligible
  for two years' training, with the opportunity of a further six
  months if this enhances their employment prospects;
— 18 year olds who were unable to enter YTS earlier because
  of custodial sentences, pregnancy or because they stayed at

school until 18 to learn English are entitled to two years' training.

All those eligible for training must enter the scheme within one year of the date they leave full-time education. This means that anyone who delays training for a full year will normally be unable to interrupt their training without reducing the duration of their standard entitlement. Those young people who were eligible for training under rules made before the introduction of the two-year scheme remain entitled to training.

Recruitment

Some young people are recruited to YTS as employees but the majority have the status of trainee and the scheme provider is under no obligation to retain them after their period of training is over.

Recruitment to 'non-premium' places on schemes is normally done through the local authority careers service or by direct recruitment by YTS itself — for example, through press advertisements. In some areas, MSC Jobcentres and Employment Offices may play a part.

Managing agents of schemes will also be free to recruit direct to premium places. Potential entrants must, however, be endorsed by the Careers Service before entry to the scheme, since the service is in the best position locally to assess which young people in the area require training through premium place programmes. Endorsement by specialist careers officers or disablement resettlement officers is also necessary for recruits to places which may be granted special additional funding.

It is not clear at the time of writing whether the new arrangements will allow the MSC to repeat its previous guarantee of a YTS place to every applicant. In the past, the Commission itself acted as managing agent for mode B schemes and in practice, scheme sponsors had little choice over who to accept to enable the guarantee to be met.

In all cases, schemes are bound by the laws concerning sexual and racial discrimination when recruiting young people, just as they are with normal employees. Nonetheless, research has uncovered strong evidence of widespread discrimination. In an effort to attract young people from ethnic minorities to YTS and overcome these difficulties, the MSC has appointed 20 YTS development officers, based with sponsoring organisations such as Community Relations Councils and local authorities.

Payments to participants

From April 1986, two rates of training allowance apply. First-year trainees receive a minimum of £27.30 a week while second-year trainees get a minimum of £35. For young people doing YTS as employees this is a wage; for others it is a training allowance.

Trainees whose schemes involve living away from home are provided with arranged accommodation funded (up to a specified limit) by the MSC, although their allowance for the period may be reduced. In addition, fares for home visits are paid. Only if they are told before joining a scheme should trainees have to pay for protective clothing or necessary special equipment.

Parents claiming child benefit may continue to do so when their child becomes a YTS trainee.

Choice of scheme and transfers

YTS is not compulsory and trainees may leave at any time. It is the case, however, that unemployed young people who repeatedly refuse offers of places on schemes or who leave their scheme 'without good reason' may face loss of supplementary benefit for up to six weeks, as would happen if they left a job under similar circumstances. In some areas, however, the careers service has been very reluctant to pass on the details of 'refusers' to the Department of Health and Social Security. Furthermore, what actually constitutes 'good reason' is unclear and may vary from person to person and place to place.

Up to two transfers between schemes are possible.

Trade unions

Young people on YTS are entitled to join a trade union if they are acceptable under its rules but, in practice, most YTS participants are non-unionised. This is in part because many YTS places are in non-unionised organisations but it is also because, with a few exceptions, the trade union movement has made little effort to meet the needs of trainees. The suspicion with which many trade unionists regard YTS may lead to virtual boycotting and consequent abandonment of a potentially large number of recruits.

Conditions of work

Trainees will not generally have to work for more than 40 hours per week excluding lunch breaks. The length of break depends on the practice of the place where the training is done but in general it will be whatever is normal for employees. Trainees do not have to do overtime and schemes are expected to abide by local bye-laws or Acts of Parliament concerning hours for young people.

In addition to bank holidays and public holidays, young people on YTS are entitled to at least 18 days' paid holiday per year (1.5 days per month on the scheme) to be agreed in advance with supervisors.

Providing the scheme's procedures are followed, trainees are entitled to receive their full allowance for periods of up to three consecutive weeks if they are off work through sickness or injury. Beyond this period they must rely on sickness or supplementary benefit.

Discipline and grievance procedures

On employer-led schemes, employers will normally extend their usual discipline and grievance procedures for employees to their YTS trainees. On other schemes, written rules and procedures have to be established, which should be given and explained to trainees as they enter the scheme.

Content of Schemes

YTS is intended to be an integrated programme of work experience, on and off-the-job training and education. The first year is intended to provide broad-based (rather than job or employer-specific) training, while the second year progresses to training which is more occupationally related and which provides the opportunity for participants to obtain or work towards vocational qualifications.

The detailed content of YTS is the responsibility of providers, reflecting the variety of schemes and training objectives. The MSC simply lays down minimum criteria as a framework in the form of 'inputs' to be expressed in a training plan and delivered through certain 'training processes' to produce specified 'outcomes'. These are summarised on the diagram below.

DESIGN FRAMEWORK FOR A TWO-YEAR YTS
Training content to be delivered through integrated
INPUTS

Planned work experience   Off-the-job
and on-the-job training   training/education

▼

expressed in a
Training plan with
competence objectives

▼

delivered through
TRAINING PROCESSES
Induction and initial assessment
Participative learning
Continuous assessment
Guidance/reviewing

▼

to produce
THESE OUTCOMES

Competence in	Competence	Ability to	Personal
a job and/or a	in a range of	transfer skills	effectiveness
range of	transferable	and knowledge	
occupational	core skills	to new	
skills		situations	

▼

which lead to
CERTIFICATION
Vocational qualifications, demonstrating
occupational competence, or credit
towards such qualifications; plus a
record of achievement

Inputs

Planned work experience and on-the-job training

All schemes must provide properly planned work experience with
appropriate supervision and instruction. They should enable
trainees to acquire and practise skills, to attain and demonstrate
agreed levels and areas of competence and to learn about the
adult world and its demands and responsibilities.

Off-the-job training/education

Schemes must provide a minimum of 20 weeks (100 working
days) off-the-job training/education over a two-year period. This

143

must be both planned, directed and integrated as far as possible with on-the-job training, even when provided by an outside organisation. The pattern of attendance for this training may be organised as day release, block release (one or more blocks) and may include residential periods. Trainees should also have the opportunity to work towards vocational qualifications awarded by recognised examining bodies.

Training plans

The incidence of on and off-the-job training should be outlined in a training plan. This document, which all schemes must produce, sets out clearly for all those involved in the programme (trainees, off-the-job tutors and work experience providers) exactly what the stages and content of training will be. Trainees and trainers are expected to be clear what competencies are expected of trainees by the end of the training, and these 'competence objectives', which should cover the four 'outcomes' of training (see below) should be written into the plan. The MSC is encouraging examining bodies to draw up authoritative modular schemes to be used as such objectives and has itself produced illustrative schemes.

Training process

Induction and initial assessment

Schemes must provide trainees with information about what will happen to them and what is expected of them at the start of their programme and at transitional stages within it. Schemes must also ensure that late entrants are adequately inducted. In order to provide a base record of a trainee's attainment on entry, initial assessment is an essential part of the training process, either during the early weeks of training or at recruitment stage. This should take into account trainees' past experience — particularly to avoid duplication if the trainee has already undertaken pre-vocational education while at school or college. In general, this assessment is intended to assist those planning schemes in the devising of an appropriate programme by establishing trainees' preferences, abilities and potential.

Participative learning

Training should seek to involve trainees in the learning process, encouraging them to learn by doing. Participation in the learning process through problem solving, experimentation, planning and negotiation are all approaches which can be used to help trainees practise their skills and apply knowledge. In assisting trainees to take responsibility for their own learning, schemes are involving young people in those decisions which affect their training.

Continuous assessment

Progress towards competence objectives should be assessed continuously and recorded for the purposes of certification. This process also provides information about trainees' emerging abilities which can be used for reviewing purposes. Assessment systems should be workable in practice and able to record adequately a trainee's progress and achievements during work experience.

Guidance and reviewing

These processes are recognised as essential parts of the training programme since they enable trainees to be fully aware of their progress and to join in decisions about their future programme. While the reviewing function may be linked to assessment, the function of guidance is intended to be rather broader, so as to encompass a wide range of practical advice and support which may be required by young people. Trainees should be clear about who they should turn to on a scheme for guidance and providers should recognise, and use as necessary, the specialist expertise of youth workers, careers officers and other external agencies.

Outcomes

Competence in a job and/or range of occupational skills

At the end of their time on YTS, trainees should be able to do real jobs — or if the job requires longer periods of training, to have acquired occupational skills which help them towards such jobs. Trainees are expected to have not only basic technical knowledge, skills and understanding but also an awareness of the context of the jobs for which they have trained, including an appreciation of the wider world of work.

Competence in a range of transferable core skills

All trainees must be given the opportunity to make progress in five core areas, identified by the MSC as:

— number and its applications
— communications
— problem solving and planning
— practical skills
— computer and information technology.

With the partial exception of the last, these are not 'subjects' to be covered separately but skills which can be learnt in a wide range of work settings as well as off the job. Since opportunities for working with computer and information technology may occur less frequently than other core areas, the MSC expects scheme providers to design specific training in this area if required.

Ability to transfer skills and knowledge to new situations

As well as providing training in specific tasks, schemes should seek to develop skills of versatility and adaptability in trainees by encouraging them to understand principles underlying tasks which can be transferred to new situations and jobs.

Personal effectiveness

This outcome involves the development of initiative and self-sufficiency, an ability to handle interpersonal relationships and acceptance of responsibility. While the MSC recognises that these qualities can be developed in a work setting, it realises that an appreciation of the world outside work is also necessary to promote full personal effectiveness.

Certification

In order that their achievements within YTS can be recognised outside the scheme, all trainees are given a standard certificate when they leave. This details the main elements of their programme and their performance in the four outcomes. They should also receive a record of achievement showing which of the competence objectives of their training plans have been fulfilled.

Monitoring

One of the major criticisms of the Youth Opportunities Programme which YTS replaced was that scheme organisers were inadequately monitored by the MSC. With YTS, the Commission is attempting to rebuff that criticism which continues to be made. Since autumn 1984, each area office has established a team of about 20 Programme Assessors who carry out quality monitoring of schemes. These are meant to be repeated at quarterly intervals. The MSC has also stated that health and safety aspects of YTS training will be the subject of careful monitoring; the Commission is extremely sensitive about this point in the face of accusations that statistics concerning YTS fatalities have not been publicised.

Programme Review Teams (PRTs)

Programme Review Teams are the MSC's suggested method for self-monitoring of schemes. The teams should consist of representatives from all sections of the scheme and its delivery agents ie sponsor, management, staff, trainees and off-the-job trainers; they can include members of the Commission's staff and other agencies such as the careers service, though this is not formally required.

The PRTs' main aim is to advise on scheme content and design, to monitor scheme progress and suggest and introduce improvements. PRTs are not at present mandatory but they could possibly become part of the YTS programme content and design for the year 1985–86. It is the PRTs' monitoring role that sets them apart from advisory or management groups.

Future Developments

YTS is likely to remain in the news in the near future as the two-year training programme develops. One issue, is whether training agreements should include a binding undertaking from the young person to complete the two-year course (at present, the MSC is calculating on an average stay of between 68 and 82 weeks — if most young people stay longer, funding available will be insufficient). The fear among many commentators is that the government would use such a binding commitment to justify the withdrawal of welfare benefits from those who leave the scheme prematurely and thus start to erode the voluntary principle of the scheme.

Women and YTS

In December 1985, the Youth Training Board endorsed a range of measures intended to broaden the participation of young women in YTS beyond traditional areas of female employment. Among the plans to be implemented are:

— Single-sex schemes: designed to encourage providers to run some schemes for young women in non-traditional occupations, such as construction or engineering, which will help break away from sex-stereotyping;
— Reserved place schemes: which would keep a proportion of places for young women on a number of schemes in areas of work not traditional to women, so as to achieve a better male/female balance;
— Job sampling or 'tasting': the MSC is to explore the feasibility of incorporating a period of tasting into some employer-led schemes to allow both male and female trainees to sample a range of occupational areas, including the non-traditional, before making final choices.

In addition, a national conference is to be mounted in 1986 to bring together a range of individuals involved in YTS at a variety of levels. The conference will cover sex-stereotyping and suggest ways of encouraging the dissemination of good practice.

Issues

More than with any other area of MSC activity, it is impossible to summarise the contentious issues concerning YTS since virtually every aspect of the scheme has come under criticism — whether justified or not. Present issues include the following.

Two-year YTS proposals

These proposals were rushed through in just three months by a working group which included representatives of the careers service, young people or voluntary organisations and which was dominated by the arguments of the Confederation of British Industry (CBI). CBI representatives managed to block proposals from the TUC and education service to set the minimum off-the-job training period at 26 weeks (twice its length in the one-year scheme). Instead they were able to win a proportionally reduced period of 20 weeks.

The dominance of the private employers' interest also lies behind the number of 'premium places' available and the size of the premium. These places, intended for areas where there are insufficient employer-led schemes and for disadvantaged young people unable to get training places with employers, are, at 43,900 for 1986–87 substantially fewer than the previous number of mode B places. Given that there is no guarantee that employers are able or willing to expand their YTS provision — indeed, many claim to have taken on as many trainees as they can handle — this appears to be something of a gamble. Furthermore, many colleges and voluntary organisations believe the premium is too low to support the costs of their schemes and many worthwhile schemes will be forced to close.

The argument against a higher premium was led by the CBI, which claimed that since any increase would be at the expense of the basic grant, fewer employers would be attracted to provide places. In addition, the CBI argued (so far without success) for premium payments for employer-providers in manufacturing industry where training costs can be high. All this is despite the fact that employer-providers benefit from a pay-off which college and voluntary organisation schemes do not — that is, the cost-free contribution of the trainees' labour power to their output and potential profits.

Other outstanding issues concerning the two-year scheme concern whether 17-year-old entrants to the two-year scheme should automatically go on to the higher rate of training allowance and whether payments to trainees should be performance-linked.

Quality monitoring

Despite the efforts of the MSC, and proposals for an inspectorate, there is still concern in some quarters over the quality of some schemes. A report by the Comptroller and Auditor General, *Vocational Education and Training for Young People* (1985) revealed that in November 1983, the MSC had found that more than a third of schemes monitored 'needed time' to bring themselves up to standard and that, over a year later, the proportion was still 32 per cent. In its haste to meet quantity targets, there can be little doubt that insufficient attention was given to quality assurance and it is unclear how the same problem is to be avoided in the rush to identify second-year training places. The Commission's response to this area of concern has been to announce, in December 1985, the establishment of a new Training Standards Advisory Service, staffed with professionals from industry and education, as well as MSC staff with direct experience of training and education. The new service, which will be similar to HM Inspectorate of Schools, will contribute to the quality and development of YTS through in depth inspections of individual schemes.

Amongst the service's objectives are the following:

— the provision of balanced and constructive feedback on the quality of training in individual schemes examined, both to the scheme manager and MSC;
— the making of a contribution towards the development of the content, design, standards and provision of vocational training within the programme, by bringing together the collective findings of the Service;
— the building up and making available of a bank of knowledge on the practices of individual schemes;
— liaison with educational and industrial bodies concerned with the evaluation of the quality of vocational education and training;
— the publication of reports identifying areas of good practice and outlining areas of concern in YTS provision.

Whether this initiative will be sufficient to dispel criticism remains to be seen.

Effectiveness

The purpose of YTS is to prepare young people for employment but the actual proportion of trainees going into paid work is disputed. The MSC claims, on the basis of surveys of leavers, that over Great Britain as a whole, some 60 per cent of trainees leave YTS to enter a full-time job and a further 10 per cent go back into further education or training. Critics claim that the voluntary sample surveys of 15 per cent of leavers are methodologically inadequate and that the real figure for trainees finding work is as low as 48 per cent. In addition, it is claimed that any overall figure glosses over wide regional variations.

The Comptroller and Auditor General's report (above) confirms the belief held by critics that job substitution occurs because of YTS, with employers preferring docile and relatively inexpensive trainees to older workers, thus increasing adult unemployment. It is only possible to speculate on the extent of this problem.

Voluntarism

Although YTS is not compulsory, there are widespread rumours that the government (rather than the MSC Commissioners) intends, as soon as possible, to end young people's entitlement to supplementary benefit in order to 'encourage' more to take up YTS or further education. Even the scheme's most ardent supporters are apprehensive about the effect of large numbers of unwilling trainees joining the scheme and are unsure whether sufficient places could be found for them without a major loss of quality.

Further Information

Proposals for schemes and information about local provision should be directed to the local Area Manpower Board, c/o Training Division Area Offices (see Chapter 2.7). Local education authority careers services, MSC Jobcentres and Employment Offices will also carry general information and many leaflets about the scheme. Information about staff training on YTS is contained in Chapter 3.25 on Accredited Centres.

The MSC also publishes a free monthly bulletin *Youth Training News*, available from the Distribution Unit (Dept YTN), Room E824, Moorfoot, Sheffield S1 4PQ.

Chapter 3.11

Information Technology Centres (ITeCs)

Introduction

ITeCs are an integral part of the YTS but with different funding arrangements, and a wider brief. They offer basic training in electronics, micro-computing and the electronic office to unemployed 16- and 17-year-old school leavers. As well as vocational training, the young people also receive (on a one-year programme) a minimum of 13 weeks' social and life skills training and they spend some time on relevant work placements. In addition, they are encouraged to provide training in information technology skills for customers other than the MSC.

History

The first ITeC allocation of 20 centres was announced by the Prime Minister in July 1981. These initial centres were sited in the inner city areas of Bristol, Glasgow, London, Liverpool, and Newcastle. In the subsequent expansion of ITeCs, allocations were based on the areas of high unemployment mainly in urban areas. The latest expansion to 174 has been demand led.

Organisation

As with all its other programmes, the MSC contracts out the running of ITeCs to sponsors, who may be any organisation with the ability to run a training programme. ITeCs have attracted sponsorship from several high technology companies such as IBM, ICL, GEC/Marconi, Ferranti, Rank Xerox and Tandy.

Trainees

At the end of December 1985 there were over 6000 young people attending ITeC courses. Under new arrangements this will rise to just under 11,000 two-year places by 1988–89. In general, ITeCs have not experienced difficulty in recruiting trainees. However, many have had some problems in attracting girls to their courses, except to the electronic office part of the training.

Where young people with disabilities are concerned, ITeC training has proved to be particularly suitable. The ITeC in Lewisham, for example, is sponsored by a training organisation for the disabled and caters mainly for disabled people. The MSC is supporting the formation of a residential training unit for disabled young people which will be attached to the ITeC in Totnes, sponsored by the Dartington Hall Trust.

Some ITeCs have become involved in selling their goods or services to the general public, that is, selling the training services or selling software, printed circuit boards, or electronic office services. In a number of cases, trainees have gone on to set up their own companies after completing their training at an ITeC. Under new arrangements, ITeCs are permitted to 'fast-stream' selected trainees through the centre from six months onwards, with the remainder of their training spent on work placements. This allows them to increase the numbers of young people trained.

Funding

In December 1985, new funding arrangements for ITeCs were announced to encourage them to take on a wider role in meeting local training needs as well as participating fully in the extended (two-year) YTS.

The centres have always had a distinctive pattern of funding. Ever since their introduction in 1981, new ITeCs have been able to attract pump-priming support from the Department of Trade and Industry amounting to £75,000 over three years. Local authorities, private industry and voluntary organisation sponsors may also provide additional support. This has allowed ITeCs to purchase capital equipment, top up staff salaries or develop products. In addition at least one centre (Bristol) has successfully applied for European Social Fund grants to enable trainees to join the centre after completing a year on other YTS schemes.

The new funding package provides ITeCs with basic and premium grants worth £270 per month for each trainee on an ITeC YTS, plus managing agent's fees of £110 per contracted place per year (see Chapter 3.10). For the next two years, ITeCs will also qualify for transitional YTS funding of up to £200 per trainee per month, reflecting the high costs of information technology training.

Under the new arrangements, ITeCs will also start to provide adult training for customers other than the MSC in order to make more intensive use of facilities and equipment and allow the training expertise of ITeCs to be used by local businesses. Support funding for up to two years will be made available to develop this work. Each centre is to prepare an individual business plan setting out its objectives over the next three years, drawing on advice and support from the MSC and the Department of Trade an Industry, with particular reference to marketing.

The balance between YTS and other work is to be decided at local level.

Evaluation

Despite the demands of having to satisfy the MSC, the Department of Trade and Industry and their sponsors, ITeCs have managed to establish themselves quickly and their record in placing trainees into jobs, further education or training is in the order of 66 per cent — higher than that of most other schemes funded under the old YTS mode B arrangements (see Chapter 3.10). To some extent this may be because the cost per trainee to the MSC is some £700 greater than other mode B1 places at £4800.

One area, however, where ITeCs have experienced difficulty is in the recruiting of young women to their courses.

Further Information

YTS L22 *A Handbook for Information Technology Centres*
ITeC Consultancy Unit
189 Freston Road
London W1O 6TH
01-969 8942
Contact: C Webb, Director

List of Information Technology Centres

The following list of ITeCs was current at January 1985.

ENGLAND

Avon

Bath ITeC, New Work Trust Ltd,
Unit 1A, The Riverside Business
Park, Lower Bristol Road, Bath
BA2 3DN
0225 337992
Contact: M Potts

Bristol (New Work) ITeC, New
Work Trust Ltd, Avondale
Workshops, Woodland Way,
Kingswood, Bristol BS15 1QH
0272 603871
Contact: M Winwood

Bristol ITeC, St Anne's House,
St Anne's Road, Bristol BS4 4AB
0272 779247
Contact: D Luck

North Bristol ITeC, Olveston
Road, Horfield, Bristol BS7 9PB
0272 517127
Contact: G Morgan

Berkshire

Bracknell ITeC, 3rd Floor,
Fitzwilliam House, Bracknell
RG12 1JX
0344 489091
Contact: J Shute

Reading ITeC, Abbey Mill
House, Abbey Square, Reading
RG1 3BE
0734 598515
Contact: D G Sellers

Slough ITeC, 5–7 Colndale
Road, Poyle Trading Estate,
Combrook, Slough SL3 0HQ
0753 684358
Contact: T Lord

Buckinghamshire

Milton Keynes ITeC, 5 Erica
Road, Stacey Bushes, Milton
Keynes MK12 6HS
0908 311526
Contact: P Loud

Cambridgeshire

Cambridge ITeC, Hooper Street,
Cambridge CB1 2NZ
0223 589777
Contact: D Battison

Peterborough ITeC, PITeC Ltd,
Park Crescent, Peterborough
PE1 4BG
0733 68931
Contact: E Dickens

Cheshire

Halton ITeC, Halton Business
Generation Centre, Waterloo
Road, Widnes WA8 0PR
051-420 4385
Contact: W Chisholm

Warrington ITeC, Barbauld
House, Barbauld Street,
Warrington WA1 2QY
0925 31431
Contact: J A Smith

Cleveland

Cleveland ITeC, 34 Albert Road,
Middlesbrough TS1 1QD
0642 221280
Contact: J Trotter

Cornwall

Cornwall ITeC, Daniel Road,
Truro TR1 2DA
0872 70964
Contact: K Rudling

Cumbria

Barrow-in-Furness ITeC, British
Ship Builders (TES) Ltd, Abbey
Road, Barrow-in-Furness
LA14 5QR
0229 23307
Contact: D H Freeman

Carlisle ITeC, Ex-Morley Street
School, Denton Holme, Carlisle
CA1 1HS
0228 49906
Contact: M Cross

West Cumbria ITeC, Kells
School, Whitehaven CA28 9AY
0946 66636
Contact: R Bristoe

Derbyshire

Derby ITeC, c/o Derby College
of Further Education,
Normanton Road Annexe,
Normanton Road, Derby
DE1 2GP
0332 380478
Contact: D Vickers

Devon

Dartington ITeC, The Old
Postern, Dartington, Totnes
TQ9 6EA
0803 866051
Contact: R Butler

Exeter ITeC, Mary Arches
Street, Exeter EX4 3AZ
0392 219038
Contact: C Moore

North Devon Microcentre,
Castle Street, Barnstable
EX31 1DR
0271 44260
Contact: B Kissock

Plymouth ITeC, Charles Cross
Centre, Constantine Street,
Plymouth PL19 9DY
0752 671110
Contact: A H C Fraser

Dorset

Dorset ITeC, Plessey Defence
Systems Ltd, Grange Road,
Christchurch BH23 4JE
04252 78795
Contact: D Carter

Durham, County

Aycliffe ITeC, Menom Road,
Aycliffe Industrial Estate,
Newtown Aycliffe DL5 6UH
0325 320052
Contact: M Ellison

Durham ITeC, Unit 13D,
Bowburn Industrial Estate,
Bowburn, Durham DH6 5AD
0385 772474
Contact: H Page

Peterlee ITeC, Neville Road,
Peterlee SRE 2AS
0783 871177
Contact: E Whitfield

Essex

Basildon ITeC, Burnt Mills
Road, Basildon SS14 1DR
0268 286929
Contact: M Bridge

Harlow ITeC, Springhills,
Hobtoe Road, Harlow
CM20 1TH
0279 446557
Contact: H Stevens

South East Essex ITeC, Hockley
Primary School, Main Road,
Hockley SS5 4RG
0702 201070
Contact: P Cooper

Gloucestershire

Gloucestershire ITeC, Larkhay
Road, Hucclecote, Gloucester
GL3 3NT
0452 63141
Contact: B Lickman

Hampshire

Portsmouth ITeC, Civic Offices,
Guildhall Square, Portsmouth
PO1 2AL
0705 834054
Contact: P D Atkinson

Southampton ITeC, 19 Duke
Street, Southampton SO1 1ES
0703 38966
Contact: G M Kearsley

Hereford and Worcester

Worcester ITeC, Cherry Orchard
School, Orchard Street,
Worcester WR5 3DY
0905 358118
Contact: P Jones

Hertfordshire

Stevenage ITeC, Ridgemond
Park, Telford Avenue, Stevenage
SG2 0QA
0438 312566
Contact: J Wheeler

Humberside

Grimsby ITeC, Compass House, Riby Street, Grimsby DN31 3HF
0472 362779
Contact: I S Jackson

Hull ITeC, Old Seaman's Mission, 84 Goulton Street, Hull HU3 4DL
0482 25576
Contact: N Frearson

Scunthorpe ITeC, Doncaster Road, Scunthorpe DN15 7DS
0724 852302
Contact: M Aykroyd

Isle of Wight

Isle of Wight ITeC, Unit 11, Riverbank Industrial Estate, Hunstake Road, Newport PO30 5UU
0983 523705
Contact: H Street

Kent

Ashford ITeC, Chart Leacon Depot, Brunswick Road, Cobbs Wood Industrial Estate, Ashford TN23 2TX
0233 21654
Contact: A Patterson

Gravesend ITeC, 102 London Road, Northfleet PA11 9LY
0474 59579
Contact: B Medhurst

Maidstone ITeC, Computotech, 2 Westree Road, Maidstone ME4 8HB
0622 686489
Contact: D Griffiths

Medway ITeC, Rodney Block,
Khyber Road, Chatham
ME4 4TT
0634 577777
Contact: J Richards

Lancashire

Blackburn ITeC, Block A/D,
Mullard Ltd, Phillips Road,
Blackburn BB1 5RZ
0254 679791
Contact: G Tattersall

Blackpool ITeC, Kingston
House, Boothley Road,
Blackpool SY1 3RS
0253 25212
Contact: R M Jones

Burnley ITeC, Ennismore Street,
Burnley BB10 3EU
0282 28210
Contact: J Tope

Lancaster ITeC, Room B37/38/
39, St Leonards House,
St Leonards Gate, Lancaster
LA1 1NN
0524 62727
Contact: H Hicks

Preston ITeC, Lancashire
House, Watery Lane, Preston
PR2 2XE
0772 735753
Contact: K Mills

Skelmersdale ITeC, Gardener's
Place, West Gillibrand,
Skelmersdale WN8 9FP
0695 23611
Contact: J Selwood

Leicestershire

Leicester ITeC, 26–28 Chancery
Street, Leicester LE1 5WD
0533 547008
Contact: L Beckreck

Loughborough ITeC, 1 Granby
Street, Loughborough LE11 3DU
0509 261763
Contact: M McNally

Lincolnshire

Boston ITeC, Boston & South
Holland ITeC Co Ltd, County
Hall, Boston PE21 6LX
0205 67123
Contact: B Skinner

East Lindsey ITeC, Tedder Hall,
Manby Park, Louth LN11 8UP
0507 601111
Contact: C F Jackson

Grantham ITeC, Isaac Newton
Way, Grantham NG3 9RT
0476 70670
Contact: B Payne

Lincoln ITeC, Unit 7 and 8
Dean Road, Lincoln LN2 4JZ
0522 43532
Contact: B Howard

Spalding ITeC, 12 Market Place,
Spalding P11 1SL
0775 66718
Contact: R Watson

London, Greater

Brent ITeC, Stonebridge
Community Project, Harrow
Road, NW10 0RG
01-965 7232
Contact: P Anderson

Croydon ITeC, Ecclesbourne
School, Ecclesbourne Road,
Thornton Heath, Croydon,
Surrey CR4 7BR
01-683 3183
Contact: R E Hasting

Haringey ITeC, Braemar Road,
N15 5EU
01-800 5689
Contact: J Kelly

Hounslow ITeC, Marlborough
Centre, London Road, Isleworth,
Middlesex UB2 4BD
01-568 5108
Contact: R Starr

Southall ITeC, Charles House,
Bridge Road, Southall,
Middlesex UB2 4BD
01-574 6565
Contact: D Beever

London, Inner

Brixton ITeC, 39 Brixton Road,
SW9 6DZ
01-735 6151
Contact: D Hacking

Camden ITeC, 7 Leighton
Place, Kentish Town NW1 2QL
01-485 3324
Contact: P Waller

Covent Garden ITeC, Central
London Youth Project, Micro
Training Centre, 99–103 Long
Acre, WC2F 9NR
01-836 9796
Contact: S Jolly

Greenwich ITeC, The MacBean
Centre, Macbean Street,
Woolwich SE18 6PW
01-854 8255
Contact: A Welch

Hackney ITeC, 5 French Place,
Shoreditch High Street, E1 6JB
01-729 3116
Contact: J Kemp

Islington ITeC, 49 Old Street,
EC1V 9HX
01-253 8069
Contact: I Irving

Lewisham ITeC, Drake House,
18 Creekside, Deptford SE8 3DZ
01-692 7141
Contact: M Ponting

Nottingdale ITeC, 191 Freston
Road, W10 6TH
01-969 0819
Contact: R Ellwood

Southwark Microtech, 194
Union Street, SE1 0LH
01-928 8434
Contact: R Anderson

Tower Hamlets ITeC, 11
Indescon Court, Millharbour,
Millwall E14 9TJ
01-987 6248
Contact: P Lyons

Manchester, Greater

Bolton ITeC, The Haulgh, Elton
Street, Bolton BL2 2RB
0242 22311 ext 491
Contact: T R Whittaker

Bury ITeC, Hillside School
Building, Limefield Brow, Bury
BL9 6QR
061-797 3630
Contact: J Gartside

Manchester (ORT GEC) ITeC,
GEC Distribution Switchgear
Ltd, Higher Openshaw ML1 1FL
061-301 2210
Contact: E Uzoegbu

Moss Side ITeC, 2 South Combe
Walk, Alexandra Precinct,
Manchester M15 5NW
061-226 6502
Contact: C Mathobi

Oldham ITeC, Orme Mill,
Crimbles Street, Waterhead,
Oldham OL4 3JA
061-624 0281
Contact: I Ingham

Rochdale ITeC, Project House,
Drake Street, Rochdale
OL16 1CA
0706 350600
Contact: M Cauldwell

Salford ITeC, ITeC Building,
50 University Road, Salford
M5 4WR
061 736 8543
Contact: B Carrington

Tameside ITeC, 48 Union Street,
Hyde SK14 1ND
061-366 0157
Contact: P Hartland

Wigan ITeC, Witec Ltd, Units 2
and 5, Clayton Street, Wigan
WN3 4DA
0942 497132
Contact: J Scattergood

Merseyside

Charles Wootton ITeC, Unit 5,
8 Myrtle Parade, Toxteth,
Liverpool L7 7EL
051-709 0340
Contact: O A Sowande

Ellesmere Port and Neston
ITeC, Meadow Lane, Ellesmere
Port, South Wirral L65 4EH
051-355 1178/0013
Contact: B Garner

Knowsley ITeC, Knowsley
House, Chorley Wood Road,
Knowsley Industrial Park,
Liverpool L33 7SH
051-546 5324
Contact: C Woodward

Marconi ITeC, Field Road,
Wallasey, Wirral L45 5BG
051-336 7000
Contact: P Burke

Merseyside ITeC, METEL (IT
UNIT), Salisbury Street,
Liverpool L8 8DR
051-207 2281
Contact: N Lindley

St Helens ITeC, 1st Floor,
Windle Pilkington School,
Waterloo Street, St Helens
WA10 1PX
0744 611365
Contact: C Reed

Sefton ITeC, Unit 9, Penpoll
Industrial Estate, Hawthorn
Road, Bootle, Liverpool L20 6LB
051-933 3100
Contact: Mr Polkowski

South Liverpool ITeC, Belle
Vale Shopping Centre, Liverpool
L25 2RF
051-488 0018
Contact: A Rice

Southport ITeC, 3rd Floor,
North House, Eastbank Street,
Southport PR8 1DS
0704 47070
Contact: J Reeves

Norfolk

Norwich ITeC, 1st Floor,
St Saviour's Lane, Norwich
NR3 1SU
0603 20341
Contact: P Scott

Northamptonshire

Corby ITeC, Deene House,
Market Square, Corby
NN17 1QB
05363 63290
Contact: V Albon

Northampton ITeC, 21–29
Hazlewood Road, Northampton
NN1 1LG
0604 24427
Contact: A Haydon

Northumberland

Cramlington ITeC, Nelson
Road, Nelson Industrial Estate,
Cramlington NE23 9BL
0670 735370
Contact: E T Rutter

Nottinghamshire

Mansfield ITeC, Thoresby Street,
Mansfield NG18 1QS
0623 650263
Contact: M Mackenzie

Nottingham ITeC, 51
Glasshouse Street, Nottingham
NG1 3LP
0602 584647
Contact: R Lovesay

Shropshire

Telford Opportunities Centre,
Halesfield 14, Telford TF7 4QR
0952 581738
Contact: A Hullyer

Somerset

Taunton ITeC, Collinson Centre,
Wellington Road, Taunton
TA1 5AX
0823 57091
Contact: S le Merle

Staffordshire

Burton ITeC, Midlands Railway
Grain Warehouse, 2 Derby
Street, Burton-on-Trent
D14 2LG
0283 37166
Contact: M Cotterill

Cannock ITeC, Chaseley House,
New Penkridge Road, Cannock
WS11 1HN
054 35 77039
Contact: R Whitlock

Hanley ITeC, Regent Road,
Hanley, Stoke-on-Trent
ST1 1EG
0782 279423
Contact: J Pout

Newcastle-under-Lyme ITeC, 1a
King Street, Newcastle-under-
Lyme ST5 1EM
0782 626354
Contact: P Kingsland

Stafford ITeC, Castle Works,
Castle Street, Stafford ST16 2EF
0785 211437
Contact: C Bailey

Suffolk

Ipswich ITeC, Argyle Street,
Ipswich IP4 2PZ
0473 55885
Contact: A Jackson

Surrey

Guildford ITeC, c/o Millmeed
House, Millmeed, Guildford
GU1 3HW
0483 505050
Contact: R Hulme

South East Surrey ITeC,
Nutfield Court, Nutfield, Redhill
RH1 2JK
073782 2978
Contact: C Bear

Spelthorne ITeC, Short Lane,
Stanwell, Middlesex TW19 7BJ
0784(2) 48801/48804
Contact: J Paschoud

Sussex, East

Brighton ITeC, Level 4, New
England House, New England
Street, Brighton BN1 4GH
0273 606089
Contact: I M Cairns

Hastings ITeC, Hastings College
of Arts and Technology, Archery
Road, St Leonards-on-Sea
TN38 0HX
0424 423847
Contact: D Faithful

Sussex, West

Crawley ITeC, Maxwell Way,
Crawley RH10 2SF
0293 34891
Contact: P J Wheaton

Tyne and Wear

Brass Tacks ITeC, Angloplas
Factory, Norham Road,
North Shields
0632 575029
Contact: I Rees

Gateshead ITeC, Victoria Works,
St James' Road, Gateshead
NE8 3EQ
0632 78096
Contact: D Milmar

Hebburn ITeC, British
Shipbuilders (Training, Education
and Safety Ltd), Ellison Street,
Hebburn NE31 1YN
0632 832221
Contact: B V Kissack

Newcastle ITeC, Unit 10,
Wincomblee Workshops, White
Street, Walker, Newcastle upon
Tyne NA6 3PJ
0632 635456
Contact: D Dyer

Sunderland ITeC, Unit BT 25–
26a, Southwick Industrial Estate,
North Hylton Road, Sunderland
SR5 3HQ
0783 492842
Contact: D J Shrimpling

Warwickshire

Bedworth ITeC, Hosiery Street,
Bedworth CV12 9DN
0203 310150
Contact: M Pitman

Rugby ITeC, 5th Floor, Myson
House, Railway Terrace, Rugby
0788 60825
Contact: B Mitchell

West Midlands

Birmingham (Aston) ITeC, c/o
TI/Tubes Ltd, Rocky Lane,
Aston, Birmingham B6 5RH
021-359 2891
Contact: C Grayson

Coventry ITeC, Casselden
House, Greyfriars Lane,
Coventry CV1 2GZ
0203 25555 ext 2255
Contact: M Stefancic

Dudley ITeC, Dudley College of
Technology, Brierley Hill
Annexe, Moor Street, Brierley
Hill DY5 3EP
0384 263535
Contact: P O'Brien

Sandwell ITeC, Sandwell
Training Agency, Tildasley
Street, West Bromwich B70 9SJ
021-553 6096
Contact: R Mills

Solihull ITeC, 2245 Coventry
Road, Sheldon, Birmingham
B26 3NT
021-742 9431
Contact: P Brown

Walsall ITeC, Willenhall Road,
Darlaston WS10 8JG
021-526 6050
Contact: W Griffiths

Wolverhampton ITeC,
Strawberry Lane, Wednesfield,
Wolverhampton WV1 3RS
0902 636170
Contact: G Cockayne

Wiltshire

Swindon ITeC, Training School,
Dean Street, Swindon SN1 3ES
0793 611808
Contact: A G Grey

Yorkshire, North

York ITeC, Woods Mill, 17
Skeldergate, York YO1 1DH
0904 28776
Contact: C Purry

Yorkshire, South

Barnsley ITeC, Barnsley
Enterprise Centre, Ceag
Building, Pontefract Road,
Barnsley SY1 1AJ
0226 298091
Contact: D C Bramall

Sheffield ITeC, Timer Works,
Thomas Street, Sheffield S1 4LE
0742 750586
Contact: J Dick

Yorkshire, West

Bradford ITeC, 7th Floor,
Arndale House, Charles Street,
Bradford BD1 1JE
0274 752896
Contact: R Armstrong

Halifax ITeC, 315 Gibbet Street,
Milethorn, Halifax HX1 4JX
0422 59026
Contact: A Jackson

Harehills ITeC, 161 Harehills
Lane, Leeds LS8 3QE
0532 499566
Contact: D Williams

Kirklees ITeC, Batley Girls
Grammar School, Batley Field
Hill, Batley
0924 441661
Contact: S Plant

Leeds (Sweet Street) ITeC, 38
Sweet Street, Leeds LS11 9AJ
0532 435511
Contact: K Berry

Shipley ITeC, Otley Road,
Shipley, Bradford BD17 1DY
0274 588488
Contact: R J Crouch

SCOTLAND

Borders

Borders ITeC, Easter Langlee
Primary School, Galashiels,
Roxburghshire TD1 2LP
0896 56517
Contact: A McCue

Central

Falkirk ITeC, Middlefield Block,
Falkirk College of Technology,
Falkirk FK2 9AD
0324 20710
Contact: A Rodger

Stirling ITeC, Pathfoot Building,
Stirling University, Stirling
FK9 4LA
0786 73171
Contact: W Gordon

Dumfries and Galloway

Dumfries ITeC, 9 Catherinefield
Industrial Estate, Dumfries
DG1 3PQ
0387 67633
Contact: J D Williams

Fife

Central Fife ITeC, Flemington
Road, Queensway Industrial
Estate, Glenrothes KY1 3NB
059 751512
Contact: G Grieves

East Fife ITeC (Levenmouth),
Banbeath Industrial Estate,
Leven KY8 5HD
0333 29825
Contact: G I Kingham

West Fife ITeC, Unit AF18,
Hillend Industrial Estate,
Dunfermline KY12 5JE
0383 824403
Contact: J Stewart

Grampian

Aberdeen ITeC, 38 Powis
Terrace, Aberdeen AB9 2LU
0224 492617
Contact: R Cook

Highland

Highland ITeC, Unit 6, 13a
Harbour Road, Inverness
IV1 1SY
0463 226505
Contact: D MacArthur

Lothian

Edinburgh ITeC, 27 York Place,
Edinburgh EH1 3HP
031-5564 533
Contact: P Innes

W Lothian ITeC, Peel House,
Ladywell, Livingstone
EH54 6AG
0506 415208
Contact: F Alexander

Strathclyde

Bellshill ITeC, Block 1, Righead
Industrial Estate, Belgrave Street,
Bellshill ML4 3JA
0698 749901 ext 501
Contact: D Ryan

Clydebank ITeC, Unit 10, 2
North Avenue, Clydebank
Business Park, Clydebank
G81 2DR
041-952 2459
Contact: G M Miller

Cranhill ITeC, 21 Bellrock
Crescent, Cranhill, Glasgow
G33 3HJ
041-774 2354
Contact: B Hunter

Cumbernauld ITeC, 19 Forth
Walk, Cumbernauld, Glasgow
G67 1BT
023 672 2111
Contact: W Mills

East Kilbride ITeC, 30 Hawbank
Road, College Milton, East
Kilbride G74 1AB
035 52 41643
Contact: D Soutar

Gear ITeC, Templeton Business
Centre, Templeton Street,
Glasgow G40 1DW
041-554 1185
Contact: J B Brodie

Govan ITeC, British
Shipbuilders (TES) Ltd,
Holmfauld Road, Linthouse,
Glasgow G15 4RY
041-445 2351
Contact: T Ritchie

INTEC (Inverclyde) Ltd, 5 East
Blackhall Street, Greenock,
Renfrewshire PA15 1HD
0475 29123
Contact: S Holt

Irvine ITeC, Intec West Ltd,
12 MacAdam Place, South
Newmoor Industrial Estate,
Irvine KA12 8EM
0294 212252
Contact: J Leckie

Tayside

Dundee and Tayside ITeC Ltd,
17 King Street, Dundee
DD1 2LD
0382 25473
Contact: G Linton

WALES

Clwyd

Deeside ITeC, The Coach
House, Kelsterston Road, Flint
CH6 5TH
0244 816 236
Contact: R Johnston

Vale of Clwyd ITeC, Fanol
Avenue, Abergele LL22 7HE
Contact: G Griffiths

Wrexham ITeC, Unit 19,
Whitegate Industrial Estate,
Wrexham LL13 8UG
0978 350575
Contact: D Glynn

Dyfed

Llanelli ITeC, 100 Trostre Road,
Llanelli SA15 2EA
0554 778321
Contact: M Truman

Glamorgan, Mid

Pontypridd ITeC, Unit G5,
Treforest Industrial Estate,
Treforest, near Pontypridd
CF37 5YL
0443 85 4133
Contact: R Howorth

Glamorgan, South

Cardiff ITeC, Frixa House, East
Canal Wharf, Cardiff CF1 5QQ
0222 493483
Contact: A Fisher

Glamorgan, West

Neath ITeC, Neath Industrial
Components, Canal Side, Neath
SA11 1PQ
0639 4141
Contact: P Vincent

Gwent

Ebbw Vale ITeC, Blaenau
Gwent Opportunities Centre,
Tafarnaubach Industrial Estate,
Tredegar NP2 3AA
049525 4311
Contact: P Phillips

Newport ITeC, Corporation
Road, Newport NP9 0YT
0633 280991
Contact: A Vaughan

Gwynedd

Caernarfon ITeC, WDA Unit 1,
Cibyn Industrial Estate,
Caernarfon LL55 2BD
0286 76477
Contact: E Hughes

Chapter 3.12

Community Industry (CI)

Introduction

The Community Industry Scheme is a long established programme which provides temporary work of benefit to the community for approximately 7000 disadvantaged young people aged between 17 and 19 years old. It seeks to improve job prospects and personal development of participants and is based in 57 inner city areas.

History

The CI scheme was introduced as a temporary measure in 1972 and therefore predates the Commission itself. It was initiated by the National Association of Youth Clubs and funded in the main by the Department of Employment. In May 1984 it became a registered charity; CI Ltd.

Organisation

The scheme is funded by grants from the Department of Employment and the European Social Fund, which are administered by the MSC's Employment Division. Places on the scheme are provided by Community Industry Ltd.

Eligibility

Participants on the programme must be between 17 and 19 years old although the number of 16 year olds is very low (approximately 140, representing about 2 per cent of the total numbers in 1984–85). Recruitment among the 16 and 17 year olds is confined to those who have declined, left or completed a YTS training. As the aim of the scheme is to prepare for employment young people who have more difficulties than their contemporaries in finding or keeping a job, it offers preferential places to those who are disadvantaged either personally, socially or physically. Since the introduction of YTS, the proportion of 18 and 19 year olds on the scheme has increased from 30 per cent in 1982–83 to 48 per cent in 1984–85 and this rise is expected to continue.

Wages

Young people on the CI scheme receive a nationally agreed wage for the job which increases with age: £33.00 at 17; £39.30 at 18; and £43.90 at 19. In addition, a London weighting allowance is paid.

The Scheme

Participants are allowed in general up to one year on the scheme, although there is the flexibility of extending this period for individuals. If it is felt that a participant would benefit from extra time in CI, an extension can be negotiated for a three- or six-month period.

Participants in CI work on projects within the local community or in workshops. Young people work in groups of eight to ten under the supervision of a team leader, known as a scheme consultant, who is usually a skilled tradesman. They undertake work projects of social value, while acquiring and practising work skills such as building trade skills, carpentry and joinery, painting and decorating, and gardening. Use is also made of placements for some young people. They can also study part time for various qualifications and receive social and life skills training.

Each centre is allocated a certain number of places depending on the needs of the community within the local area; some centres offer 50 places, others 100 and some 150 places.

The official method of recruitment is via the careers office and Jobcentre, although unofficially people are referred from youth clubs, probation offices and other organisations.

Future Developments

The MSC plans to maintain the level of provision, ie 7000 places, over the coming years.

Funding

In 1984–85 approximately £25.2 million was spent on Community Industry, of which £1.8 million was allocated by the ESF.

Further Information

Community Industry
24 Highbury Crescent
London N5 1RX
01-226 6663

MSC
Special Employment Measures Branch
Moorfoot
Sheffield S1 4PQ
0742 753275

Chapter 3.13

Technical and Vocational Education Initiative (TVEI)

Introduction

The Technical and Vocational Education Initiative was set up in 1983 for an initial period of five years, to provide local education authorities (LEAs) with direct grant funding to stimulate the development of general technical and job-related education for young people aged between 14 and 18. As such it represents the first and, so far, the only venture of the MSC to influence and fund the school curriculum directly.

History

The Initiative was first announced in November 1982, in a surprise statement by the Prime Minister. Since then it has progressed in a number of stages. The first 14 pilot projects started in September 1983, a further 46 projects were approved in February 1984 for a September start and in November 1984 funds were made available for all LEAs to mount programmes under the initiative.

Originally all LEAs in England and Wales were invited to submit plans. Of those which responded to the request, 14 were successful. The LEAs selected initially were: Barnsley; Bedfordshire; Birmingham; Bradford; Clwyd; Devon; Enfield; Hereford and Worcester; Hertfordshire; Leicestershire; Sandwell; Staffordshire; Wirral; Wigan.

The extension to the initial programme, coming into operation from September 1984, brought in more authorities and by June 1985, there were 62 TVEI projects including five in Scotland and involving every kind of local authority:

— 4 London boroughs
— 6 Welsh counties
— 4 Scottish education authorities (5 projects)

183

— 29 English counties
— 18 Metropolitan boroughs.

Organisation

The MSC was charged with managing the initiative by the
Secretary of State for Employment and allocated funds for
distribution. A National Steering Group (see Chapter 2.4) was set
up to establish working criteria and to monitor progress. In
addition there are assessors from the Department of Education
and Science, Her Majesty's Inspectorate of Schools, the
Department of Employment and the Scottish Education
Department. TVEI is admnistered by a special unit of the MSC
based in London.

The national criteria, decided by the steering group but within
which the individual projects can experiment, state that
programmes should be 'broad based to encourage initiative,
problem solving and other aspects of personal development'.
Technical and vocational elements have to be broadly related to
employment trends and general education remains an essential
part of the child's curriculum. Other guidelines ensure that TVEI
projects:

— provide equal opportunities for young people of both sexes
and avoid sex stereotyping;
— provide a four-year curriculum from 14 to 18 designed to
prepare students for working and adult life in a rapidly
changing society;
— provide planned work experience from age 15 onwards;
— assess each student regularly;
— provide adequate educational and careers counselling;
— cater for children from a broad range of abilities.

Each LEA project has a co-ordinator to bring together the
educational institutions involved and also other interested parties
such as parents, local industry and commerce, teachers and
lecturers. LEAs rather than the MSC are responsible for the day-
to-day running of programmes and, since each project is designed
to meet local needs and circumstances, there are wide differences
between projects. Some LEA schemes are based on existing
facilities, others use TVEI funding for new ones.

Projects

Each project provides a comprehensive four-year course of full-time technical, vocational and general education, including the opportunity to gain a recognised qualification. Most projects bring together a number of secondary schools in a locality, together with one or more further education colleges and have designed new curricula (although TVEI is not an 'exam' but a catalyst of change). Projects provide LEAs with the funding to experiment with new ways of organising, planning and managing education, as well as an opportunity to introduce new subjects. Some LEAs have developed modular courses to broaden children's subject range, others have integrated TVEI elements with the existing curriculum.

The changes in what and how children are taught have had implications for those doing the teaching. In March 1985, the MSC agreed to establish and fund a new interim programme of TVEI-related in-service training for teachers (TRIST), for a period of two years. A total of £25 million will be made available, over this period, to all education authorities in England, Scotland and Wales to make provision for secondary school and further education teachers.

The number of institutions in any one project varies from three (two schools and a college of further education) to 17 (eight schools, six colleges of further education, two sixth form colleges and a college of art and design).

Numbers

Each of the 62 projects has funding for approximately 250 students per year, giving a total number of participants over the four years of about 1000. The original 14 LEAs, which ran the first projects, tend to have more pupils doing TVEI courses since there were fewer authorities among which to share the available funding. By July 1985, some 20,900 students were taking part in the scheme. TVEI currently covers about 3 per cent of all 14 year olds, spread over about 8 per cent of secondary schools.

Pupils at participating schools can choose whether or not to take TVEI options as part of their third-year subject choice — participation is voluntary. Some LEAs have also started some 16 year olds on TVEI courses. Some TVEI projects tend to cater for the more academically able, others attract the less academic.

Qualifications

Students participating in the TVEI programme may study for a wide range of nationally recognised qualifications. These can include certificates given by City and Guilds, Business and Technical Education Council, and the Royal Society of Arts, depending on each individual project. There is also the possibility of study for the Certificate of Pre-Vocational Education as well as GCE O and A levels and CSE. In some cases new O level and CSE courses have been designed and validated by the appropriate boards to cover the skills needed by some of the high technology businesses.

As well as preparing young people for these examinations, all projects intend to provide some system of recording and reviewing progress of individual students. This record of profiling should be available to students on completion of their programme to enable them to show it to prospective employers.

Funding

The 14 original pilot projects were promised £46 million for five years. For the 48 projects in the second stage, £100 million was provided for the five years. This means that each project has up to £2 million of funding available — £400,000 a year for five years. MSC cash is intended to meet the extra costs incurred by the LEA in running the project. Overall, most money (some 60 per cent) goes on additional staffing and about a quarter on new premises and equipment. At least 1 per cent of MSC funds must be spent by the LEA on evaluation of the project.

The extra funding TVEI pumps into schools and colleges does mean that teacher/pupil ratios are lower than the normal secondary school level and also means that pupils have access to a wider range of up-to-date equipment — particularly in the field of new technology.

Issues

As TVEI is the MSC's first venture into funding the school curriculum, it is not surprising that many LEAs were initially suspicious of its intentions. In most cases, the prospect of extra funding has overcome any reservations but a number (including the Inner London Education Authority) remain unwilling to accept MSC intervention and are not participating in the project.

It is perhaps too early to evaluate the success of the project although TVEI has been called 'the most monitored scheme in educational history'. Preliminary research as part of the national evaluation appears to indicate slightly higher levels of mathematical achievement among pupils involved in TVEI compared to non-TVEI pupils. The question remains, whatever results are achieved, as to what the outcome would have been if the education service had been given the extra funding directly, rather than through the Department of Employment, with MSC strings attached.

A final issue concerns the future development of TVEI projects. At present, TVEI is not seen as a permanent programme and it will soon be taking on pupils who will be in the middle of their programme when the committed money runs out. Whether LEAs will be able or willing to assume the extra costs in the long term remains to be seen.

Further Information

TVEI Unit
Room 10/13
MSC
236 Gray's Inn Road
London WC1X 8HL

TVEI Insight: Free magazine published by MSC and available from MSC, Distribution Unit (Dept TVEI), Room E824, Moorfoot, Sheffield S1 4PQ.

List of Authorities Running Projects

TVEI projects are running in the following LEAs. Those LEAs in metropolitan areas are listed under that authority.

ENGLAND

Bedfordshire
TVEI Project Co-ordinator, Bedfordshire County Council, Education Department, County Hall, Bedford MK42 9AP
0234 63222
Co-ordinator: H Carr-Archer

Berkshire
TVEI Project Co-ordinator, TVEI Office, Alfred Sutton Boys
School, Crescent Road, Reading RG1 5SR
0734 661331
Co-ordinator: M C Smyth

Buckinghamshire
TVEI Project Co-ordinator, Milton Keynes Area Education
Office, Wolverton House, Stratford Road, Wolverton Mill, Milton
Keynes MK12 5NY
0908 563731
Co-ordinator: G Vincent

Cambridgeshire
TVEI Project Director, Peterborough Educational Development
Centre, Cottesmore Close, Peterborough PE3 6TP
0733 261968
Co-ordinator: A Nicholl

Cheshire
TVEI Project Co-ordinator, TVEI Centre, Bedford Street, Crewe
CW2 6JQ
0270 213706
Co-ordinator: R Lister

Cleveland
TVEI Project Co-ordinator, Brackenhoe School, Marton Road,
Middlesbrough TS4 3RX
0642 326802
Co-ordinator: M K Anderson

Cornwall
TVEI Project Co-ordinator, TVEI Centre, Cornwall Technical
College of Further Education, Trevenson Campus, Trevenson
Road, Pool, Redruth TR15 3RD
0209 714280
Co-ordinator: P L Millington

Cumbria
TVEI Project Director, Cumbria County Council, Education
Department, 5 Portland Square, Carlisle CA1 1PU
0228 32161
Co-ordinator: B A Wind

Derbyshire
TVEI Project Co-ordinator, South East Derbyshire College, Field
Road, Ilkeston
0602 324212

Devon
TVEI Project Co-ordinator, Exeter TVEI Centre, St Hilda's, York
Road, Exeter EX4 6PG
0392 219615
Co-ordinator: G Philpotts

Durham
TVEI Project Co-ordinator, Durham County Council, Howletch
JMI School, Penine Drive, Peterlee SR8 2NQ
0783 872537
Co-ordinator: Dr A Stoker

Essex
TVEI Project Director, Essex County TVEI Centre, Barn Hall
School, Alderney Gardens, Wickford
03744 69646
Co-ordinator: N Hunt

Gloucestershire
TVEI Project Co-ordinator, Gloucestershire County Council,
Education Department, Archdeacon Centre, Archdeacon Street,
Gloucester
0452 33588
Co-ordinator: S L Brown

Hampshire
TVEI Project Co-ordinator, Hampshire County Council, Oak
Park School, Leigh Road, Havant PO9 2EX
0705 453302
Co-ordinator: R W Lloyd-Jones

Hereford and Worcester
TVEI Project Co-ordinator, TVEI Centre, Hereford and Worcester
County Council, Widemarsh Street, Hereford HP4 9HA
0432 57377
Co-ordinator: D Botterill

Hertfordshire
TVEI Project Co-ordinator, Divisional Education Office, The
Grange, High Street, Stevenage SG1 3BD
0438 60331
Co-ordinator: Dr R G Wallace

Isle of Wight
TVEI Project Co-ordinator, Teachers' Centre, Seely House, Upper
St James' Street, Newport PO30 1LL
0983 524233
Co-ordinator: B Sutton

Leicestershire
TVEI Project Co-ordinator, Leicestershire County Council,
Education Department, Room 138, County Hall, Glenfield,
Leicester LE3 8RF
0533 871313 ext 503
Co-ordinator: D D'Hooghe

Lincolnshire
TVEI Project Co-ordinator, c/o Gainsborough College of Further
Education, Morton Terrace, Gainsborough DN21 2SU
0427 611591/4585
Co-ordinator: D Jennings

London, Greater

Croydon
TVEI Project Co-ordinator, London Borough of Croydon,
Davidson Centre, Davidson Road, Croydon CR0 6DD
01-654 9701
Co-ordinator: R F Pickup

Enfield
TVEI Project Co-ordinator, London Borough of Enfield,
Education Department, PO Box 56, Civic Centre, Silver Street,
Enfield EN1 3XQ
01-366 6565 ext 9336
Co-ordinator: M Hearn

Havering
TVEI Project Co-ordinator, London Borough of Havering,
Mercury House, Mercury Gardens, Romford RM1 3DR
0708 66999 ext 304
Co-ordinator: R Croucher

Richmond upon Thames
TVEI Project Director, London Borough of Richmond upon
Thames, 56–58 York Street, Twickenham TW1 3LT
01-892 0033
Co-ordinator: D Edwards

Manchester, Greater

Bolton
TVEI Project Co-ordinator, Bolton Metropolitan Borough,
Paderborn House, PO Box 53, Civic Centre, Bolton BL1 1JW
0204 22311 ext 510
Co-ordinator: C M Ellin

Bury
TVEI Project Director, Metropolitan Borough of Bury, Education
Development Centre, Broadoak High School, Seedfield Building,
Parkinson Street, Bury BL9 8LP
061-797 2331
Co-ordinator: H Meredith

Stockport
TVEI Project Co-ordinator, Stockport Teachers' Centre, Lisburne
Lane, Offerton, Stockport SK2 7LL
061-456 8985
Co-ordinator: A W Cross

Tameside
TVEI Project Co-ordinator (Acting), Tameside Metropolitan
Borough, Education Department, Council Office, Wellington
Road, Ashton under Lyne OL6 6DL
061-330 8355 ext 3219
Co-ordinator: R Moxon

Wigan
TVEI Project Co-ordinator, TVEI Centre, Wigan Metropolitan
Borough Council, Education Department, Gateway House,
Standishgate, Wigan WN1 1XL
0942 884606
Co-ordinator: S R Cooper

Merseyside

Wirral
TVEI Project Co-ordinator, Wirral Technology Centre, Ilford
Avenue, Wallasey L44 4BU
051-639 8232
Co-ordinator: C G B Farwell

Norfolk
TVEI Project Co-ordinator, Norfolk County Council, Room 051,
Education Department, County Hall, Martineau Lane, Norwich
NR1 2DL
0603 611122 ext 5339
Co-ordinator: M V Smith

Northamptonshire
TVEI Project Co-ordinator, TVEI Project Office, Cliftonville
Middle School, Cliftonville Road, Northampton NN1 5BW
0604 24900
Co-ordinator: P B Smith

Northumberland
TVEI Project Co-ordinator, Northumberland County Council,
Morpeth Teachers' Centre, Witton House, Cottingwood Lane,
Morpeth NE61 1BU
0670 511324
Co-ordinator: R Morris

Shropshire
TVEI Project Co-ordinator, TVEI Unit, Listley Street Avenue,
Bridgnorth WV15 6AL
07462 66835
Co-ordinator: M Webster

Somerset
TVEI Project Co-ordinator, Holyrood School, Zembard Lane,
Chard TA20 1JL
046 06 3831
Co-ordinator: J Henderson

Staffordshire
TVEI Project Co-ordinator, Staffordshire County Council,
Education Offices, PO Box 23, Unity House, Hanley, Stoke-on-
Trent ST1 4QP
0782 29611 ext 2359
Co-ordinator: K Wild

Suffolk
TVEI Project Co-ordinator, Northern Area, Education Offices,
Suffolk House, London Road North, Lowestoft NR32 1BH
0502 62262
Co-ordinator: R Loose

Surrey
TVEI Project Co-ordinator, Camberley Teachers' Centre,
118 Upper Chobham Road, Camberley GU15 1ES
0276 26681
Co-ordinator: D M Owen

Sussex, East
TVEI Project Director Designate, East Sussex County Council,
PO Box 4, County Hall, St Anne's Crescent, Lewes BN7 1SG
0273 475400 ext 374
Co-ordinator: G Jebson

Tyne and Wear

Newcastle upon Tyne
TVEI Project Co-ordinator, City of Newcastle upon Tyne,
Pendower Hall Teachers' Centre, West Road, Newcastle upon
Tyne NE15 6PP
091 274 3620
Co-ordinator: P Jones

North Tyneside
TVEI Project Co-ordinator Designate, North Tyneside TVEI
Centre, West Tower, Queen Victoria Training Centre, Coach
Lane, North Shields
0632 587335
Co-ordinator: P Parish

South Tyneside
TVEI Project Co-ordinator, Resource Centre, St Michael's
Avenue, The Honnen, South Shields
0632 563603
Co-ordinator: W Graham

Sunderland
TVEI Project Co-ordinator, Metropolitan Borough of Sunderland,
Thorney Close School, Telford Road, Sunderland
0783 201833
Co-ordinator: K Smith

Warwickshire
TVEI Project Co-ordinator, Warwickshire County Council,
22 Northgate Street, Warwick CV34 4SR
0926 493431 ext 2113
Co-ordinator: G Jones

West Midlands

Birmingham
TVEI Project Co-ordinator, City of Birmingham Education
Department, Bordesley Centre, Camp Hill, Stratford Road,
Birmingham B11 1AR
021-771 4667
Co-ordinator: C Lea

Coventry
TVEI Project Co-ordinator, TOPSHOP, Greyfriars Lane,
Coventry CV1 2GY
0203 553241/2 ext 4
Co-ordinator: A Booth

Dudley
TVEI Project Co-ordinator, Dudley Teachers' Education and
Development Centre, Kingswinford DY6 8EH
0384 288864
Co-ordinator: Dr P N Smith

Sandwell
TVEI Project Co-ordinator, Metropolitan Borough of Sandwell,
Langley High School Annexe, Popes Lane, Oldbury, Warley
B69 4RJ
021-544 7077
Co-ordinator: K Granger

Solihull
TVEI Project Co-ordinator, Education Industry Centre,
Woodlands School, Sanda Croft, Chelmsley Wood B36 0NF
021-770 4140
Co-ordinator: M Schofield

Yorkshire, South

Barnsley
TVEI Project Co-ordinator, Barnsley Metropolitan Borough
Council, Education Department, Bernslai Close, Barnsley
S70 2HS
0226 287621 ext 283
Co-ordinator: J MacRory

Doncaster
TVEI Project Director, TVEI Centre, Sycamore School,
St Wilfred's Road, Cantley DN4 6AH
0302 532740
Co-ordinator: J G Hughes

Yorkshire, West

Bradford
TVEI Project Co-ordinator, City of Bradford Metropolitan
Council, The Consortium Centre, Tong Campus, Westgage Hill,
Tong BD4 6NR
0274 689199
Co-ordinator: P Brindle

WALES

Clwyd
TVEI Project Co-ordinator, Clwyd County Council, Room 3123,
Shire Hall, Mold CH7 6ND
0352 2121 ext 2569
Co-ordinator: A Farlam

Glamorgan, Mid
TVEI Project Co-ordinator, TVEI Unit, Cymmer Comprehensive
Lower School, Grawen Street, Porth, Rhondda CF39 9HA
0443 687606
Co-ordinator: D Layton

Glamorgan, West
TVEI Project Co-ordinator, West Glamorgan County Council,
Dwr-y-felin Comprehensive School, Dwr-y-felin Road, Neath
SA10 7RE
0639 55161
Co-ordinator: P G Fabian

Gwent
TVEI Project Co-ordinator, Pontypool College, Blaendanre Road, Pontypool NP4 5YE
04955 55141 ext 130
Co-ordinator: K Fuge

Gwynedd
TVEI Project Co-ordinator, Gwynedd County Council, TVEI Unit, Teachers' Centre, Bridge Street, Llangefli, Isle of Anglesey LL77 7HL
0248 724929
Co-ordinator: T Brockley

Powys
TVEI Project Co-ordinator (Acting), Powys County Council, Education Department, The Lindens, Spa Road, Llandrindod Wells LD1 5HA
0597 3711
Co-ordinator: Dr M E Brooks

SCOTLAND

Borders
TVEI Project Co-ordinator, TVEI Centre, Langlands Mill, Hawick TD9 7DS
0450 78666
Co-ordinator: W Geddes

Central

Dumfries and Galloway
TVEI Project Co-ordinator, Lincluden Primary School, Lincluden DG2 0PU
0387 69589
Co-ordinator: J B Collier

Fife
TVEI Project Co-ordinator, Fife Regional Council, Education Department, Regional Offices, Wemyssfield, Kirkcaldy KY1 1XS
0592 756554
Co-ordinator: W Kirkpatrick

Strathclyde

Glasgow
St Leonard's RC Secondary School, 62 Lochend Road,
Easterhouse, Glasgow G34 0NY
041-773 2706
Co-ordinator: G Warnock

Renfrew
TVEI Project Co-ordinator, James Watt College, Finnart Street,
Greenock PA16 8HF
0475 24433
Co-ordinator: J Travers

Chapter 3.14

Adult Training — The 1985 Changes

On 15 July 1985, the Manpower Services Commission announced a major restructuring of its adult training services. This short section explains how the material in the following five chapters links together.

The changes meant that the long-established Training Opportunities Scheme (TOPS) was replaced by two new programmes, one of which is broken into a number of separate schemes.

The reason for the change was to create 'more flexible provision that responds to local needs'. Since many individual *courses* offered under TOPS are retained intact or with modifications, and since Area Manpower Boards will continue to determine with Training Division Area Offices which courses are run where, it might not be immediately clear what changes have occurred beyond the introduction of new names for courses. In fact, the key changes include:

— new eligibility criteria which allow 18 year olds to apply for courses (the minimum age for TOPS was 19);
— an increase in the number of adults helped to train by the MSC (220,000 in 1985–86 and a planned 250,000 in 1986–87 including Open Tech participants);
— a cut in the number of full-time courses (which attract a training allowance) and a sharp rise in the number of part-time opportunities for which participants are not paid. While it is difficult to put a precise figure on the number of full-time places lost, it is likely to be in the order of 10,000.

Provision is now grouped into two programmes:

— *Job Training Programme:* aimed at helping to meet known employment needs, and the creation and growth of businesses through a variety of schemes;
— *Wider Opportunities Training Programme:* aimed at helping unemployed people who lack basic skills and confidence

improve their work-related skills, retain employability and cope with the changing content of jobs and work.

The following diagram explains provision:

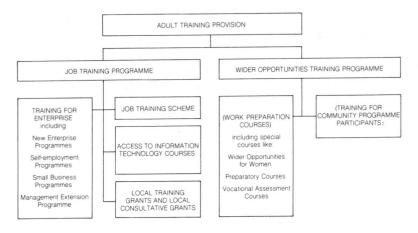

Material in brackets means there is no specific title for the provision

Chapter 3.15

Job Training Scheme

Introduction

This new scheme, introduced in July 1985 as part of the Job Training Programme (see Chapter 3.14) carries on the occupational skill-training element of the old Training Opportunities Scheme which it replaces. It helps to meet identified employment needs by providing training for adults who are unemployed or willing to give up work for training which will improve their prospects. There are opportunities for people to update existing skills or learn new ones. The scheme does not cover courses leading to first degrees, normal training for the professions or training for a specific employer. It is not intended to supplant employers' own responsibilities for training.

Types of Training

A wide range of courses is offered under the JTS umbrella. Courses range from craft work and office skills through to computing and technician and technologist courses. They include basic skills training for work in industries like construction, engineering, electronics and the automotive trade as well as training for commercial and retailing jobs. There are courses at various levels.

The emphasis of the scheme is firmly upon training for skills where there are real job prospects — not training 'for stock'. This means patterns of courses will vary from area to area, according to local employment patterns.

Where Courses are Held

Courses are run throughout Great Britain in a variety of training establishments. The MSC's Skillcentres (see Chapter 2.3) provided about one-third of occupational training under TOPS and this is likely to continue at the same level. Industries for which they provide practical training include: construction trades (such as carpentry, bricklaying and plumbing); electrical and electronic industries and other new technologies; general servicing (such as video, TV and typewriter repair); hotel and catering; hairdressing; HGV driving; and plant and automotive trades.

Some Skillcentre courses allow trainees to study for City and Guilds qualifications but many courses offer only Skillcentre 'Certificates of Completion' rather than more widely recognised qualifications. Two Skillcentres provide residential accommodation for trainees if required; others have lists of local accommodation for trainees living beyond daily travelling distance.

As well as Skillcentre courses, Training Division also funds courses run by various educational establishments and other organisations. Some are exclusively for trainees; others have been 'infill' courses where TD sponsors (funds) a trainee to do an existing course run by an institution.

Under TOPS it was occasionally possible for a learner to find a suitable course and then apply for infill sponsorship — although places were strictly limited and dependent both on the individual's employment prospects on completion of training, and on the funds available to the area office at the time of application. If accepted, the MSC paid course fees and a normal training allowance. It is not yet clear if or how the infill arrangements have survived the ending of TOPS and the establishment of the Job Training Scheme.

Occupational training courses for adults run by further education colleges for Training Division, tend to be geared towards office and commercial skill training. They include typing, shorthand, bookkeeping, accounting and computing courses. Other areas include health and welfare occupational training.

Length of Courses

Generally courses last from three to six months. No course is longer than a year. Most courses are full time but a few are part time.

Eligibility Criteria

The eligibility rules for the Job Training Scheme are more flex-

ible than those which applied to TOPS. Before applying for a place, would-be trainees must:
- be unemployed, or prepared to give up their job to train;
- have been away from full-time education for at least two years;
- be at least 18 years old on the day the course starts;
- intend to look for a job which uses the new skills learned in training;
- normally live and be allowed to work in Great Britain.

In addition, there is a one-year maximum limit to the amount of MSC funding any person can have within a three-year period under this scheme or the Training for Enterprise Scheme (see next chapter). Equivalent TOPS courses taken in the past may count against this limit. People who have been on relevant training courses for less than one year can apply for the balance of MSC support. There are exceptions to these criteria for disabled people.

There are no maximum age limits for taking a course but, in practice, younger trainees are more likely to be accepted if suitable, since their working lives after training are potentially greater. This means that people over 55 may find difficulties in getting a place.

Other people meeting the eligibility criteria may not get places either — there is no right to JTS training. For some courses there are written or practical tests and for all courses there is an interview.

Allowances

People accepted on to courses pay no fees and most full-time courses attract a training allowance. This varies depending on individual circumstances and commitments. The basic allowance for 1985–86 was £38. There are extra payments for adult dependants, travelling expenses, meals and a living away from home allowance where necessary. In addition, trainees may be entitled to housing and supplementary benefit in certain circumstances. Current rates of allowances are given in leaflet AT14, available from Jobcentres.

Trainees on the few part-time courses under the Job Training Scheme do not receive an allowance.

Numbers and Funding

About 54,000 individuals are expected to enter training on this scheme in 1985–86, the cost of which is expected to be in the region of £159 million. This compares with the 68,200 people planned for TOPS training in 1983–84 but does not take into account the numbers on the other new schemes in the Job Training Programme, such as Training for Enterprise, or those on the Wider Opportunities Training Programme.

How to Apply

Details of Job Training Scheme courses are available from Jobcentres. Employment advisers in the Jobcentre will also supply application forms and other information but the decision on who to accept is made by training advisers based at TD area offices on the basis of tests and an interview. Some high-level courses may be advertised in the national press or through Professional and Executive Recruitment and have a different application procedure.

Disabled People and JTS

People with disabilities can take advantage of the full range of JTS training. In addition, applications are given special consideration and standard rules for eligibility may be relaxed for suitable courses. People with disabilities may also qualify for training beyond the scope of JTS (see Chapter 3.6).

Further Information

As this is a new scheme, many people may not be familiar with it. Jobcentre and Employment Office staff will have up-to-date information; a useful starting point is leaflet ATL9.

Chapter 3.16

Training for Enterprise

Introduction

This new scheme, introduced in July 1985 as part of the Job Training Programme (see Chapter 3.14) carries forward a number of courses available under the old Training Opportunities Scheme which it replaces. There are, however, changes and modifications. The four main types of course available under Training for Enterprise are described separately below but they, and other programmes, share a common goal of trying to teach and promote the management skills needed to start, run and develop a small business.

Self-employment Programmes

These are short programmes for people running or planning to start a one-person business without employing others. Courses cover useful and basic business skills such as assessing a product or service, identifying demand, pricing and determining true costs and profits. Once basic principles have been explained, work on the programme is based on participants' own businesses or ideas. People on the courses learn how to prepare business plans to attract loans and to make cash-flow and sales forecasts. Some programmes may also offer other practical training for particular business ideas.

Self-employment Programmes may be full time (often preferred by those yet to start up) or part time (convenient for those already in business). They give the equivalent of between five and ten days' learning time.

Small Business Programmes

Known formerly as Small Business Courses, these are intended to help people whose business idea is likely to employ three or more staff. They include help in three main areas:

— managing the business
— market research
— launching the business.

The first area covers much the same ground as for the Self-employment Courses (above) but in more detail and with additional subjects such as employment practice. The second area, research, is so vital to a new business that the Programme provides access to a budget of up to £500 as well as giving advice and training. For the third element, participants are given individual review sessions with the programme organiser to go over key decisions for the first few weeks when the business is launched.

Courses are both full and part time. Full-time courses last about eight weeks — 15 days' learning about management followed by about five weeks' total contact time, over a period of months, for individual review sessions. Part-time courses provide the same content spread over a longer period.

New Enterprise Programme

This programme, which is run at five leading university business schools, is for people launching businesses with significant growth and employment potential. The courses, each with some 16 participants, start with four weeks' intensive residential tuition at a business school in London, Warwick, Manchester, Durham or Glasgow to learn all the techniques of professional business management. Market research is given considerable emphasis as participants formulate their business plans and they have access to a budget of up to £1250 for their own research. This residential period is followed by 12 weeks during which time participants start their enterprises, but return to the business school once a month to review progress and discuss any problems with a panel of experts.

A few part-time programmes are also available for shorter periods, including weekends, suitable for people who have not yet given up their employment or who have started in business already. In the past more than 80 per cent of trainees have succeeded in establishing new and growing companies.

Management Extension Programme

This programme offers practical help and advice to owners and managers of existing businesses with growth potential but lacking in management resources. The aim of the programme is to match up the ideas and needs of small businesses with the skills of experienced executives, seconded to the small firm. The programme uses redundant managers with several years' senior management experience, plus expertise in specialist areas such as marketing, finance, production or engineering. They have also undergone an intensive MSC training course.

The programme, which is run on the MSC's behalf by university business schools, regional management centres, polytechnics and consultancies, costs nothing to the host firm and the participating manager receives a weekly training allowance.

After the small business has outlined its proposals and requirements, these are matched with the skills and experience of participating managers. Before starting secondment with the host firm, the manager spends a week getting to know the business and its personnel. Managers are then seconded for a period of up to three months after which the firm has acquired useful skills and knowledge. In many cases, host firms have offered permanent employment to their participating manager although they are under no obligation to do so.

Other Programmes

Training for Enterprise also includes other small schemes such as the Action Learning Programme, which brings together groups of owners or managers of small businesses to learn from each other's experiences under guidance. There is also Owner/Manager Training — programmes designed to improve performance in such fields as planning, finance and marketing.

Eligibility Criteria

For individuals, entry criteria resemble those of the Job Training Scheme; that is, applicants must:

— be unemployed or prepared to give up their job to train on full-time courses. Applicants marginally in business may

also be accepted;
— have been out of full-time education for at least two years;
— be at least 18 years old when the course starts;
— normally live and be allowed to work in Great Britain.

In addition, there is a maximum one-year limit to the amount of MSC funding a person can have within a three-year period under this scheme or the Job Training Scheme (previous chapter). Equivalent TOPS courses may count against this limit. People who have been on relevant training courses for less than a year can apply for the balance of MSC support. Relaxation of these rules may be allowed for disabled people.

There is no set maximum age but the MSC is likely to take into account the length of an applicant's working life after training.

Entry to courses is competitive and applicants have to convince an interviewing panel of their determination and commitment, that their business idea is viable and that they have the necessary skill and knowledge to make it work. For the New Enterprise Programme, for example, only 25 per cent of applicants emerge from the selection interviews with a place.

Companies wishing to use the Management Extension Programme must employ no more than 200 people.

Allowances

People accepted on to courses pay no fees and full-time courses attract a training allowance of the same level as for the job training scheme, with a similar system of extra payments for travel, dependants and living away from home.

Numbers and Funding

For 1985–86, there are expected to be 7000 places available on Self Employment Courses, 4000 places on Small Business Courses, 2000 places on the New Enterprise Programme and 4000 on the Management Extension Programme and other schemes like Action Learning and Owner/Manager Training. There are plans to expand these programmes in 1986–87 to support up to 25,000 training placements.

Enterprise Training programmes will cost £14.3 million in 1985–86 and £19.5 million in 1986–87. The cost to the taxpayer for each person trained under the most intensive scheme — the New Enterprise Programme — is £5130.

Evaluation

Management training of this sort appears to increase prospects of survival for new businesses quite considerably. The MSC estimates that jobs created under Enterprise Training programmes cost the taxpayer less than £1000 per job created. In addition, follow-up of participants suggests that the failure rate of their businesses is low — less than 2 per cent in the case of New Enterprise Programme participants.

How to Apply

Although Jobcentres may carry leaflets about the programmes, applications and full details are available from Training Division area offices (see Chapter 2.5). Applications and enquiries for the New Enterprise Programme should be made directly to the MSC's central Enterprise Training section at the Head Office, Moorfoot, Sheffield.

Further Information

Ask for leaflets ATL 47 *Setting Up Your Own Business*; ATL 33 *Management Extension Programme* (for host firms) and ATL 50 (for unemployed managers).

Access to Information Technology (AIT) Courses

Introduction

These are new courses, introduced in July 1985 as part of the Job Training Programme (see Chapter 3.14), following earlier pilot projects. The courses are intended to give adults the opportunity to gain an awareness of new technology as it affects them in their working environment through part-time courses.

Eligibility

AIT courses are open to anyone over the age of 17 and under retirement age who is not in full-time education or on a YTS scheme. Participants may be employed, unemployed or self-employed.

The Courses

These courses will provide up to 30 hours' tuition, generally in the evenings and/or at weekends. The courses are structured so that the most inexperienced person can become familiar with handling computers. They are practical courses with learning done mainly by direct 'hands-on' experience with individuals working at their own pace on computers.

A typical AIT course includes a general introduction to information technology and the basic operation of a micro-computer and then looks at different applications of the technology for operations such as accounting or file handling, computer aided manufacture, robotics and static control devices and computer aided design and simulation. The emphasis between commercial and industrial applications will vary from course to course, depending on the provider and on local needs.

Cost

AIT courses cost 50p per hour, payable in advance; the charge will be waived for unemployed people.

Providers

Courses are provided by colleges, training centres, ITeCs and other organisations.

Numbers and Funding

The MSC plans to provide opportunities for up to 35,000 people during 1985–86 at a cost of £1.5 million.

Further Information

See leaflet ATL 35 from Jobcentres and Employment Offices which will also provide details of local courses, as will TD area offices.

Chapter 3.18

Local Consultancy Grants and Local Training Grants

Introduction

These are new schemes, introduced in July 1985 as part of the Job Training Programme (see Chapter 3.14), following earlier pilot projects. They offer financial assistance in the form of grants to employers seeking to improve or plan their own or bought-in training. They are aimed particularly at smaller companies faced with changes in their operations which require assistance.

Eligibility for Consultancy

To qualify for a consultancy grant, the company must show that:

— it is in the process of changes which are likely to put new demands on its workforce and have training implications;
— it is unable to manage the change successfully without the financial assistance to purchase specialist advice.

Purpose of consultancy grant

These grants are intended to help employers obtain professional assistance from agencies like private consultancy firms, colleges, the Skillcentre Training Agency and industrial training organisations, in order to analyse training needs likely to arise from changes within the company. Companies can commission the organisation of their choice.

Amount of consultancy grant

If accepted, the company can claim a grant of two-thirds of the cost of the consultancy fee up to a maximum limit of £1000 per employer. A consultancy should normally be completed within three months of the date for which the grant is approved.

Eligibility for Training Grant

To qualify for a grant, employers must:

— show that training is the most appropriate way of meeting
their objectives;
— be unable to undertake training at the speed or at the
standard required without financial assistance from the
MSC;
— show that the training programme has been properly
planned.

In addition, if the training is for new recruits, employers must
also show that:

— the vacancies are hard to fill;
— local people, with some training, would consider the
vacancies.

Training grants cannot be spent on people under the age of 17 or
on the Youth Training Scheme. Apart from this, employers may
choose whom they wish although they should not discriminate on
grounds of race, religion, sex, marital status or disability.

Funding for training grants is limited and they are allocated at
the discretion of Training Division Area Offices. Employers are
more likely to be assisted if they are smaller firms intending to
make major changes by introducing new products or bringing in
new technology. Special rules apply to companies which have
received previous local training grants from the MSC.

Purpose of training grant

This scheme seeks to help companies improve their efficiency by
introducing or developing adult training to update, upgrade or
broaden the skills of existing employees or fill hard-to-fill
vacancies by taking on new recruits requiring training to meet the
standards required. The grant can be spent on in-house training
or on bought-in training from Skillcentres, colleges, polytechnics
or private training companies.

Amount of training grant

If awarded, the grant is a flat rate contribution of £25 per person
per day's training up to a maximum of £1000 per trainee and
£30,000 per employer. Special rules apply, however, for employers

buying in open learning packages (such as those of the Open Tech — see Chapter 3.20). Employers are free to set the length of training although support is only available to a maximum of 40 days per employee and should normally be completed within a year.

Further Information

Full details and application forms for both grant schemes are available from Training Division Area Offices (see Chapter 2.5). Details of other MSC funded training grants are given in Chapter 3.22. See also leaflets ATL 46 and ATL 60.

Chapter 3.19

Wider Opportunities Training Programme

Introduction

This is a new, nationwide programme, introduced in July 1985 as one of two initiatives brought in to replace the Training Opportunities scheme (see Chapter 3.14 for explanation). It has been developed to meet the needs of unemployed adults by helping them to:

— retain employability
— improve their work-related skills
— cope with changing conditions and patterns of work

There is also additional training provision for long-term unemployed adults on the Community Programme.

Compared to other MSC training for adults, there have been few concrete details released concerning this programme at the time of writing.

Eligibility

The only publicised eligibility criteria announced at July 1985 are that participants must be at least 18 years old and unemployed. They must not have done a TOPS course in the previous three years. Clarification and further details should be obtainable from Jobcentres and Employment Offices.

Participation on a wider opportunities courses is not counted against an individual's training entitlement under the Job Training Scheme (Chapter 3.15) or Training for Enterprise Courses (Chapter 3.16).

Courses Available

Courses may be full time or, more likely, part time and may last from a few days to several weeks. Trainees on full-time courses will be paid a training allowance similar to that of the Job Training Scheme. Participants on part-time courses may require some assistance with fares and should usually remain eligible for any benefits being claimed.

Courses may be offered by colleges, MSC Skillcentres, employers or private training organisations. The actual content and range will vary according to the state of the local labour market, but will not be limited to job-specific skills and may include new technology and computer familiarisation. There will also be courses in self-assessment, job-hunting skills, skill sampling and where necessary, help will be given with basic education. Information and advice on further education and training will also be available.

Some of the courses build on the various work preparation courses run previously under TOPS and include (whether under the old titles or new names) courses like:

— *Wider Opportunities for Women (WOW) courses:* These courses are aimed specifically at women re-entering the labour market after a break. They are single sex courses, permitted under section 47 of the 1975 Sex Discrimination Act. Courses include elements of job sampling, confidence building and familiarisation with the local labour market.

In 1984–85, WOW courses ran at about 20 centres nationwide, and offered about 500 places. A further 90 places were offered on WOW courses for women returning to high-level management/supervisory jobs or jobs affected by the recent introduction of new technology. For 1985–86, the MSC plans to offer 1600 places for these courses. Details of their availability should be obtainable from Training Division Area Offices or Jobcentres.

— *Preparatory Courses:* These courses focus on work-related literacy and numeracy as well as job-seeking and occupational skills. About a quarter of preparatory courses seek to improve the employability of people for whom English is a second language (ESL courses); these concentrate on spoken as well as written English. Courses are usually based in further education colleges or adult education centres. Course length varies according to individual need up to a maximum of about 15 weeks. In at least one area, this provision is publicised under the title

'Job Link Work Preparation'.

The number of planned starts on these courses in 1985–86 is likely to be over 5000.

— *Work Related Skills and Assessment Courses:* These modular courses are designed to give people with narrow or obsolete skills training an assessment in broader-based occupational skills — including those necessary for work in new technology and for self-employment. Run in Skillcentres, the training can last from a few days to several weeks.

The MSC plans to fund 15,000 starts on these courses in 1985–86.

In addition to these specific courses, it is likely that others will run under a variety of names and may include management-level work preparation courses, concentrating on self-assessment and presentation, such as the Career Review and Development Courses and Bridge Programmes run under TOPS.

As well as courses for unemployed people, Wider Opportunities Training will be available to participants on Community Programme schemes (see Chapter 3.7). By 1986–87, the MSC hopes to offer training to 50,000 CP workers in addition to any in-house training provided by scheme sponsors during work time. Training within the Wider Opportunities programme is voluntary and will be provided free of charge for a maximum total of 13 weeks. Following the success of pilot projects in early 1985, people on CP can undertake training (when not working) in subjects like new technology, graphic design, retailing and basic skills. This type of training provision does not yet have a distinctive name and is mentioned in MSC literature under the ponderous title, Link with the Wider Opportunities Programme.

Numbers

In 1985–86, the entire programme is expected to provide training for over 40,000 people.

Issues

Compared to the other elements of the MSC's adult training provision announced at the same time (see Chapters 3.15 to 3.18), there are relatively few hard facts available about Wider Opportunities Training Programme courses. It is possible that this is because the programme will be genuinely flexible and responsive to local needs, but a suspicion remains that it was launched prematurely, before details had been fully worked out. Certainly, staff in a number of Jobcentres and Employment Offices appear to have been sketchily briefed on the programme. As a consequence, it was, at the time of writing, unclear how, or even if, the quality of training under this programme will be monitored; how eligible applicants will be selected; on what grounds effectiveness will be measured; how the variety of courses will be promoted (and to whom); and where they will be run.

Further Information

Jobcentres and Employment Offices will have details of local opportunities. There is also a very general leaflet: ATL 45.

Chapter 3.20

Open Tech Programme (OTP)

Introduction

Open Tech is not an institution but a programme of MSC funded projects which attempt to increase the training and retraining opportunities of adults employed in technician and supervisory positions through open learning methods. In some projects, any individual able to find the fees can enrol on an Open Tech course, but it is expected that the majority of users will enrol via their employer who will pay projects for materials.

The OTP provides one part of the framework of the MSC's New Training Initiative; it is a strand of the Adult Training Strategy.

History

The OTP was launched in August 1982, and is managed by the Open Tech Unit based at Training Division headquarters in Sheffield. Projects are offered in England, Scotland and Wales. The OTP is funded by the MSC until Spring 1987.

Aims of the Programme

The aim of the programme is to extend the training opportunities available to adults in England, Scotland and Wales by filling gaps in existing provision, supplementing rather than replacing or duplicating facilities. The main focus is on the training needs both of employers and individuals at technician and supervisory level. These needs are met through a programme of 'open learning', enabling people to learn at a time and/or place which suits them best. Learning may take several forms. It can be self-study at home or work; in specifically designed workshop sessions; at training centres or colleges; it may include access to equipment and use of tapes, videos, or computer based material.

Intended Market

The programme is designed primarily for adults employed at technician or supervisory level or those seeking to return to employment. There are no age criteria for entering the programme but it is not seen as suitable for immediate school leavers. Most participants will have had some work experience and have left full-time education or training.

Most employed students on the project are supported wholly or in part by their employer. Unemployed students or those who attend as individuals have the usual sources of finance available to them.

Fee levels are the responsibility of the training providers and relevant authorities.

Operation

Open Tech consists of the Open Tech Unit in Sheffield plus over 100 free-standing projects created and operated by outside organisations using MSC funds.

Projects may be run by:

— industrial and commercial companies
— further and higher education colleges
— local authorities
— industrial training boards and other training organisations.

In determining which projects to fund the MSC is guided by the Open Tech Steering Group (see Chapter 2.5 'Elements of Interest').

During the first year of operation, 60 per cent of the operational projects were college based, 30 per cent industry based and 10 per cent provided by the local authorities, trade unions, and miscellaneous education and training bodies. The second year of operation showed a similar pattern.

Some programmes offered by projects provide the opportunity for participants to gain a national qualification. Others are entirely new training courses.

The projects cover a wide range of activities but are basically of two kinds:

— *Operational:* developing learning materials and/or facilities and making them more widely available;

— *Supporting:* providing information services, helping with training of staff involved in open learning projects, evaluation.

Most projects (about 80 per cent) are concerned with the design, production and/or delivery of open learning materials and setting up open and distance learning systems. They create or buy the materials and deliver them directly to the users.

Most of the operational projects are concerned with technician level skills offering either training at initial qualification level and/or updating. The remaining operational projects are at supervisory and management skills level. Some projects offer learning at both levels.

There are also a number of support projects, two of which are described below.

Open Tech Training and Support Unit (OTTSU)

The Council for Educational Technology Open Learning Unit has a three-year contract (1984–87) to provide a specialised consultancy service for the operational side of OTP. It has a panel of consultants from a wide variety of backgrounds, all of whom have considerable expertise in problem-solving consultancy, as well as experience in most aspects of the development, operation and promotion of open learning systems. Organisers of Open Tech Projects seeking support may apply to the OTTSU which matches the customers' needs with the expertise and experience of consultants who then visit projects, run training workshops, or give advice. The initial discussion, written report and the proposal for action are provided free of charge. In addition to the OTTSU panel, CET holds an open register of a further 100 consultants who can be drawn upon if required. OTTSU covers England and Wales.

CET Open Learning Unit
Rooms 24–27, Prudential Building (above Bar Street)
Southampton SO1 0FG
0703 36429/38368

Contact: D Chase or J Coffey

In Scotland there is a sister unit called SCOTTSU

SCOTTSU
Dundee College of Education
Gardyne Road
Broughty Ferry
Dundee DD5 1NY
0382 453433
Contact: W Fyfe

Materials and Resources Information Service (MARIS)

This service is managed for the MSC by the National Extension
College. It collects information about materials and resources
suitable for use in open learning schemes so that Open Tech
providers can find out about existing material which might be
usable or adaptable. The service is free and not limited to those
running or planning schemes under the OTP. Materials collected
by MARIS may be in forms such as print, tape, video,
computer program, film or a variety of these resources. They are
available to people in the United Kingdom. The service also
produces a comprehensive Open Tech Directory and operates
'MARIS-NET', a nationally networked computer database to
disseminate information on open learning materials.

MARIS
Bank House
1 St Mary's Street
Ely
Cambridgeshire CB7 4ER
0353 61284
Contact: T MacCormack

MARIS (Scotland)
Scottish Council for Educational Technology
Dowanhill
74 Victoria Crescent Road
Glasgow G12 9JN
041-334 9314
Contact: K Fraser

MARIS (Scotland) has been operational from March 1984 and
offers a similar service to its sister organisation in England in
Open Tech areas of interest.

Practical Training Facilities (PTFs)

First established in the summer of 1984, PTFs are intended to provide distance learning students with 'hands-on' experience of information technology, computing and engineering equipment. Based in colleges and polytechnics, PTFs have been given 'pump-priming' funding but are expected to become financially independent. They do not run specific set courses or lectures, although tutors will be on hand if needed. PTFs exist in the following institutions:

Computer Assisted Training Services
9–10 Flemington Road, Queensway Estate, Glenrothes KY7 5QW
0592 759447

Contact: D Thomas

Dorset Microsystems Centre
Dorset Institute of Higher Education
2nd Floor, Norwich Union House, The Lansdowne, Bournemouth, Dorset BH1 3NG
0202 26349

Contact: M Deeley

Dudley Open Access Centre
Dudley College of Technology, The Broadway, Dudley, West Midlands DY1 4AS
0384 237940

Contact: B Green

East Lancs Tech Unit
Accrington and Rossendale College, Sandy Lane, Accrington, Lancashire BB5 2AW
0254 31392

Contact: P Moseley

Flexitec (Bannockburn)
Hill Park Education Centre, Bannockburn, Stirling FK7 2BR
0786 81655

Contact: W Sutherland

Flexitec (Galashiels)
Lang Lee Centre, Marigold Drive, Galashiels TD1 2LP
0896 56512

Contact: T Jones

Flexitec (Glasgow)
Dowanhill, 74 Victoria Crescent Road, Glasgow G12 9JN
041-357 0340

Contact: D Paterson

Gwent College of Higher Education
Open Learning Unit
Faculty of Engineering and Science
Allt-yr-yn Avenue, Newport, Gwent NP9 5XA
0633 51525

Contact: L Oelman

Mid-Kent College
Horsted, Maidstone Road, Chatham, Kent ME5 9UQ
0634 41001 ext 235

Contact: P Clarke

National Computing Centre
Micro Systems Administration Unit
Bracken House, Charles Street, Manchester M1 7BD
061-273 5173

Contact: J Turnbull

Sheffield Skillcentre
Open Tech PTF, Richmond Park Road, Sheffield S13 8HT
0742 446471

Contact: W Baker

Swindon Technology Unit
The College, Regent Circus, Swindon, Wiltshire SN1 1PT
0793 66178

Contact: C Kerr

Tamar Tech PTF
Plymouth Skillcentre, Strode Road, Plympton, Devon PL7 4BG
0752 341521

Contact: J Humphreys

Washington Micro Technology Centre
Armstrong House, District 2, Washington,
Tyne and Wear NE37 1PO
091-417 8517

Contact: G Brown

Watford College
Hempstead Road, Watford, Hertfordshire WD1 3EZ
0923 43141

Contact: J Lythgoe

Funding

The cost to the MSC of running the Open Tech Programme was
£8.2 million in 1983–84 and is expected to be £14.6 million in
1984–85 and £15.2 million in 1985–86. The programme will be
funded until spring 1987.

This is seen as pump-priming to enable projects to get off the
ground. After a set period of time, usually three years, projects are
expected to be self-financing. Although most of the funding
available is allocated to the operational projects, the OTP budget
is not intended to be spent directly on supporting students.

Further Information

The Open Tech Unit produces a free quarterly magazine *Open
Tech Programme News* discussing issues of interest. In addition, the
unit produces a series of occasional papers on matters relating to
its work and the development of open learning. These are
available free of charge on request. Details of all Open Tech
materials are given in *The Open Tech Directory* published at £7.95
by the National Extension College, Cambridge.

The two lists below are of Open Tech materials projects and
regional schemes and delivery systems under way at July 1985

Open Tech Materials Projects

Accrington and Rossendale College
Footwear OTU, Lea Bank Lodge, Hareholme Lane, Rossendale
BB4 7JZ
0706 211181

Contact: F Jones, Training Advisor

Project: Technological developments in the footwear industry —
materials for technicians and supervisors

Agricola-Lincolnshire
Lincolnshire College of Agriculture and Horticulture, Riseholme
Hall, Lincoln LN2 2LG
0522 44756

Contact: J Goodman

Project: Crop management technology

Agricultural Training Board
Bourne House, 32–34 Beckenham Road, Beckenham, Kent
BR3 4PB
01-650 4890

Contact: G P Allen

Project: Mushroom production

Air Transport Industry Training Association
125 London Road, High Wycombe, Buckinghamshire HP11 1BT
0494 445262

Contact: J E Boden, Technical Advisor

Project: Open learning materials in avionics

Amalgamated Union of Engineering Workers
110 Peckham Road, London SE15 5EL
01-703 4231

Contact: P Clarke, Open Learning Education Administrator

Project: New technology training

Austin Rover Group
Haseley Training and Conference Centre, Haseley Manor,
Hatton, near Warwick CV35 7LX
092 687511

Contact: D Yeamans

Projects: Electronic and mechanical skills, interpersonal and
management skills training, computer literacy and programming

Barnet College
26 Danbury Street, London N1 8JU
01-354 3718

Contact: G Johnson

Project: Basic and updating nurse training

British Fibreboard and Packaging Association
Sutherland House, 5 Argyle Street, London W1V 1AD
01-434 3851

Contact: J Collett, Training Advisor

Project: Technicians in the fibreboard industry

British Institute of Cleaning Science
Suite 75–76 Central Buildings, Southwark Street, London
SE1 1TY
01-403 7461

Contact: J Butler, Project Leader

Project: Open learning for supervisors and managers in the
cleaning industry

British Institute of Innkeepers
42 Portman Square, London W1V 1AD
01-486 4831

Contact: C Connell

Project: Business aspects of licensed house management

Buckinghamshire College of Higher Education
Newlands Park, Gore Lane, Chalfont St Giles, Buckinghamshire
HP8 4AD
02407 4441

Contact: M Lansman, Director of Training

Project: Development of an open learning course in export
marketing management

Business and Technician Education Council
Berkshire House, 168–173 High Holborn, London WC1V 7AG
01-379 7088

Contact: H Goodman

Project: 'Updating for business': business applications of
information technology

Capel Manor Institute of Horticulture
Bullsmoor Lane, Waltham Cross, Hertfordshire EN7 5HR
0992 763849

Contact: Dr S Dowbiggin

Project: Leisure and amenity horticulture

Central Manchester College
Cornbrook Annexe, Barrack Street, Manchester M15 4ER
061-833 9858

Contact: G Bell

Project: Open learning materials for the transport industry

Centre for the Study of Management Learning
School of Management and Organisational Studies, University of
Lancaster, Lancaster LA1 4YX
0524 65201

Contact: D S Binstead

Project: Management learning

City and Guilds of London Institute
46 Britannia Street, Kings Cross, London WC1 9RG
01-278 2468

Contact: A Hutchings

Project: Progammable controller training, process maintenance
skills

City of Bath Technical College
Highways OPT, 8–9 Broad Street, Bath BA1 5LJ
0225 60850

Contact: C Woolin, Project Manager

Project: The development and production of open access learning
materials and their delivery for technical, supervisory and
managerial staff employed in highways and public works

CNJ Systems Ltd
102 Station Parade, Harrogate, North Yorkshire HG1 1HQ
0423 522461

Contact: Dr T Bentley

Project: Development of an embedded computer-based training
system for Stewart Wrightson Ltd

Computeach Open Tech Ltd
113 Tennant Street, Edgbaston, Birmingham B15 1EY
021-632 5776

Contact: R Montgomery

Project: Computing

Comtech
Wigan College of Technology, Parsons Walk, Wigan WN1 1RR
0942 494911

Contact: H Beeley

Project: Management skills for technologists

Consultative Group for Training and Education in Agriculture
c/o ATB, Bourne House, Beckenham Road, Beckenham, Kent
BR3 4PB
01-650 4890

Contact: J St J Groom

Project: Support and co-ordination for the agricultural projects

Construction Industry Training Board
Bircham Newton Training Centre, Kings Lynn, Norfolk
PE31 6RH
048 523 291

Contact: D J Bishop, Head of Management Services

Project: The development and testing of open access learning
materials and their delivery for site managers in the construction
industry

Cranfield Institute of Technology
Department of Social Policy, Cranfield Institute of Technology,
Cranfield, Bedford MK43 0AL
0234 750111

Contact: J Paley

Project: Open learning for direct care workers

Cranfield Quality Assurance Training Ltd
Cranfield Institute of Technology, Cranfield, Bedford MK43 0AL
0234 752786

Contact: Dr J H Rogerson

Project: Quality management for supervisors in the fabrication
and related industries

Dairy Trade Federation
19 Cornwall Terrace, London NW1 4QP
01-486 7244

Contact: J Calnan

Project: Supervisory training in the dairy industry

Dyfed County Council
Education Department, Pibwrlwyd, Carmarthen, Dyfed
SA31 2NH
0267 4591

Contact: B Mee

Project: Farm management

East Devon Microelectronics Open Learning Unit
Twyford House, Kennedy Way, Tiverton, Devon BX16 6RZ
0884 255625

Contact: T Cork, Project Manager

Project: Microelectronics for agricultural machinery

East Surrey College
Gatton Point, Redhill, Surrey RH1 2JX
0737 62684

Contact: G Allen

Project: Aviation studies

Electrical, Electronic, Telecommunication and Plumbing Union
(EEPTU)
Cudham Hall Training Centre, near Sevenoaks, Kent TN14 7QB
0959 71888

Contact: D Roger, Technical Advisor
Project: Updating for technicians

Engineering ITB
PO Box 176, 54 Clarendon Road, Watford, Hertfordshire
WD1 1LB
0923 38441

Contact: A Stenner

Project: Engineering design

Fielden House Productivity Centre Ltd
856 Wilmslow Road, Didsbury, Manchester M20 8RY
061-445 2426

Contact: G Jones, Chief Executive

Project: To develop and promote the use of open access learning
materials in textiles and colouration for craft and technician
trainees and personnel

Glass Training Ltd
BGIRA Building, Northumberland Road, Sheffield S10 2AU
0742 661494

Contact: J Thornton

Project: Glass manufacture

Gwent College of Higher Education
Allt-yr-yn Avenue, Newport, Gwent NP2 5XA
0633 51525/8

Contact: L Oelman

Project: The development, testing and delivery of open learning
materials in plant and energy management

Henley Distance Learning Ltd
Henley Management College, Greenlands, Henley-on-Thames,
Oxfordshire RG9 3AU
0491 571552

Contact: Dr A Cooper, Education Director

Project: To provide training in the development of information
technology and management for supervisors and managers

Hotel and Catering Industry Training Board
Ramsey House, Central Square, Wembley, Middlesex HA9 7AP
01-902 8865

Contact: Dr P W Critten

Project: Open learning for supervisors and managers in the hotel
and catering industry

Humberside College of Higher Education
(1) Nuns Corner, Grimsby, South Humberside DN34 5BQ
0472 74140

Contact: Dr C Whitfield

Project: Open learning system for refrigeration engineering and
air conditioning

(2) Humber Lodge, 61 Bargate, Grimsby, South Humberside
DN34 5BQ
0472 74140

Contact: G Whitaker

Project: Process technology, plant and control engineering

Imperial Chemical Industries Ltd
Personnel and Training Section, ICI Agricultural Division,
Billingham, Cleveland TS23 1LE
0642 553601 ext 3524

Contact: Dr T Foggo

Project: Chemical plant operation and maintenance, engineering

Institution of Electrical and Electronics Incorporated Engineers
(1) University of Bristol, c/o Queens Building, University, Bristol
BS8 1TR
0272 299550

Contact: D J Higham, Open Tech Manager

Project: Mathematics for computing and data analysis

(2) Savoy Hill House, Savoy Hill, London WC2R 0BS
01-836 3357

Contact: G T Richardson

Project: Telecommunications and electronics

Kingston Regional Management Centre
Kingston Polytechnic, Gypsy Hill Centre, Kingston Hill,
Kingston-upon-Thames KT2 7LB
01-549 1141

Contact: P J Thurbin

Project: Flexible supervisory/management development systems

Leicester Polytechnic
PO Box 143, Leicester LE1 9BH
0533 551551

Contact: J Clarke

Project: Pollution control

Leith Nautical College
24 Milton Road East, Edinburgh EH15 2PP
031-669 8028

Contact: J Ford, Principal

Project: Open learning courses for personnel in the offshore and
maritime industries

LIKAT
Hinckley College of Further Education, London Road, Hinckley,
Leicestershire LE10 1HQ
0455 632388

Contact: A W Timson

Project: Leicestershire Institute for the Knitting and Allied Trades

Local Government Training Board
4th Floor, Arndale House, The Arndale Centre, Luton,
Bedfordshire LU1 2TS
0582 451166

Contact: K Henfrey

Project: Administration in the public services

Loughborough University
Department of Mechanical Engineering, Loughborough
University, Leicestershire LE11 3TU
0509 263171 ext 5116

Contact: I Wright

Project: Managing CAE

Lucas Industries
Lucas Group Services Ltd, Dog Kennel Lane, Shirley, Solihull,
West Midlands B90 4JJ
021-744 9101

Contact: J Garner, Open Tech Project Manager

Project: Design, develop and test open learning materials and
delivery systems to meet identified needs among supervisors,
technicians, engineers and managers

Luton College of Higher Education
Park Square, Luton, Bedfordshire LU1 3JU
0582 457446

Contact: N Wellings, Open Learning Unit Co-ordinator

Project: Open learning studies to the Institute of Motor Industry's
final certificate, and related studies

MEDC
Paisley College of Technology, High Street, Paisley, Strathclyde
PA1 2BE
041-887 0962

Contact: L Beynon

Project: Microprocessor systems servicing

Midland Independent Steel Training Association
Springvale House, Millfields Road, Bilson, West Midlands
WV14 0QJ
0902 43598

Contact: P Gaukroger

Project: Supervision in the process industry

National Association of Goldsmiths
St Dunstan's House, Carey Lane, London EC2V 8AB
01-726 4374

Contact: C Lenan, Executive Director

Project: Open learning materials for the retail jewellery trade

National Association of Lift Makers
Leicester House, 8 Leicester Street, London WC2H 7BN
01-437 0678

Contact: D M Fazakerley, Director

Project: Development of open access learning in lift technology
for technicians in the lift manufacturing industry and the
establishment of a pilot delivery system

National Examinations Board for Supervisory Studies
76 Portland Place, London W1N 4AA
01-580 3050

Contact: P Sear

Project: National delivery of supervisory learning packages

North East Wales Institute of Higher Education
Connah's Quay, Deeside, Clwyd CH5 4BR
0244 817531

Contact: R Wilson

Project: Small business development and administration

North Manchester College
Moston College, Ashley Lane, Moston, Manchester M9 1WU
061-205 7525

Contact: D Tyldesley, Head of Department of Engineering and
Science

Project: Development, testing and delivery of open learning
materials in a broad range of basic engineering and supporting
science subjects

North West Consortium
Division of Educational Studies and Technology, Lancashire
Polytechnic, Corporation Street, Preston, Lancashire PR1 2TQ
0772 22141 ext 2379

Contact: R Wilson

Project: Training technology for trainers

Northern Regional Management Centre
Derwent House, Washington Centre, Washington New Town
NE38 7ST
091-417 1150

Contact: H Pardue

Project: Open learning for supervisors

Open Learning Support for the Road Transport Industry
Capitol House, Empire Way, Wembley, Middlesex HA9 0NG
0656 645011

Contact: E Bowden

Project: Open learning support for the road transport industry

Organisation for Rehabilitation through Training (ORT)
Open Tech Department, ORT House, Sumpter Close, Finchley
Road, London NW3 5HR
01-431 1333

Contact: Dr D Sharon

Project: To design, develop and test open learning materials on
robotics literacy for pilot operation to meet the identified needs of
technicians and supervisors in a variety of industries

Oxfordshire County Council
OPTIS, Gosford Hill School, Oxford Road, Kidlington, Oxford
OX5 2NT
0865 4170

Contact: Dr R Webberley, Further Education Curriculum
Development Officer

Project: Open learning training for Youth Training Scheme
instructors

PACNET
Plymouth Polytechnic, Drake Circus, Plymouth, Devon PL4 8AA
0752 662806

Contact: R Winders

Project: Teleconferencing

Paintmakers Association of Great Britain Ltd
Alembic House, 93 Albert Embankment, London SE1 7TY
01-582 1185

Contact: D Clements, Project Manager

Project: Development and testing of open access learning
materials and their delivery to personnel involved in or
concerned with the paint industry

Paper and Board Industry Federation
Plough Place, Fetter Lane, London EC4A 1AL
01-353 5222

Contact: T A Linley, Head of Education and Training

Project: Development, testing and delivery of open learning
materials

Plastics Processing Industry Training Board
Brent House, 950 Great West Road, Brentford, Middlesex
TW8 9ES
01-568 0731

Contact: D Ramsey, Chief Training Manager

Project: To design, develop and test an open learning system for
scientists, engineers and managers in the polymer industries and
for the technical, supervisory, scientific and managerial staff in
the polymer processing industries

Plymouth College of Further Education
Kings Road, Davenport, Plymouth, Devon PL1 1UP
0752 264762

Contact: J Carr

Project: Open learning materials for technicians

Polymer Open Tech
Dowanhill, 74 Victoria Crescent, Glasgow G12 9JN
041-357 3099

Contact: D Ramsay, Project Manager

Project: Open learning materials for the polymer industry

Polytechnic of the South Bank
(1) Department of Nursing, Borough Road, London SE1 0AA
01-228 2015 ext 257

Contact: K Robinson, Head of Department of Nursing and
Community Studies

Project: Post-experience nursing

(2) Manor House, 58 Clapham Common North Side, London
SW4 9RZ
01-228 2015

Contact: L Antill

Project: Development, testing and delivery of open learning
materials in office technology

Polytechnic of Wales
Department of Mechanical and Production Engineering,
Polytechnic of Wales, Pontypridd, Mid Glamorgan CF37 1DL
0443 405133

Contact: Dr M Basset

Project: Computer-aided manufacturing systems

Portsmouth Polytechnic
Hasard Centre, King Henry the First Street, Portsmouth,
Hampshire PO1 2DY
0705 827681

Contact: Prof J Powell

Project: Health and safety at work

Radiography Open Tech Project
Storey Institute, Meeting House Lane, Lancaster, Lancashire
LA1 1TH
0524 383015

Contact: V Challen

Project: Open learning materials for radiographers

Retail Consortium
Commonwealth House, 1–19 New Oxford Street, London
WC1A 1PA
01-404 4622

Contact: C Benson

Projects: Information technology and supervisory skills for
departmental managers and small shopkeepers, management
skills for first and second line supervisors and the self-employed

Scitech
Canterbury College of Technology, New Dover Road, Canterbury,
Kent CT1 3AJ
0227 451603

Contact: Dr M Harper

Project: Open learning for school laboratory technicians

SCOTBEC
38 Queen Street, Glasgow G1 3DY
041-557 4555

Contact: Dr M Johnstone

Project: Management for tourism

Scot West Training Services Ltd
Unit 20, Stevenston Industrial Estate, Stevenston, Ayrshire
KA20 3LS
0294 68003

Contact: F Brown

Project: Maintenance of control systems/hydraulics and
pneumatics

Sea Fish Industry Authority
Industrial Development Unit, St Andrew's Dock, Hull HU3 4QE
0482 28034

Contact: E Barnett

Project: Open learning for the sea fish industry

Sheffield City Polytechnic
(1) Pond Street, Sheffield S1 1WB
0742 20911 ext 2309

Contact: K Shearstone, Project Director, Department of Applied
Statistics

Project: Development and piloting of open learning materials in
quality assurance

(2) Lowfield Hall, Totley Hall Lane, Sheffield S17 4AB
0742 20911 ext 246

Contact: J Sparrow

Project: Energy control for supervisors

Southtek Consortium
Learning Resources, A Block, Brighton Polytechnic,
Moulsecoomb, Brighton BN2 4GJ
0273 607164

Contact: J Cairns

Project: The development of open learning materials and a
delivery system for technical training in industry

Stevenson College of Further Education
Bankhead Avenue, Sighthill, Edinburgh EH11 4DE
031-453 6161

Contact: J Dalziel

Project: Open learning materials for the fire service

Strathclyde Business School
University of Strathclyde, 130 Rottenrow, Glasgow G4 0GE
041-552 7141

Contact: R Graham

Project: Flexible management development programme

Telford College of Further Education
Crewe Toll, Edinburgh EH4 2NZ
031-332 2491 ext 310

Contact: S McCulloch

Project: Library and information science

Teltec
Telford College of Further Education
Crewe Toll, Edinburgh EH4 2NZ
031-332 2491 ext 309

Contact: D Simpson

Projects: Computing, microelectronics and electronics, oil-related
technologies, process technology, pneumatics/hydraulics

Thames Polytechnic
Department of Chemistry, Wellington Street, London SE18 6PF
01-854 2030

Contact: Dr B Currell, Head of Chemistry

Project: Analytical science

Trainer Support Services
5 Baring Road, Beaconsfield, Buckinghamshire HP9 2NX
04946 77179

Contact: C R Thorpe

Project: Support system for the training of trainers through open
learning

Warley College of Technology
Pound Road, Oldbury, Warley, Sandwell, West Midlands
B68 8NA
021-558 4121

Contact: P Lucas

Project: Open access learning packages in computer aided
engineering

Watford College
Hempstead Road, Watford, Hertfordshire WD1 3EZ
0923 41211

Contact: A Jamieson, Head of Department

Project: The development of open learning materials for technical training of adult personnel in the printing and graphic communications industry

Watt Committee on Energy Ltd
Savoy Hill House, Savoy Hill, London WC2R 0BU
01-379 6875

Contact: G Mordue

Project: Support and information for open tech energy projects

Welsh Agricultural College
Llanbadarn Fawr, Aberystwyth, Dyfed SY23 3AL
0970 4471

Contact: R E Goodfellow

Project: Grassland production utilisation

Weld-Link
School of Industrial Science, Cranfield Institute of Technology, Cranfield, Bedfordshire MK43 0AL
0234 752786

Contact: P Craig

Project: Welding technology

West Suffolk College of Further Education
Out Rigsbygate, Bury St Edmunds, Suffolk IP33 3RT
0284 701301

Contact: F Cooper, Head of Mechanical Engineering Department

Project: Agricultural mechanics

Open Tech Regional Schemes and Delivery Systems

These projects are concerned with delivering a wide range of open learning materials for a particular locality or providing practical experience in support of open learning.

Amalgamated Union of Engineering Workers
110 Peckham Road, London SE15 5EL
01-703 4231

Contact: P Clark

Project: Union-based (pilot) delivery system

Birmingham Open Learning Development Unit
Garretts Green Lane, Garretts Green, Birmingham B33 0TS
021-743 5236

Contact: P Duncan

Project: Delivery system for the city of Birmingham

Central Manchester College
Lower Hardman Street, Manchester M33 3ER
061-833 9858

Contact: G A Rowlands

Project: Delivery system for the city of Manchester

Coventry Open Tech Unit
Topshop, Greyfriars Lane, Coventry CV1 2GY
0203 553241

Contact: H Temple

Project: Delivery system covering the Coventry area

Cheshire Open Tech Project
Hall 9, Padgate Campus, Fernhead, Warrington, Cheshire
WA2 0DB
0925 818244

Contact: I Taylor

Project: Regional delivery system covering Cheshire

Dyfed County Council Open Tech Unit
Education Department, Pibwrlwyd, Carmarthen, Dyfed
SA31 2NH
0267 233333 ext 4512

Contact: D Owen

Project: Regional delivery system covering Dyfed, South and West
Wales

Eastek
32a High Street, Hadleigh, Ipswich, Suffolk IP7 5AP
0473 823400

Contact: D Moore

Project: Regional delivery system covering Essex, Suffolk and Norfolk

Enfield Local Education Authority
PO Box 56, Civic Centre, Silver Street, Enfield, Middlesex
EN1 3XQ
01-366 9442

Contact: D Willetts

Project: Delivery system covering the London Borough of Enfield

Hereford and Worcester Open Tech Project
Henwick House, Henwick Grove, Worcester WR2 6AJ
0905 429836

Contact: R Dean

Project: Regional delivery system covering Hereford, Worcester and Powys

Institution of Mechanical Engineers
1 Birdcage Walk, Westminster, London SW1H 9JJ
01-222 7899

Contact: P F Ashcroft

Project: Delivery system and resource centre for professional engineers

Mid and North Wales Training Group Ltd
Castle Works, Hendomen, Montgomery, Powys SY15 6EZ
068681 670

Contact: P Haycock

Project: Regional delivery system covering Mid and North Wales

Midtech Open Learning
Project Office, Letchworth Skillcentre, Pixmore Avenue,
Letchworth, Hertfordshire SG6 1JP
0462 671113

Contact: C E Allen

Project: Regional delivery system covering Bedfordshire, Cambridgeshire, Hertfordshire and Milton Keynes

North East Open Learning Network
3rd Floor, Erick House, Princess Square, Newcastle upon Tyne
NE1 8ER
0632 614072

Contact: E Polden

Project: Regional delivery system covering North East England

North East Wales Institute of Higher Education
Connah's Quay, Deeside, Clwyd CH5 4BR
0244 817531

Contact: Dr J Musson

Project: Regional delivery system covering North Wales

North of Scotland Open Tech Development Unit
HIDB Offices, 62 High Street, Invergordon, Scotland IV18 0DH
0349 853337

Contact: G Grandison

Project: Regional delivery system covering the North of Scotland

Open Learning Support for the Road Transport Industry
Capitol House, Empire Way, Wembley, Middlesex HA9 0NG
0656 645011

Contact: E Bowden

Project: Open learning delivery and support for the road
transport industry

Rochdale Open Tech
Floor 2, Octagon House, 25 Yorkshire Street, Rochdale
OL16 1BW
0706 527102

Contact: A Donald

Project: Delivery system covering Rochdale

Southtek Ltd
A Block, Brighton Polytechnic, Moulescoomb, Brighton, East
Sussex BN2 4GJ
0273 607164

Contact: J Cairns

Project: National support centre network

Taytec Ltd
Gardyne Road, Dundee, Tayside DD5 1NY
0382 459606

Contact: S Gilmore

Project: Regional delivery system covering Tayside

Chapter 3.21

Local Collaborative Projects (LCPs)

Introduction

A local collaborative project (LCP) is a pilot programme set up in 1984 to help employers define and tackle their training needs at local level, in collaboration with the providers of training or education, and decide how to tackle them.

The £1.3 million pilot programme was announced in April 1984 and is part of the government's strategy for improving adult training arrangements — the third objective of the New Training Initiative.

Organisation

The programme is run jointly by MSC and the three Education Departments in England, Scotland and Wales. In England, the programme will be managed in conjunction with the Department of Education and Science's 'PICKUP' programme, building on the experience or local collaboration gained during the progress of the PICKUP programme.

Aims

The scheme was designed to help groups of local employers assess their training needs more accurately by working closely with training providers such as Skillcentres, colleges, universities, polytechnics and private training providers, and to help them take appropriate action to meet those needs. So, for example, a group of engineering companies might work with a local polytechnic to investigate the need for robotics training and prepare suitable courses.

Financial Support

The pilot programme is estimated as costing the MSC £1.35

million. There are two types of financial assistance:

— small-scale support, offering up to £15,000 per project to build on existing collaboration. The MSC is expected to support 70 projects in this way in the year 1984–85;
— large-scale support, offering up to £50,000 per project to allow for the starting of a new collaboration in an area where no such efforts exist already, but where there are problems which could be solved by a joint approach. The area could be defined in geographical terms, but also by industrial sector, size of firms and so on.

Financial assistance will normally be available for up to one year and will be expected to meet costs associated with establishing a joint approach. Funds will not be available towards the actual costs of training.

To receive support, projects must involve genuine collaboration, with active commitment from both the employers and the providers, including the commitment of substantial resources.

Example of a Project

In November 1984, a one-year LCP to identify training needs in the chemical process industry started in Manchester. Run under the auspices of Manchester Polytechnic, it involves manufacturing companies; the Electrical, Electronics, Telecommunications and Plumbing Union; the Chemical Industries Association and two local colleges.

The project involved over 250 hour-long one-to-one interviews with operatives, supervisors and managers from a range of companies to examine attitudes to previous training and present job and to identify training for future career needs. Information gathered will be processed and analysed by computer at the polytechnic. Then a framework will be devised to assist all levels of management to identify and assess training needs and priorities.

Further Information

Further details about collaborative projects, including how to apply for financial support, are available from Education

Departments and from the MSC's regional offices of the Training Division.

See also leaflet ATL 18.

List of Contacts

MSC regional contacts

These are based in the MSC's nine regional offices, addresses listed in Chapter 2.5.

C Rigg, London region
M Malpas, Midlands region
R Marshall, Northern region
B Winterbottom, North West region
C Hurd, South East region
N Harrington, South West region
D Naylor, Yorkshire and Humberside region
J Ferrier, Scottish region
J R R Evans, Welsh region

Education contacts

Eastern Counties Regional Agent, PICKUP Office
Cambridge College of Arts and Technology, Collier Road, Cambridge CB1 2AJ
0223 352900

Contact: A Winkless

East Midlands Regional Agent, PICKUP Office
Room 20, Spur F, Block 5, Government Buildings, Chalfont Drive, Nottingham NG8 3SY

Contact: R Arnfield

London and Thames Valley Regional Office, PICKUP Office
Oxford Polytechnic, Headington, Oxford OX3 0BP
0865 60264

Contact: D Thomas

North East and Cumbria Regional Agent, PICKUP Office
Allendale, Newcastle Polytechnic, Coach Lane Campus, Coach Lane, Newcastle upon Tyne NE7 7XA
0632 663345

Contact: N Ellidge

North West Regional Agent, PICKUP Office
Woodlands Centre, Southport Road, Chorley, Lancashire
PR7 1QR
02572 75474

Contact: D Esther

South East Regional Agent, PICKUP Office
Kingston Regional Management Centre, Kingston Polytechnic,
Kingston Hill, Kingston-upon-Thames KT2 7LB
01-541 0209

Contact: D Jarvis

South West Regional Agent, PICKUP Office,
Bristol Polytechnic, Coldharbour Lane, Frenchay, Bristol
BS16 1QY
0272 659075

Contact: R Hadfield

West Midlands Regional Agent, PICKUP Office
University of Aston, Birmingham B4 7ET
0902 714771

Contact: P Wilson

Yorkshire and Humberside Regional Agent, PICKUP Office
Yorkshire and Humberside Association for Further and Higher
Education, Bowling Green Terrace, Leeds LS11 9SX
0532 438634

Contact: J Geale

Scottish Education Department
New St Andrews House, St James Centre, Edinburgh EH1 3SY

Contact: F Hunter

Welsh Office Education Department
Cathays Park, Cardiff CF1 3NQ

Contact: J Edwards

Chapter 3.22

Industrial Training

Introduction

Industrial training in Britain is administered by a number of statutory Industrial Training Boards (ITBs) and over 100 voluntary Industrial Training Organisations (ITOs). Many administer a variety of small specialist schemes for the MSC.

History

Industrial Training Boards were first set up in 1964 by the Industrial Training Act, to make better provision for and to encourage the adequate training of people over 16 for employment in any activities of industry and/or commerce. They are now the responsibility of the Training Division of the MSC although the Secretary of State for Employment, after consultation with the MSC, has the power to establish new ITBs or to abolish existing ones. During 1982–83 the majority of the 25 statutory ITBs were wound up and voluntary organisations established in their place. There are currently only seven statutory ITBs in operation.

ITBs and ITOs work with firms to develop their own training programmes rather than with individuals who want training. MSC support is primarily financial but the boards and organisations also impose a levy on employers within the industry to meet the costs of training.

MSC Aided Schemes

Sandwich course students: industrial placements

Grants may be available to employers who can provide formal, structured training to a college-based student having difficulty in finding an industrial placement. The employer must ensure that the training is approved by the college or university concerned and by the relevant Industry Training Organisation. The student must be following engineering or technology related disciplines or courses in computer studies at first degree or higher diploma level.

Computer skills

To encourage additional training in computer skills, grants are offered under the following headings:

— programming
— real-time programming
— systems analysis
— higher level computer skills
— small business systems.

To qualify for a grant, courses must cover a basic core of training. Extra grant-aided modules can be chosen from a wide range. The MSC maintains a register of approved providers of courses but will also consider proposals for supporting in-house training.

National priority skills training

Funds are available to support initiatives which:

— update or upgrade skills and knowledge, provide training in multi-skills and convert skills in priority economic and occupational areas;
— provide training in new emerging skills where rapid development is needed;
— provide training to meet existing and future skill shortage needs, both in quantity and quality.

Priority is given to proposals which widen either training or job opportunities for adults, and those which offer training in skills which can be applied outside the sector in which they are learned.

Training for the management of change

This scheme funds training for managers to initiate and implement change, better understand the potential of new technology, improve company performance and develop skill in managing the organisational and human consequences of change.

Projects which are problem centred, opportunity centred and which use training methods with potential for wider applications are given priority.

Training for women

Funds are available for experimental training schemes, action research projects, and other development and pump-priming activities which encourage the potential contribution of women to be fully developed. Proposals should show how it is expected that lasting improvements can be achieved after MSC funding is completed.

Ethnic minorities

Support will be considered for training schemes which enable members of ethnic minorities to enter occupations in which they are under-represented and which are of key importance to the economy.

Training of trainers to help carry through and support change

This is a scheme which seeks to maintain and improve the standards and quality of training for trainers of all kinds. Priority is given to proposals for assisting trainers to use new technology in training and learning, for example computer based learning, and to cope with other forms of open access to learning. Development programmes which have wider application will be preferred.

Development of new training materials and methods of delivering and measuring learning

This is designed to provide support for projects not eligible for support under the Open Tech Programme. They should be concerned with improving the flexibility, efficiency and responsiveness of training through the development and piloting of new training methods, training packages, materials and methods of delivery, and with ways of testing, assessing and measuring learning. Projects should also have potential for the wider application of the results of development and piloting.

Redundant apprentices: adoption grants

Adoption grants are available for those redundant apprentices who have completed at least nine months of a training programme recognised by the appropriate joint industry body, so that they may be placed with employers willing to complete the training, where the industry and the appropriate ITO have been unable to find a placement. The employer must not have made an apprentice redundant in the same occupation within the six months preceding the proposed adoption. Apprentices made redundant during their final six months' apprenticeship are not eligible, nor are those who remain unemployed and unplaced six months after the date of redundancy.

Further Information

Employers who wish to apply for a grant for any of the schemes should contact the ITO for their industry. In the case of computer skills training where no ITO exists, applications for grant support should be made to:

Computer Grants Unit
MSC
Room E627
Moorfoot
Sheffield S1 4PQ

For details of ITOs contact MSC, Room E621, at Moorfoot, Sheffield (0742 704025).

List of Industrial Training Boards

The following list gives details of the seven ITBs.

Clothing and Allied Products
10th Floor, Tower House, Merrion Way, Leeds LS2 8NY
0532 441331

Construction
Radnor House, 1272 London Road, Norbury, London SW16 4EL
01-764 5060

Engineering
41 Clarendon Road, Watford, Hertfordshire WD1 1HS
0923 44322
(includes the Foundry Industry Training Committee)

Hotel and Catering
PO Box 18, Ramsey House, Central Square, Wembley,
Middlesex HA9 7AP
01-902 8865

Offshore Petroleum
Forties Road, Montrose, Angus DD10 9ET
0674 72230

Plastics Processing
Brent House, 950 Great West Road, Brentford,
Middlesex TW8 9ES
01-568 0731

Road Transport
Capitol House, Empire Way, Wembley, Middlesex HA9 0NG
01-902 8880

The Agricultural Training Board is a separate entity from the
other training boards and is responsible to the Agricultural
Minister. The provisions governing the Board are set out in the
Agricultural Training Board Act 1982.

Agricultural Training Board
Bourne House, 32–34 Beckenham Road, Beckenham,
Kent BR3 4PB
01-650 4890

Chapter 3.23

The Industrial Language Training Service

Introduction and Organisation

This service provides English language training in the workplace for members of ethnic minorities. In addition it trains managers, supervisors, trade union officials and others in communication skills and gives them an awareness of cultural differences of ethnic minority workers. It arranges training at the request of employing organisations.

Though funded by the MSC, the service is operated by a number of local education authorities who employ a total of more than 100 full-time trainers between them. There are over 30 Industrial Language Training Units (ILTUs) situated in areas of high ethnic minority settlement (where the need for this service is greatest). Their work is co-ordinated and supported by a National Centre.

Courses

ILTUs run classes in spoken and written English for workers born abroad. Each unit designs its courses round the needs of a particular group of workers, the emphasis being on the language needed at work. They also run courses for managers, supervisors, teachers, social workers and others who come into contact with people whose first language is not English. Courses are held either completely in work time or in half work and half non-work time.

Funding and Numbers

The service, which operates on a partial fee recovery basis charging firms, is funded by the MSC's Training Division and cost the Commission £1.9 million during 1984–85.

During the 1984–85 period some 11,300 people received training.

Industrial Language Training Units

The following is a list of current Industrial Language Training Units.

National Office
Pathway Industrial Unit, The Havelock Centre, Havelock Road, Southall, Middlesex UB2 4NZ
01-571 2241
Contact: D Gubbay

LOCAL UNITS

Bedfordshire
Bedfordshire Industrial Language Training Unit, The Westbourne Centre, Westbourne Road, Bedford MK40 4PQ
0234 53481
Contact: W Gray

Berkshire
Slough Industrial Language Centre, Slough College of Higher Education, Wellington Street, Farnham Road, Slough SL1 1YG
0753 25004/71821
Contact: S Khan

Hertfordshire
Industrial Language Training Unit, Department of Adult Education, North Hertfordshire College, Cambridge Road, Hitchin SG4 0JD
0462 32351/2/3 ext 66
Contact: V Fitzgerald

Callowland Adult Education Centre, Leavesden Road, Watford
0923 20270
Contact: V Fitzgerald

Lancashire

Lancashire Industrial Language Training Unit, 54–56 Blackburn Road, Accrington BB5 1LE
0254 393316

Contact: R Munns

Burnley College of Arts and Technology, Ormerod Road, Burnley BB11 2RX
0282 36111

Contact: C Histon

Leicestershire

Industrial Language Unit, Charles Keene College of Further Education, Painter Street, Leicester LE1 3WA
0533 56037 ext 23

Contact: W Dillon

London, Greater

Barking

Industrial Language Training Unit, Department of Humanities, Barking College of Technology, Dagenham Road, Romford, Essex RM7 0XU
0708 27943

Contact: C Blissett or P Lamb

Brent

Brent Industrial Language Training Unit, Ashley Gardens, Preston Road, Wembley, Middlesex HA9 8NP
01-908 1708/2905

Contact: J White

Ealing and Hounslow

Pathway Industrial Unit, Havelock Centre, Havelock Road, Southall, Middlesex UB2 4NZ
01-571 2241

Contact: D Gubbay

Enfield	(post to) Industrial Language Training Unit, Edmonton College of Further Education, Montague Road, Edmonton, London N18 2LY 01-805 5694 Contact: A Beattie (Visitors) Hut D, Middlesex Polytechnic Site, Queensway, Enfield
Newham	Industrial Language Training Unit, Room 24, London Borough of Newham, The Chief Executive's Department, East Ham Town Hall, London E6 2RP 01-472 1430 ext 3475/6 Contact: E Christmas
London, North of the River	North London Industrial Language Training Unit, Jack Ashley Buildings, 3 Prah Road, London N4 2RA 01-354 0303 Contact: M Kia-Nejand
London, South of the River	Industrial Language Training Unit, Southwark Institute, Hunter Close, Weston Street, London SE1 4UU 01-403 0463 and 01-407 8986 Contact: D Hooper
Manchester, Greater Bolton	Bolton Industrial Language Training Unit, Faculty of Open Education, Clarence Street Centre, Bolton Metropolitan College, Bolton BL1 2ET 0204 34455 Contact: A Gough

Manchester	Industrial Language Training Unit, Room 2, College of Adult Education, Cavendish Street, All Saints, Manchester M15 6BP 061-273 8610 Contact: D Chator
Oldham	Language Training Unit, Greenacres Centre, Galland Street, Greenacres, Oldham OL4 3EU 061-624 3668 Contact: D Morgan
Rochdale	Industrial Language Unit, Room 8, Teachers Centre, Baillie Street, Rochdale OL6 1JJ 0706 359700 Contact: G Loughlin
Tameside	Industrial Language Training Unit, Warrington House, Church Street, Ashton under Lyne, Tameside OL6 7PR 061-330 8888 Contact: P Trumper
Northamptonshire	Industrial Language Training Unit, The Lodge, Rickyard Road, The Arbours, Northampton NN3 3QZ 0604 410236 Contact: M Constantine
Tyne and Wear (Newcastle)	Industrial Language Training Unit, Newcastle upon Tyne College of Arts and Technology, Ryehill House, Maple Terrace, Newcastle upon Tyne NE4 7SA 091-273 8866 (this will be changed soon) Contact: D Watkis

West Midlands

Birmingham	Industrial Language Training Unit, Handsworth Technical College, The Council House, Soho Road, Birmingham B21 9DP 021-551 6031 ext 222 Contact: C Brierley
Coventry and Warwickshire	Industrial Language Training Service, Stoke School Site, Briton Road, Coventry CV2 4LF 0203 455947 Contact: H Pidgon
Dudley	Language and Literacy Centre, Dudley College of Technology, The Broadway, Dudley DY1 4AS 0384 23867 Contact: B Devsi
Sandwell	Sandwell Industrial Language Service, Warley College of Technology, Crocketts Lane, Smethwick, Warley B66 3BU 021-558 6077 Contact: T Brooks
Walsall	Industrial Language Training Unit, Butts Centre, Butts Road, Walsall WS4 2AY 0922 34953/615280 Contact: R Chandola
Wolverhampton	Industrial Language Training Unit, The Annexe, Bilston College of Further Education, Mount Pleasant, Bilston, Wolverhampton WV14 6EW 0902 402861 Contact: S Sangha

Warwickshire

Coventry & Warwickshire Unit,
Industrial Language Service,
Stoke School Site, Briton Road,
Coventry CV2 4LS
0203 455947

Contact: R Paget

Yorkshire, South
Sheffield

Industrial Language Training, St
Barnabas Centre, Alderson
Road, Sheffield S2 4UD
0742 52366

Contact: J Sahota

Yorkshire, West
Bradford

West Yorkshire Language Link,
3rd Floor, Auburn House, The
Wool Exchange, Upper
Piccadilly, Bradford BD1 3NU
0274 305625

Contact: P Raper

Calderdale

Bermerside Hall, Skircoat
Green, Halifax HX3 0RZ
0422 62552/53144

Contact: J Ferris or D McAll

Kirklees

West Yorkshire Language Link,
Marsh Adult Education Centre,
2 St James Road, Marsh,
Huddersfield HD1 4QA
0484 38418

Contact: J C Clark

Leeds

West Yorkshire Language Link,
2 Woodhouse Square, Leeds
LS3 1AD
0532 449603/450245

Contact: C Robbins

Chapter 3.24
The Careers and Occupational Information Centre (COIC)

Introduction

The Careers and Occupational Information Centre exists to provide and stimulate the growth of information covering the whole world of work including careers education, youth training and job change.

History

COIC was originally established as part of the Careers Service network, directly accountable to the Department of Employment and existed before the Manpower Services Commission itself. Since the establishment of the MSC in 1974, COIC has increased its scope and range of publications. It is now an important arm of the Personnel and Central Services Division and is based at the head office of MSC at Moorfoot, Sheffield. It has a sister organisation, COIC Scotland, which promotes and markets COIC products and provides a full Scottish dimension to them.

Function

The function of COIC is to encourage the widest dissemination possible of careers and occupational information. Its publications serve students within the educational system (secondary schools and colleges) at every academic level, trainees on YTS and people of all ages in work and out of work. This is done through publication and distribution of materials, in a wide variety of forms: books, leaflets, teaching packs, games, videos and more recently, computer software. Most of the information is priced but a lot of free literature is also produced. This includes *Newscheck*, a monthly magazine for careers teachers, careers officers, educational guidance workers and, increasingly, people working within the YTS.

Schemes and Services

A distribution service for free careers materials produced outside the MSC is also provided by COIC and, in addition, it maintains its own 'bookshops' through many local county careers services.

COIC is not an enquiry or advice service for the public, although its sales force puts on exhibitions and demonstrations of their material for people working in the field.

COIC's roots have always been strongly based in the development of an objective and comprehensive range of occupational information within its current resources. It was set up because people involved in careers education, guidance and counselling needed authoritative information. COIC works to three main criteria in meeting this objective:

— *Accuracy:* all information is checked before being published, and most material is regularly updated or new editions produced;
— *Innovation:* to keep pace with the new technology, and new ideas;
— *Design* (with the user in mind): based on feedback received from strong links with schools, careers services, and the Basic Skills Unit.

To help meet this last objective COIC chairs a Careers Materials Advisory Committee (CMAC) which meets three or four times a year to discuss the needs of practitioners working in the field. It acts as a two-way feedback forum for members to pass on information. The committee consists of 16 members who represent COIC, the Careers Service, careers education in schools and other interested organisations.

Market

Until recently all the occupational information produced by COIC was directed mainly towards young people, particularly those involved in secondary school careers education programmes. More recently, information specifically for adult jobseekers, career changers and those within the YTS has been added to its publication list.

During 1985, joint publishing ventures with the private sector were started.

Data on Occupations Retrieval System (DOORS)

DOORS is COIC's computerised information base which uses the resources of new technology to store and deliver comprehensive careers information in a more flexible and efficient form than is possible using other methods. The system was installed in April 1984, and is still in its infancy. It will eventually consist of some 800 occupational records, covering jobs from the professional to the unskilled in a wide variety of industries and services, in both the public and private sector. Currently, it contains 150 occupational records.

Its purpose is to provide comprehensive, updated and easily understood occupational information and is currently being used as a source of material for COIC products such as the *Occupations '86 Guide*. In time it is hoped that it will be expanded for general use by the Careers Service and by the public through Jobcentres.

Further Information

Further information on publications is available from the COIC catalogue or the marketing section at Moorfoot (0742 704563).

Chapter 3.25

Accredited Centres (ACs)

Introduction

Accredited Centres (for training) are a national network of organisations funded by Training Division and providing staff development and training services for adult staff working with young people on the Youth Training Scheme (see Chapter 3.10). There are 55 of these centres throughout England, Scotland and Wales, one for each MSC area. The first ones were established in 1982–83 to help ensure the success of the YTS. The remainder were established on a rolling basis throughout 1983. General information about ACs can be found in leaflet L36 from Training Division area offices.

Organisation

The centres operate autonomously and are organised in different ways. Some are based in industry, others in educational establishments or existing training organisations. Each centre has a staff training co-ordinator (STC), and some administrative support. Training is provided by a network of individuals or agencies whose staff have appropriate expertise, such as college lecturers or private trainers.

Courses

The ACs provide a variety of in-service and full- and part-time courses for new YTS staff and those needing refresher courses, ranging from half-day modules to courses lasting several weeks, including residential courses.

The approach is flexible to meet the different needs of individuals and locations. All the facilities of the Accredited Centres are free to staff working in YTS schemes and courses are locally based, using the centre's own premises or other premises. Centres may offer courses leading to certain qualifications such as the RSA Certification for Vocational Preparation Tutors and the City and Guilds of London Institute (CGLI) 924 Youth Trainers Award. Some offer other qualifications and most will also offer courses to non-YTS personnel to whom they charge an appropriate fee.

Other Services

Centres also provide an information bank of resources containing up-to-date information on YTS and play a consultancy role to help providers ensure that the latest and most cost effective techniques are used in the scheme.

Models of Operation

There are a great many different ways of operating within the 55 centres. There is a standard MSC model which sets out eight modules of training, namely:

— Introduction
— Management and administration
— Design
— An integrated scheme
— Working with young people
— Assessment and review
— Trainee-centred learning
— Health and safety.

However, each centre has a lot of autonomy in deciding how and when to do the training and who should do it. There is also flexibility in deciding on the balance of the work, although the current contract states that 80 per cent of the training must be covered within the MSC modules and 20 per cent can be outside them. For example, one Accredited Centre which has responsibility for two adjoining counties has an STC based in a college in one county and a second member of staff based in another college in the second county. Their field of operation covers four main activities:

1. An open programme of events on a whole range of topics, each of which usally lasts for a short length of time and to which participants are invited.
2. In-house training whereby staff from the AC will visit an

agency and work out with that agency its own particular training needs. The AC does not necessarily do the whole of the training programme but often complements and supports the internal staff of the agency. Courses can last a few weeks or could spread over a two-year period.
3. Consultancy work whereby the AC staff are called in to look at schemes and offer advice and suggestions.
4. Resources/information collection and dissemination. The AC is responsible for collecting and housing a large selection of appropriate materials for use within YTS and offers them for loan to YTS workers. It also distributes MSC publications.

The training is done by a team of workers, staff tutors and appointed agents who are identified by the STC and agreed by the TD area manager. They have a variety of backgrounds and are 'bought in' by, and give different lengths of time to, the Centre. Most of them are locally based but trainers with particular expertise may be called in from other areas when need demands their services.

Support for AC Staff

Staff Training Co-ordinators meet together regularly in their MSC regions. This regional networking is set up, encouraged and convened by the MSC regional staff and is the vehicle by which STCs normally pass requests and information up to MSC headquarters in Sheffield, via their link regional MSC personnel (the RDO[AC]). There is some joint networking between adjoining regions but at present, no national system for STCs to come together to share and exchange views exists.

Funding

Accredited Centres have been financed by MSC on a yearly contract basis. At present the centres offer their services free to clients as MSC underwrites the total cost. In the longer term, the aim is 'to support staff training in YTS at the point of delivery by funding the individual through the employer rather than funding Accredited Centres direct'.

Each centre received up to £150,000 in the year 1983–84 and £175,000 in 1984–85 worked out on the basis of an equal share of

273

the total budget for each year per Accredited Centre. In 1985–86, the MSC did not fund the existence of centres as such but related the funding more directly to delivery. Accredited Centres and Training Division areas jointly planned scheme staff training requirements. Central development funding for 1985–86 was almost all used for local collaborative quality improvement projects. Arrangements for 1986–87 are to be broadly similar but were not available at the time of writing.

Issues

The primary issue facing the AC network is that of uncertainty in terms of funding and the future beyond 1987–88. As YTS becomes established the pressure for out-of-house staff training becomes less urgent as scheme staff become better able to induct new colleagues and draw upon a growing body of knowledge and skill. One possible response would be to widen the remit of ACs beyond YTS staff training but this would doubtless be seen with concern by in-service trainers in education and other industrial and management training organisations.

If changing funding arrangements led to ACs having to sell their services is an open market, there would be a danger of competition within the network which may threaten cooperation and good practice.

List of Accredited Centres and Staff Training Co-ordinators

This list of centres and co-ordinators was current in November 1985.

ENGLAND

Avon AC
Bristol Polytechnic
Redland Hill House, Bristol BS6 6UZ
0272 741251
STC: D Brockington

Berkshire and Oxfordshire AC
Slough College of Higher Education
Department of Management Development
Wellington Street, Slough SL1 1YG
0753 820611

Birmingham and Solihull AC
City of Birmingham Polytechnic
9 Westbourne Road, Birmingham B15 3TN
021-454 5106
STC: D Kamp

Bradford, Calderdale and Kirklees AC
Yorkshire and Humberside Association for Further and Higher
  Education
Bowling Green Terrace, Leeds, West Yorkshire LS11 9SX
0532 440751
STC: A Hardy

Buckinghamshire and Hertfordshire AC
MSC TD Instructor Training College
Pixmore Avenue, Letchworth, Hertfordshire SG6 1JP
04626 72872
STC: W Lawrence

Cambridgeshire and Bedfordshire AC
National Extension College
Bank House, 1 St Mary Street, Ely, Cambridgeshire CB7 4ER
0353 61146
STC: A Rossetti

Cheshire AC
Skillcentre
Castle Rise, Runcorn, Cheshire WA7 5XR
09285 65921
STC: K Jones

Cleveland AC
11th Floor, Corporation House, 73 Albert Road,
Middlesbrough TS1 2RU
0642 248575
STC: C G Fraser

Coventry AC
Coventry Management Training Centre
Woodland Grange, Blackdown, Leamington Spa CV32 6RN
0926 36621
STC: G Russell

Cumbria AC
Brathay Hall, Ambleside, Cumbria LA22 0HP
0966 32888
STC: D Spragg

Derbyshire AC
Derby College of Further Education
Wilmorton, London Road, Derby DE2 8UG
0332 73012
STC: E R Hawkins

Devon and Cornwall AC
Cornwall College of Further and Higher Education
Redruth, Cornwall TR15 3RD
0209 712911
STC: R Ford

Dudley and Sandwell AC
Wolverhampton Polytechnic
Faculty of Education, Castle View, Dudley,
West Midlands DY1 3HR
0384 59741/59642
STC: T Withington

Durham Area AC
New College, Neville's Cross Centre, Darlington Road,
Durham DH1 4SY
0385 47325
STC: R Thomson

Essex AC
Marconi Staff Development Centre
102 Arbour Lane, Springfield, Chelmsford, Essex CM1 5RN
0245 350011
STC: P Kyne

Gloucestershire and Wiltshire AC
Christchurch Annexe
Gloucester Road, Cheltenham, Gloucestershire, GL51 8PB
0242 584879
STC: H Norman

Hampshire AC
Portsmouth Polytechnic
Locksway Road, Milton, Southsea, Hampshire PO4 8JF
0705 732650
STC: E G Parker

Humberside AC
Alderson House
Humberside College of Higher Education
Inglemire Avenue, Hull, Humberside HU6 7LU
0482 42157
STC: B P Sauer

Kent AC
Mid-Kent College of Further and Higher Education
Horsted, Maidstone Road, Chatham, Kent ME5 9UQ
0634 408104
STC: R Spain

Lancashire AC
Lancashire College of Adult Education
Southport Road, Chorley, Lancashire PR7 1AD
02572 69596
STC: A Barton

Leeds and North Yorkshire AC
Education for Industrial Society
Wira House, Clayton Wood Rise, Leeds LS16 6RF
0532 780521
STC: D Bell

Leicestershire and Northamptonshire AC
Loddington Hall
Loddington, Kettering, Northamptonshire NN14 1LS
0536 712630
STC: J Jameson

Lincolnshire AC
Lincoln College of Technology
Cathedral Street, Lincoln LN2 5HQ
0522 44441
STC: A Middleton

London North AC
Standard Telephones and Cables Telecommunications Ltd
Oakleigh Road South
New Southgate, London N11 1HB
01-368 1234
STC: I M Mackay

London North East AC
East Ham College of Technology
High Street South, Eastham, London E6 4ER
01-472 1480
STC: B E Thomas

London South and West AC
Garnett College
Manresa House, Holybourne Avenue, London SW15 4JF
01-789 6533
STC: G H Powell

London South East AC
Croydon College
College Road, Fairfield, Croydon CR9 1DX
01-688 1272
STC: D Jenkins

Manchester Central AC
Fielden House Productivity Centre
856 Wilmslow Road, Didsbury, Manchester M20 8RY
061-445 0111
STC: P Burkinshaw

Manchester East AC
Tameside College of Technology
Beaufort Road, Ashton under Lyne,
Greater Manchester OL6 6NX
061-339 8683
STC: N Mackie

Manchester North AC
The Management Centre
Ashfield House, Standish, Wigan WN6 0EQ
0257 425662
STC: J Lover

Merseyside Inner AC
Fielden House Productivity Centre Ltd
Duchy House, 24 Sir Thomas Street, Liverpool L1 6PH
051-236 8701
STC: D Smith

Merseyside Outer AC
St Helens College of Technology
Water Street, St Helens, Merseyside WA10 1PZ
0744 33766
STC: T Fairclough

Newcastle AC
Newcastle upon Tyne Polytechnic
Coach Lane Campus, Newcastle upon Tyne NE7 7XA
0632 663344
STC: A Grosvenor

Norfolk and Suffolk AC
Norwich City College of Further and Higher Education
Ipswich Road, Norwich, Norfolk NR2 2LJ
0603 621575
STC: I L Brown

Nottinghamshire AC
Trent Polytechnic
Burton Street, Nottingham NG1 4BU
0602 413823
STC: A Heaton

Sheffield AC
Sheffield City Council
Education Offices
PO Box 67, Leopold Street, Sheffield, South Yorkshire S1 1RJ
0742 26341 ext 365
STC: M Threlfall

Somerset and Dorset AC
Somerset Education Centre
Park Road, Bridgwater, Somerset TA6 7HS
0278 421069
STC: H Lloyd-Jones

Staffordshire AC
Stoke-on-Trent Technical College
Tunstall Annexe, The Boulevard, Stoke-on-Trent,
Staffordshire ST6 1JJ
0782 811114
STC: R Faulkner

Sunderland AC
Sunderland Polytechnic
St Mary's Annexe, Chester Road, Sunderland,
Tyne and Wear SR1 3SD
0783 650436
STC: D Gilhespy

Surrey and Sussex AC
Education for Industrial Society
144 West Street, Havant, Hampshire PO9 1LP
0705 470604
STC: P Mardell

Telford AC
Telford College of Arts and Technology
Walker Annexe
Hartsbridge Road, Oakengates, Telford, Salop TF1 2NP
0952 612505
STC: J Spratling

Wolverhampton AC
Walsall Chamber of Commerce and Industry
St Paul's Road, Wednesbury, West Midlands WS10 9QX
021-556 3517
STC: K Woodward

SCOTLAND

Ayrshire, Dumfries and Galloway AC
Scot-West Training Services Ltd
Unit 40
ICI Industrial Estate
Stevenston, Ayrshire KA20 3LS
0294 68003
STC: M King

Central and Fife AC
Glenrothes and Buckhaven Technical College
Stenton Road, Glenrothes, South Fife KY6 2RA
0592 772233
STC: R Mullin

Glasgow City AC
MSC TD Instructor Training College
Hillington Industrial Estate
Queen Elizabeth Avenue, Glasgow G52 4TL
041-810 3111
STC: J Budge

Grampian and Tayside AC
Bridge of Don Old Academy
Hutcheon Gardens, Bridge of Don, Aberdeen
0224 823010
STC: C Malcolm

Highlands and Islands AC
Hitts Ltd
Unit 8, Invergordon Industrial Estate, Invergordon,
Ross-shire IV18 0QP
0349 853645
STC: M Meighan

Lanarkshire AC
Finning Ltd
Baillieston, Glasgow G69 7TX
0236 20111
STC: B Ball

Lothian and Borders AC
Stevenson College of Further Education
Bankhead Avenue, Sighthill, Edinburgh EH11 4DE
031-453 6161 ext 207
STC: W Davidson

Renfrew, Dumbarton and Argyll AC
MSC TD Instructor Training College
Hillington Industrial Estate
Queen Elizabeth Avenue, Glasgow G52 4TL
041-810 3111
STC: R Paterson

WALES

Gwent AC
Gwent Staff Training Centre
Gwent College of Higher Education
Allt-yr-yn-Site, Allt-yr-yn Avenue, Newport, Gwent NPT 5XA
0633 50131
STC: J Jordan

Mid and South Glamorgan AC
Room 328, Companies House, Crown Way, Maindy,
Cardiff CF4 3UT
0222 388588 ext 2626
STC: B J Davies

North Wales AC
North East Wales Institute of Higher Education
Cartrefle College
Cefn Road, Wrexham, Clwyd LL13 9NL
0978 359221
STC: A M Wood

West Wales AC
West Glamorgan County Council
Gors Avenue, Cockett, Swansea, West Glamorgan SA1 6SF
0792 579997
STC: R L Barnes

Appendix A

Employment Offices and Jobcentres

ENGLAND

Avon

Avonmouth EO, 20 Gloucester Road, Avonmouth, Bristol BS11 9AF
0272 823456

Bath JC, Strahan House, James Street West, Bath BA1 1ZI
0225 312025

Bedminster JC, St Catherine's Place, Bedminster BS3 4HT
0272 660445/8

Bristol JC (Tier 2), Tower Lane, Bristol BS1 2HZ
0272 215371

Bristol JC (Tier 1), 79–81 Fairfax Street, Bristol BS1 3DJ
0272 215371

Clevedon JC, 28 Old Street, Clevedon BS21 6OF
0272 872273/874674

Filton EO, Conygre House, Conygre Road, Filton, Bristol BS12 7DE
0272 692338

Fishponds JC, Beacon Tower, Fishponds Road, Fishponds, Bristol BS6 3HA
0272 65612

Keynsham JC, 11 The Centre, Keynsham, Bristol BS18 1ED
027 56 61430

Kingswood JC, The Laurels, Hanham Road, Kingswood, Bristol BS15 2PQ
0272 670781

Midsomer Norton JC, 124 High Street, Midsomer Norton, Bath BA3 3YN
0761 413251/413501

Westbury on Trym JC, 53–55 Westbury Hill, Westbury on Trym, Bristol BS9 3AD
0272 629124

Weston-super-Mare JC, 4 High Street, Weston-super-Mare BS23 1HY
0934 412010

Yate JC, 30 West Walk, Yate, Bristol BS17 4XF
0454 312319/318026

Bedfordshire

Bedford JC, Allhallows, Bedford MK10 1LM
0234 41122

Biggleswade JC, 55–57 High Street, Biggleswade SG18 0AX
0767 312719

Dunstable JC, 41 High Street North, Dunstable LU6 1JE
0582 67886

Leighton Buzzard JC, 17–17a Market Place, Leighton Buzzard LU7 7EU
0525 371852

Luton JC, 14–16 Chapel Street,
Luton LU1 2SU
0582 37551

Berkshire

Bracknell JC, 12 High Street,
Bracknell RG12 1AY
0344 52025

Maidenhead JC, 22–24 King
Street, Maidenhead SL6 1DS
0628 76711/5

Newbury JC, 1–3 The Broadway,
Newbury RG13 1AS
0635 48801

Reading JC, 20 The Butts
Centre, Reading RG1 7QE
0734 583721

Slough JC (Tier 1), 72 High
Street, Slough SL1 1EL
0753 37711

Slough JC (Tier 2), 42–44 High
Street, Slough SL1 1HW
0753 37711

Windsor JC, 3 Queen Anne's
Court, Peascod Street, Windsor
SL4 1DG
075 35 55123

Wokingham JC, 13 Peach Street,
Wokingham RG11 1XJ
0734 787279

Buckinghamshire

Aylesbury JC, 67 High Street,
Aylesbury HP10 1SA
0296 89741

Buckingham EO, Old National
School, School Lane,
Buckingham, Milton Keynes
MK18 1HA
0908 813241

Chesham JC, 31 Red Lion
Street, Chesham HP5 1LD
0494 772856

Gerrards Cross EO, 2 Packhorse
Road, Gerrards Cross SL9 7QF
0753 887953

High Wycombe JC, 44–45
Oxford Street, High Wycombe
HP11 2EY
0494 30834

Milton Keynes Central JC,
736 Silbury Boulevard, Milton
Keynes MK9 3LD
0908 663131

Milton Keynes North
(Wolverton) JC, 47–53 Church
Street, The Agora, Wolverton,
Milton Keynes MK12 5LH
0908 317709

Milton Keynes South (Bletchley)
JC, Wetherburn Ct, The Brunel
Centre, Bletchley, Milton Keynes
MK2 2UH
0908 79241

Cambridgeshire

Cambridge JC, Guildhall
Chambers, Guildhall Place,
Cambridge CB2 3QU
0223 64941

Ely JC, 2 Coronation Parade,
High Street, Ely CB7 4LB
0353 3528

Huntingdon JC, Government
Buildings, Chequers Court,
Huntingdon PE18 6LS
0480 57323

March JC, Government Offices,
High Street, March PE15 9LL
035 42 3931

Peterborough JC, Midgate
House, 10 Midgate,
Peterborough PE1 1SX
0733 64371

St Neots JC, 54 Market Square,
St Neots PE19 2BD
0480 76051

Wisbech JC, 13 Market Place,
Wisbech PE13 1DT
0945 582188

Cheshire

Chester JC, Gateway House, 86
Northgate Street, Chester CH1 2HT
0244 312881

Congleton EO, 6 Wagg Street,
Congleton CW12 4BD
026 02 71739

Crewe JC, 32–34 Market Street,
Crewe CW1 2LJ
0270 214251

Knutsford JC, 11 Tatton Street,
Knutsford WA1 66AE
0565 2706

Macclesfield JC, 17–19 Market
Place, Macclesfield SK10 1EB
0625 616161

Middlewich JC, 36 Wheelock
Street, Middlewich CW10 9AA
060 684 3865

Nantwich JC, 44 Beam Street,
Nantwich CW5 5LQ
0270 63135/6

Northwich EO, Dane House,
Chester Way, Northwich CW9 5JQ
0606 44411/4

Runcorn JC, Rutland House,
Shopping City, Runcorn
WA7 2ET
0928 713232

Sandbach EO, Congleton Road,
Sandbach CW11 0DH
093 67 2126/7444

Warrington EO, 66 Sankey
Street, Warrington WA1 1SD
0925 32311

Widnes JC, 7 Albert Square,
Widnes WA8 6JJ
051-423 4771

Wilmslow JC, 22 Alderley Road,
Wilmslow SK9 1PE
0625 525253

Winsford JC, 1–3 Jubilee Way,
Winsford CW7 1BG
060 65 57215

Cleveland

Billingham JC, Crown Buildings,
Queensway, Billingham TS23 2LS
0642 555901/558712

Eston JC, Hadrian House, 81
High Street, Eston TS6 9EH
0642 455561

Guisborough JC, 17 Market
Place, Guisborough TS14 6BN
0287 35362/35777

Hartlepool JC, Titan House,
York Road, Hartlepool TS26 9HH
0429 65261

Loftus EO, Market Place, Loftus,
Saltburn-by-Sea TS13 4HA
0287 40553

Middlesbrough JC, Rede House,
Corporation Road,
Middlesbrough TS1 1TN
0642 248191

Redcar JC, Craigton House,
West Terrace, Redcar TS10 1LN
0642 482508

Saltburn-by-Sea EO, 6 Dundas
Street, Saltburn-by-Sea TS12 1AH
0287 22969/22647

Stockton EO, 159 High Street,
Stockton-on-Tees TS18 1PL
0642 675146

Yarm JC, 48 High Street, Yarm
TS15 9AH
0642 784542/3

Cornwall

Bodmin JC, 71a Fore Street,
Bodmin PL31 2JZ
0208 3333/3791

Bude JC, Summerleaze Crescent,
Bude EX23 8BT
0288 2866

Camborne JC, Trevithick,
Camborne TR14 8LQ
0209 712093

Camelford JC, Cleveland House,
Fore Street, Camelford PL32 9PF
0840 213517

Falmouth JC, The Moor,
Falmouth TR11 3QA
0326 311650

Hayle JC, 52 Fore Street, Hayle
TR27 4DY
0736 753030

Helston JC, 5 Coinagehall Street,
Helston TR13 8HX
032 65 3721

Launceston JC, 2 Church Street,
Launceston PL15 8AP
0566 3387

Liskeard JC, 14 Pike Street,
Liskeard PL14 6BR
0579 42110

Looe JC, Lisandra House, Fore
Street, East Looe PL13 1AN
050 36 2235/3415

Newquay JC, 11 Trevena
Terrace, Newquay TR7 1NW
063 73 6234/7

Penzance JC, 87 Market Jew
Street, Penzance TR18 2NH
0736 66491

Redruth JC, Alma Place,
Redruth TR15 1JN
0209 213375/9

St Austell JC, Carlyon House, 20
Carlyon Road, St Austell PL25 4BU
0726 74422

St Ives JC, 2 Chapel Street,
St Ives TR26 2NF
0736 794091

Saltash JC, 32 Fore Street,
Saltash PL12 6JH
075 55 6295

Truro JC, Circuit House,
St Clement Street, Truro TR1 1DX
0872 73186

Wadebridge EO, 2 Brooklyn,
Fernleigh Road, Wadebridge
PL27 7AT
020 881 2761

Cumbria

Aspatria JC (part-time office),
Market Hall, Market Square,
Aspatria, Carlisle CA5 3HT
0965 20227

Barrow JC, 36 Cornwallis Street,
Barrow-in-Furness LA14 2LL
0229 27272

Carlisle JC, Stockland House,
Castle Street, Carlisle CA3 8SU
0228 39611

Cleator Moor JC, 81 High Street,
Cleator Moor, CA25 5BS
0946 812136

Cockermouth EO, Station Street,
Cockermouth CA13 9QL
0900 823513

Kendal EO, Station Road,
Kendal LA9 6BT
0539 29220

Keswick JC, Unit 5, Herries
Thwaite Centre, Main Street,
Keswick CA12 5DZ
0596 73737

Maryport JC, 88 Senhouse
Street, Maryport CA15 6BS
090 081 5655/6

Millom JC, Government
Buildings, St George's Road,
Millom LA18 5DN
0657 2326

Penrith EO, Voreda House, Portland Place, Penrith CA11 7QH
0768 64321

Ulverston JC, Glynis House, 25-27 Brogden Street, Ulverston LA12 7AS
0229 52801

Whitehaven EO, 83 Lowther Street, Whitehaven CA28 7RH
0946 2455

Windermere EO, District Bank House, High Street, Windermere LA23 1AF
096 62 3218/5657

Workington JC, Finkle Street, Workington CA14 2DH
0900 4334

Derbyshire

Alfreton JC, Institute Lane, Alfreton DE5 7BQ
0773 834821

Bakewell JC, Catcliffe House, King Street, Bakewell DE4 1DZ
062 981 2641

Belper JC, 54 King Street, Belper DE5 1PN
077 382 5551

Buxton JC, 34 Spring Gardens, Buxton SK17 6BZ
0298 6248

Chesterfield JC, 63 Low Pavement, Chesterfield S40 1ES
0246 72161

Clay Cross JC, Bridge Street, Clay Cross, Chesterfield S45 9EF
0246 863822

Derby JC (Tier 1), 4-8 Osmaston Road, Derby DE1 2HQ
0332 372631

Derby JC (Tier 2), Gower House, Gower Street, Derby DE1 1JU
0332 372631

Dronfield JC, 29 Chesterfield Road, Dronfield S18 6XA
0246 414870/415952

Glossop JC, 43-45 High Street West, Glossop SK13 8AZ
045 74 62411

Heanor JC, 18 Market Street, Heanor DE7 7NP
077 37 761216

Ilkeston EO, Nesfield Road, Ilkeston DE7 8TW
0602 325191

Matlock JC, Firs Parade, Matlock DE4 3AE
0629 55721

Staveley JC, 26 High Street, Staveley, Chesterfield S43 3UX
0246 474051

Devon

Ashburton EO, Penrhyn House, 81 East Street, Ashburton, Newton Abbot TQ13 7AS
0364 52282

Axminster JC, Chard Street, Axminster EX13 5DZ
0297 32169

Bideford JC, Northbank House, North Road, Bideford EX39 2NR
023 72 2631

Barnstable JC, 90-91 Boughtport Street, Barnstaple EX31 2DW
0271 73241/4

Bovey Tracey JC, Courtenay House, 74 Fore Street, Bovey Tracey, Newton Abbot TQ13 9AE
0626 833269

Brixham JC, 5 Fore Street, Brixham TQ5 8AL
080 45 6651/2

Dartmouth JC, 5 Higher Street, Dartmouth TQ6 9RB
080 43 2728/3250

Devonport JC, Queen's House,
St Levans Road, Devonport,
Plymouth PL2 3LO
0752 59111

Exeter JC, 25 Guildhall Centre,
Exeter EX1 1AZ
0392 33851

Exmouth EO, 2 Chapel Street,
Exmouth EX8 1PD
039 52 72430

Honiton JC, 6 New Street,
Honiton EX14 8TY
0404 41151

Ilfracombe JC, 1–2 High Street,
Ilfracombe EX34 9DX
0271 63090

Kingsbridge EO, 20 Fore Street,
Kingsbridge TQ7 1PA
0548 2084

Newton Abbot JC, 36–38 Market
Walk, Newton Abbot TQ12 2RY
0626 3671/2

Okehampton JC, 23 Fore Street,
Okehampton EX20 1AI
0837 2447/8

Paignton JC, 4 Palace Avenue,
Paignton TQ3 3HU
0803 552103

Plymouth JC, Cobourg House,
Mayflower Street, Plymouth
PL1 1QJ
0752 24292

Plympton JC, 62 The Ridgeway,
Plympton, Plymouth PL7 3AX
0752 336800/336469

Seaton JC, Montpellier House,
78 Queen Street, Seaton EX12 2RJ
0297 22577

Sidmouth JC, 1 Mill Street,
Sidmouth EX10 8DT
039 55 6509

Tavistock JC, Pearl Assurance
House, Duke Street, Tavistock
PL19 0BE
0822 2251/2212

Teignmouth JC, 13 Regent
Street, Teignmouth TQ14 8SJ
062 67 6367

Tiverton JC, Coggan's Well
House, Phoenix Lane, Tiverton
EX16 6LU
0884 57646/7

Torquay JC, 2 Market Street,
Torquay TQ1 3BT
0803 212811

Totnes JC, 4 Birdwood Court,
High Street, Totnes TQ9 5SC
0803 862144

Dorset

Blandford JC, 50 East Street,
Blandford Forum DT10 7UE
0258 54669

Bournemouth JC, 185–187 Old
Christchurch Road,
Bournemouth BH1 1JT
0202 293551

Bridport JC, 35a South Street,
Bridport DT6 3JS
0308 56184

Christchurch JC, 38a High
Street, Christchurch BH23 1DJ
0202 477221

Dorchester JC, 12–13 Trinity
Street, Dorchester DT1 1TH
0305 67844/5

Poole JC, 2nd Floor, Brownsea
House, 10 Arndale Centre, Poole
BH15 1SW
0202 679101/7

Shaftesbury JC, 5 High Street,
Shaftesbury SP7 8HZ
0747 2121

Sherborne EO, The Fairfield,
Coldharbour, Sherborne DT9 4JH
0935 2039

Swanage JC, 1–3 Mermond
Place, Swanage BH19 1DG
0929 2274/422274

Wareham JC, 4 North Street,
Wareham BH20 4LE
092 95 2417/8

Weymouth JC, 9–10 St Thomas
Street, Weymouth DT4 8EW
0305 784701

Wimborne EO, 61 West
Borough, Wimborne BH21 1LZ
0202 884876

Durham, County

Barnard Castle JC, Mission Hall,
5 The Bank, Barnard Castle
DL12 8PL
0833 37731

Birtley JC, Co-operative
Buildings, Durham Road, Birtley,
Chester-le-Street DH3 2QP
091 4105317/8

Bishop Auckland JC, 106–108
Newgate Street, Bishop
Auckland DL14 7EQ
0388 661401

Chester-le-Street JC, 92 Front
Street, Chester-le-Street DH3 3QD
0385 887066

Consett JC, Derwent Centre,
Consett DH8 5ES
0207 507071

Crook JC, 68 Hope Street, Crook
DL15 9JS
0388 3751

Darlington JC, Bondgate House,
90 Bondgate, Darlington DL3 7JY
0325 460677

Durham JC, 25 North Road,
Durham DH1 4SS
0385 45323·

Newton Aycliffe JC, 1 Upper
Beveridge Way, Newton Aycliffe
DL5 4EB
0325 314581

Peterlee JC, 58 Yoden Way,
Peterlee SR8 1BL
0783 867661

Seaham JC, St John's Square,
Seaham SR7 7JE
0783 814014

Spennymoor JC, 1–2 Parkwood
Precinct, Spennymoor
DL16 6AB
0388 814328/814353

Stanley JC, 88 Front Street,
Stanley DH9 0AT
0207 235711

Wingate JC, 27 Front Street,
Wingate TS28 5DD
0429 838762

Essex

Basildon JC, Great Oaks House,
Great Oaks, Basildon SS14 1JB
0268 286681

Braintree JC, 74a High Street,
Braintree CM7 7NA
0376 40101

Brentwood JC, 98 High Street,
Brentwood CM14 4AP
0277 214469

Burnham on Couch EO (part-
time office), 4 Devonshire Road,
Burnham on Crouch CM0 8BH
0621 782164

Canvey Island JC, 140 Furtherwick
Road, Canvey Island SS8 7AL
0268 694222

Chelmsford JC, 5 New London
Road, Chelmsford CM2 0LZ
0245 84641

Clacton JC, 92 Station Road,
Clacton-on-Sea CO15 1SG
0255 420886

Colchester JC, Greytown House,
High Street, Colchester CO1 1YJ
0206 563361

Epping EO, Crown Building,
Crows Road, Epping CM16 5DB
0378 77087

Grays EO, 50 London Road,
Grays RM17 5YA
0375 30351

Halstead EO, The Centre, High
Street, Halstead CO9 2AJ
0787 473164

Harlow EO, Aylmer House,
Linkway, Harlow CM20 1DJ
0279 20461

Harwich JC, 268 High Street,
Dovercourt, Harwich CO12 2BD
025 55 502261

Maldon JC, 112a High Street,
Maldon CM9 7ET
0621 52954

Rayleigh JC, 69 High Street,
Rayleigh SS6 7EX
0268 774343

Saffron Walden JC, 62 High
Street, Saffron Walden CB10 1EE
0799 22103

Southend JC, 99 Southchurch
Road, Southend-on-Sea SS1 2NQ
0702 610211

Stanford-le-Hope JC, 20 King
Street, Stanford-le-Hope SS17 0HL
0375 670281

Tilbury JC, Calcutta Road,
Tilbury RM18 7QR
037 52 4221

Witham EO, Iceni House,
Newland Road, Witham CM8 2AU
0376 512821

Gloucestershire

Cheltenham EO, 100
Winchcombe Street, Cheltenham
GL52 2PF
0242 525762

Cinderford EO, 32 Market
Street, Cinderford GL14 2RX
0594 23679

Cirencester JC, Forum House,
Southway, Cirencester GL7 1LT
0285 2447/3446

Coleford EO, Lords Hill,
Coleford GL16 8BD
0594 33130

Dursley JC, 31 Parsonage Street,
Dursley GL11 4BW
0453 2278/46383

Gloucester JC, 33 Southgate
Street, Gloucester GL1 1UA
0452 28303

Lydney JC, Regent Street,
Lydney GL15 5RW
0594 42288/9

Nailsworth JC, Old Market,
Nailsworth GL6 0DU
045 383 3184/5

Stroud JC, 1st Floor, 54–56
London Road, Stroud GL5 2AD
045 36 2374/7

Tewkesbury JC, 99–100 High
Street, Tewkesbury GL20 5JZ
0684 293276

Hampshire
Aldershot JC, 77–79 Victoria
Road, Aldershot GU11 1SH
0252 21342

Andover EO, Chantry House,
Chantry Way, Andover SP10 1NA
0264 24361

Alton JC, 8–9 Cross and Pillory
Lane, Alton GU34 1HJ
0420 87016

Andover JC, 45 Bridge Street,
Andover SP10 1LZ
0264 57644

Basingstoke JC, 45 Wote Street,
Basingstoke RG21 1EP
0256 50333

Eastleigh JC, 42–50 High Street,
Eastleigh SO5 5LE
0703 619233

Fareham JC, 175–177 West
Street, Fareham PO16 0HH
0329 231551

Farnborough JC, 89 Queensmead,
Farnborough GU14 7RZ
0252 548818

Fleet JC, 185 Fleet Road, Fleet,
Aldershot GU13 8BB
025 14 23123

Gosport JC, 12 High Street,
Gosport PO12 1BX
070 17 588231

Havant JC, 33 East Street,
Havant PO9 1HP
0705 471012

Hythe JC, 18 Marsh Parade,
Hythe, Southampton SO4 6AN
0703 848721

Liphook EO, Headley Road,
Liphook GU30 7NS
0428 723148/724732

Lymington JC, Coronation
House, Queens Street,
Lymington SO9 8NH
0590 77811/3

Petersfield JC, 14a Chapel Street,
Petersfield GU31 3DP
0730 2851/2

Portsmouth JC, Lake Road,
Portsmouth PO1 4DU
0705 827311

Ringwood JC, 54 High Street,
Ringwood BH24 1DE
042 54 78008

Romsey JC, 3–4 Dukes Mill
Centre, Romsey SO5 8PJ
0794 516626

Southampton JC (Ind), 119 High
Street, Southampton SO9 2EF
0703 29900

Southampton JC (Comm),
26 Hanover Buildings,
Southampton SO9 2EH
0703 29900

Tidworth JC, Kirkee Road,
Tidworth SP9 7DZ
0980 43863

Winchester JC, 91–92 High
Street, Winchester SO23 9AP
0962 51736

Hereford and Worcester

Bromsgrove EO, Recreation
Road, Bromsgrove B61 8DT
0527 75176/8

Droitwich JC, Clarendon House,
16 St Andrew Street, Droitwich
WR9 8DY
0905 779412

Evesham EO, 36 Swan Lane,
Evesham WR11 4PG
0386 6186/2991

Hereford EO, 6a St Peter's
Street, Hereford HR1 2LG
0432 54111

Kidderminster JC, The Bull
Ring, Kidderminster DY10 2JQ
0562 68321/4

Ledbury JC, Bye Street, Ledbury
HR8 2AB
0531 3711/2

Leominster JC, 1st Floor, Corn
Square, Leominster HR6 8LD
0568 4222/3

Malvern EO, Rockcliffe, Church
Street, Malvern WR14 2AZ
068 45 62457/8

Pershore JC, Head Street,
Pershore WR10 1DD
0386 554991

Redditch JC, 8 Evesham Walk,
Redditch B97 4EX
0527 65231

Ross-on-Wye JC, 11 George
Place, Ross-on-Wye HR9 5BZ
0989 64426

Stourport JC, 29 Bridge Street,
Stourport on Severn DY13 8UR
029 93 78111/3

Worcester JC, Haswell House,
St Nicholas Street, Worcester
WR1 1UW
0905 26481

Hertfordshire

Berkhamsted JC, 300 High
Street, Berkhamsted HP4 3DS
04427 3969

Bishops Stortford JC, 90 High
Street, Bishops Stortford CM23 3LD
0729 55688

Borehamwood JC, 144 Shenley
Road, Borehamwood WD6 1EL
01-207 0722

Harpenden EO, Clayton House,
7 Vaughan Road, Harpenden
AL5 4EF
058 27 2173

Hatfield JC, 100 Town Centre,
Hatfield AL10 0NW
070 72 71261

Hemel Hempstead JC, 20 Bridge
Street, Hemel Hempstead HP1 1LZ
0442 212066

Hertford JC, 12–14 Parliament
Square, Hertford SG14 1LF
0992 551927

Hitchin JC, Crown House,
Bridge Street, Hitchin SG5 2DG
0462 54921

Hoddesdon JC, 22 Tower Centre,
Hoddesdon EN11 8UP
0992 442077

Letchworth JC, The People's
House, 2 Station Road,
Letchworth SG6 3AZ
046 26 2691

Rickmansworth JC, 3 Penn
Place, Rickmansworth WD1 1RE
0923 78189

Royston JC, Market Hill,
Royston SG8 9JY
0763 42147

St Albans EO, Beauver House,
6 Bricket Road, St Albans AL1 3JP
0727 59271

Stevenage JC, 32 The Forum,
Stevenage SG1 1EZ
0438 316611

Watford JC, Senior House, 53
Queens Road, Watford WD1 2PX
0923 47344

Welwyn Garden City JC,
15 Howardsgate, Welwyn
Garden City AL8 6BU
070 73 30545

Humberside

Barton-on-Humber JC, King
Street, Barton-on-Humber
DN18 5ER
0652 33697

Beverley EO, Morton Lane,
Beverley HU17 9DE
0482 869382

Bransholme JC, 51c Goodhart Road, Bransholme, Hull HU7 4OF
0482 834411

Bridlington JC, 19–20 Queen Street, Bridlington YO15 2SR
0262 70231

Driffield JC, Bourne House, 8 King Street, Driffield YO25 7QW
0377 46777

Goole JC, 71–73 Boothferry Road, Goole DN14 5BB
0405 69735

Grimsby JC, 43 Freeman Street, Grimsby DN32 7AE
0472 55293

Hessle EO, 26 The Weir, Hessle HU13 0RX
0482 6492221/3

Hull JC, Queens House, 44–46 Paragon Street, Hull HU1 3NZ
0482 27065

Scunthorpe JC, 1 Gilliatt Street, Scunthorpe DN15 6EY
0724 868522

Isle of Man

Employment services in the Isle of Man are provided by the Isle of Man Government.

Isle of Man Government Employment Exchange, Nobles Hall, Westmoreland Road, Douglas
0624 26262

Isle of Man Government Jobcentre, 2 Wells Road Hill, Douglas
0624 26262 ext 2709/2710

Isle of Wight

Cowes JC, 10 Birmingham Road, Cowes PO31 7JB
0983 297611/2

Freshwater JC (part-time office), Tennyson Road, Freshwater PO40 9AB
0983 754151

Newport JC, 130–132 High Street, Newport PO30 1TU
0983 524831

Ryde JC, 44 High Street, Ryde PO33 2RB
0983 63777

Shanklin JC, 66 High Street, Shanklin PO37 6NH
0983 866211

Kent
Ashford JC, 22 High Street, Ashford TN34 8SL
0233 35151

Canterbury JC, St Johns Lane, Canterbury CT1 2QQ
0227 62201

Chatham JC, 249–251 High Street, Chatham ME4 4AQ
0634 44588

Cranbrook JC, 'Clermont', High Street, Cranbrook TN17 3DH
0580 712294

Deal JC, 6 Broad Street, Deal CT14 6ER
030 43 373311

Dover JC, King Street, Dover CT16 1NS
0304 210837

Edenbridge JC, 25 High Street, Edenbridge TN8 5DP
0732 865234

Faversham JC, 3 Queens Parade, East Street, Faversham ME13 8AM
0795 532871/2

Folkestone JC, 18 Bouverie Place, Folkestone CT20 1AX
0303 59461

Gillingham JC, 37–45 Balmoral Road, Gillingham ME7 4PQ
0634 576721

Gravesend JC, 8–9 Berkeley Crescent, Gravesend DA12 2AF
0474 22151

Herne Bay JC, 22 Bank Street, Herne Bay CT6 5EA
022 72 3811/2

Hythe JC, 137–139 High Street, Hythe CT21 5JF
0303 60264

Maidstone JC, 38–40 Gabriels Hill, Maidstone ME15 6JF
0622 678361

Margate JC, Cecil House, Cecil Square, Margate CT9 1BP
0634 28585

New Romney JC, 75 High Street, New Romney TN28 8AC
0679 64611

Ramsgate JC, Argyle Centre, 7 York Street, Ramsgate CT11 9DS
0843 581541

Sandwich JC, 11 Market Street, Sandwich CT13 9DB
0304 613774

Sevenoaks JC, 72 High Street, Sevenoaks TN13 1JS
0732 450808

Sheerness JC, 1 Bank House, Broadway, Sheerness ME12 1TT
0795 661341

Sittingbourne JC, 5 Roman Square, Sittingbourne ME10 4BY
0795 75244

Strood JC, 141–141a High Street, Strood, Rochester ME2 4AN
0634 722161

Tonbridge JC, Crown Buildings, Bradford Street, Tonbridge TN9 1DN
0732 356377

Tunbridge Wells JC, 85 Mount Pleasant Road, Tunbridge Wells TN1 1PX
0892 37577

Whitstable JC, 13 High Street, Whitstable CT5 1AP
0227 261424

Lancashire

Accrington JC, 10–12 St James Street, Accrington BB5 1PJ
0254 384136

Ashton-in-Makerfield EO, Warrington Road, Ashton-in-Makerfield, Wigan WN4 9PN
0942 727456

Ashton-under-Lyne JC, 66 Old Street, Ashton-under-Lyne OL6 6BQ
061-339 3224

Bacup EO, 9 Gladstone Street, Bacup OL13 9JZ
0706 874177/876177

Bamber Bridge JC, Station Road, Bamber Bridge, Preston PR5 6TT
0772 35278

Barnoldswick JC, 1 York House, Church Street, Barnoldswick, Colne BB8 5UT
0282 812192

Blackburn JC, 12 Lord Street, Blackburn BB2 1LP
0254 678911

Blackpool JC, 52–54 Waterloo Road, Blackpool FY4 1TQ
0253 49411

Blackpool EO, 73–75 Talbot Road, Blackpool FY1 1LL
0253 294444

Burnley JC, St James House,
Hargreaves Street, Burnley
BB11 1LR
0282 38721

Chorley EO, Hamilton Road,
Chorley PR7 2HB
025 72 79631/7

Clitheroe JC, 31 Lowergate,
Clitheroe BB7 1AE
0200 22564

Colne JC, 68–70 Market Street,
Colne BB8 0HS
0282 867380

Darwen JC, 10 Market Street,
Darwen BB3 1AZ
0254 771121

Fleetwood EO, 140 Lord Street,
Fleetwood FY7 6RL
039 17 78211

Great Harwood JC, 34 Queen
Street, Great Harwood,
Blackburn BB6 7QQ
0254 888000

Haslingden JC, 13 Manchester
Road, Haslingden, Rossendale
BB4 5SL
0706 229421

Heywood JC, Church Street,
Heywood OL10 1LS
0706 64141

Hindley JC, Liverpool Road,
Hindley, Wigan WN2 3HH
0942 55326

Kirkham JC, 25 Poulton Street,
Kirkham, Preston PR4 2AA
0772 684179

Lancaster EO, 7 Gage Street,
Lancaster LA1 1UL
0524 64331

Leigh JC, 116 Bradshawgate,
Leigh WN7 4NP
0942 675331

Leyland EO, Golden Hill Lane,
Leyland, Preston PR5 2LS
0772 421271

Littleborough JC (PTO), Barehill
Street, Littleborough OL15 9BB
0706 70013

Morecambe JC, Heron House,
2 Central Drive, Morecambe
LA4 5NT
0524 419024

Nelson JC, 25 Manchester Road,
Nelson BB9 9YP
0282 694713

Ormskirk EO, Park Road,
Ormskirk L39 3LA
0695 74381/75459

Padiham EO, Victoria Road,
Padiham, Burnley BB12 8RE
0282 72222

Preston JC (Comm), Crystal
House, Birley Street, Preston
0772 59616

Preston JC (Ind), Duchy House,
96 Lancaster Road, Preston
PR1 1DB
0772 59393

Rawtenstall JC, 2 The Centre,
Rawtenstall, Rossendale BB4 7QF
0706 214556

St Anne's on Sea JC, 23–25 St
Anne's Road West, Lytham St
Anne's FY8 1QB
0253 729431

Skelmersdale JC, Whelmar
House, Southway, Skelmersdale
WN8 6NR
0695 21441

Thornton EO, 21–23 Fleetwood
Road North, Thornton
Cleveleys, Blackpool FY5 4AB
0253 823251

Todmorden JC, 15 Bridge Street,
Todmorden OL14 5DF
070 681 2531

Leicestershire

Coalville JC, 24 New Broadway,
Coalville, Leicester LE6 3FB
0530 36101

Hinckley EO, Holliers Walk,
Hinckley LE10 1QP
0455 632571/2

Leicester JC, Charles Street,
Leicester LE1 3JD
0533 531221

Loughborough JC, 17 Biggin
Street, Loughborough LE11 1UA
0509 232661

Market Harborough JC,
6 Church Square, Market
Harborough LE16 7NB
0858 64249

Melton Mowbray JC, 57
Sherrard Street, Melton
Mowbray LE13 1XH
0664 67444

Oakham JC, 2 Gaol Street,
Oakham LE15 6AQ
0572 2252

Wigston JC, 27 Leicester Road,
Wigston, Leicester LE8 1LT
0533 887431

Lincolnshire

Boston JC, 3–4 Market Place,
Boston PE21 6EA
0205 67615

Bourne EO, 1 North Road,
Bourne PE10 9AL
0778 422024

Gainsborough JC, 19 Church
Street, Gainsborough DN21 2JJ
0427 610113/5

Grantham JC, St Peter's Hill,
Grantham NG31 6QB
0476 67333

Holbeach JC, 55 High Street,
Holbeach, Spalding PE12 7HF
0406 24041

Horncastle EO, The Old
Courthouse, North Street,
Horncastle LN9 5EA
065 82 2227

Lincoln JC, 280–281 High Street,
Lincoln LN2 1LL
0522 40511

Louth JC, 17 Eastgate, Louth
LN11 9NB
0507 601461

Mablethorpe JC, Tennyson
Road, Mablethorpe LN12 1HG
052 137 3591

Skegness JC, 3 Briarway,
Skegness PE25 3PB
0754 2354

Sleaford JC, 12 Southgate,
Sleaford NG34 7YZ
0529 304060

Spalding JC, 18 Hall Place,
Spalding PE11 1SQ
0775 66271

Stamford JC, 13 St John Street,
Stamford PE9 2HQ
0780 52071

London, Greater

Acton JC, 164 High Street, Acton
W3 9NN
01-993 0831

Balham JC, 122–126 Balham
High Road, SW12 9AA
01-673 2193/9

Barking JC, 60 East Street,
Barking IG11 8EQ
01-591 0666

Barnet JC, 74 High Street,
Barnet EN5 1AS
01-441 3456

Beckenham EO, 2 Beckenham
Road, Beckenham, Kent BR3 4PH
01-650 5055

Becontree JC, 714–720 Green
Lane, Dagenham RM8 1YJ
01-597 2121

Bermondsey EO, Brunel Road,
Rotherhithe SE16 1HX
01-237 2864

Bexleyheath JC, 196 The
Broadway, Bexleyheath, Kent
DA6 7BL
01-304 5121

Borough JC, 92–94 Borough
High Street, Southwark SE1 1LJ
01-403 2055

Brixton JC, 422 Brixton Road,
Brixton SW9 7AE
01-733 5522

Bromley JC, 1 Westmoreland
Road, Bromley, Kent BR2 0TB
01-460 9911

Burnt Oak JC, 93–95 The
Broadway, Burnt Oak, Edgware,
Middlesex HA8 5EP
01-951 0411

Camberwell EO, Collyer Place,
Peckham SE15 5DS
01-639 4377

Caterham EO, 102 Godstone
Road, Caterham, Surrey CR3 6RB
0883 42368/9

Cathedral Place JC, 43
Cathedral Place EC4N 7ES
01-248 2141

Catford JC, 62–66 Rushey
Green, Catford SE6 4JD
01-690 9811

Chiswick JC, 319–327 Chiswick
High Road W4 4HH
01-995 4071

City EO, Atlantic House,
Farringdon Street EC4A 4DA
01-583 5020

Clapham Junction JC, Woburn
House, 155 Falcon Road SW11 1PD
01-223 5283

Croydon JC (Comm), 135 North
End, Croydon CR0 1TN
01-680 4124

Croydon EO, 17 Dingwell Road,
Croydon CR9 2TN
01-688 3881

Dagenham EO, Chequers Lane,
Dagenham, Essex RM9 6PS
01-592 4533

Dartford JC, 29–31 Lowfield
Street, Dartford, Kent DA1 1JY
0322 25412

Dartford DP Section, 208
Lowfield Street, Dartford, Kent
DA1 1JY
0322 25412

Deptford JC, 124 Deptford High
Street SE8 4NP
01-691 8723

Downham JC, 413–417 Bromley
Road, Bromley, Kent BR1 4PL
01-698 1114

Ealing JC, 39 High Street, Ealing
W5 5DB
01-579 9342

East Finchley JC, 99–101 High
Road, East Finchley N2 8AG
01-444 5131

East Ham JC, Heron House,
2 Heigham Road, East Ham
E6 2JG
01-552 5631

Edgware Road JC, 182 Edgware
Road W2 1ET
01-724 1351/2

Edmonton JC, 135 Fore Street,
Edmonton N18 2XF
01-803 0066

Eltham JC, 4–9 Pound Place
SE9 5DS
01-850 0101

Enfield EO, 318 High Street,
Ponders End, Enfield, Middlesex
EN3 4HQ
01-805 6060

Enfield Town JC, 36 The Town,
Enfield, Middlesex EN2 6LA
01-367 5251

Erith EO, 7 Queens Road, Erith,
Kent DA8 1TW
0322 348111

Feltham JC, 76 The Centre,
Feltham, Middlesex TW13 4BJ
01-890 6665/7

Finchley JC, 60 Ballards Lane,
Finchley N3 2BY
01-349 2033

Fulham EO, Wyfold Road,
Fulham SW6 6SH
01-385 2241

Fulham JC, 376 North End
Road, Fulham SW6 1NP
01-381 1900/1

Golders Green JC, 11–13 Golders
Green Road NW11 8DY
01-458 8366

Hackney EO, Spustowe Terrace,
Dalston Lane, Hackney E8 1LY
01-254 6171

Hackney JC, 394-396 Mare
Street, Hackney E8 1HP
01-533 1121

Hainault EO (OH), 19 New
North Road, Hainault, Essex
IG6 2UA
01-500 0095

Hammersmith EO, Hythe
House, 200 Shepherds Bush
Road, Hammersmith W6 7NR
01-603 3456

Hammersmith JC, 73 King Street
W6 7NR
01-741 1525

Harrow EO, Milton Road,
Wealdstone, Harrow, Middlesex
HA1 1XQ
01-427 7755

Harrow JC, 7 Manor Parade,
Sheepcote Road, Harrow,
Middlesex HA1 2JN
01-863 8566

Hayes JC, 50 Station Road,
Hayes, Middlesex UB3 4RX
01-848 3761

Heathrow JC, Building No 865,
Heathrow Airport, Norwood
Crescent, Bath Road, Hounslow,
Middlesex TW6 2DP
01-759 9718

Holborn JC, 275–277 High
Holborn WC1V 7EE
01-242 9256

Holloway EO, Medina Road,
Holloway N7 7JX
01-607 4431

Hornchurch JC, 182–184 High
Street, Hornchurch, Essex
RM12 6QP
040 24 74922

Hotel and Catering Trades JC,
3 Denmark Street WC2H 8LR
01-836 6622

Hotel and Catering Trades JC,
35 Mortimer Street W1 8DJ
01-836 6622

Hounslow EO, 20 Montague Road, Hounslow, Middlesex TW3 1LE
01-572 2561

Hounslow JC, 216–218 High Street, Hounslow, Middlesex TW3 1LE
01-572 2561

Ilford JC, 88 High Road, Ilford, Essex IG1 1EG
01-514 2727

Kensington JC, 198–200 Kensington High Street, Kensington W8 6BA
01-937 6976/2501

Kensington (Westway) JC, 150 Ladbroke Grove W10 5NE
01-969 0914

Kentish Town JC, 178 Kentish Town Road NW5 2BN
01-267 9551

Kilburn JC, 292–294 Kilburn High Road, Kilburn NW6 2DB
01-328 6543

Kings Cross EO, 1 Barnsbury Road, Penton Street N1 0EX
01-837 8811

Kingston JC, 19–23 Fife Road, Kingston-upon-Thames Surrey KT1 1SX
01-549 5921

Lewisham JC, 97–99 High Street, Lewisham SE13 6AT
01-318 7174/4411

Leyton JC, Grosvenor Park Road, Leyton E17 9PF
01-520 5500

Leyton JC, Markhouse Road, Leyton E17 8BD
01-520 3835

Leytonstone JC, 616 High Road, Leytonstone E11 3DA
01-558 0941

Loughton JC, 284 High Road, Loughton, Essex IG10 1RM
01-508 6181

Mitcham JC, 246–248 London Road, Mitcham, Surrey CR4 3XN
01-640 7221/5

Morden JC, 41 London Road, Morden, Surrey SM4 5HZ
01-640 2953

Orpington JC, The Walnuts, High Street, Orpington, Kent BR6 0TL
0689 73121

Palmers Green JC, 348 Green Lane, Palmers Green N13 5TJ
01-882 4666

Plaistow JC, 3–9 Balaam Street, Barking Road, Plaistow E13 8EB
01-476 2000

Poplar EO, 313–317 Burdett Road, Limehouse E14 7DR
01-987 4101

Richmond JC, 17–19 Kew Road, Richmond, Surrey TW9 2NS
01-948 5351

Romford JC, 16 North Street, Romford, Essex RM1 1BL
0708 44201

Ruislip JC, 126 High Street, Ruislip, Middlesex HA4 8LY
089 56 76455

St Marylebone EO, 46 Lisson Grove NW1 6TZ
01-262 3477

Shepherds Bush JC, 164 Uxbridge Road, Shepherds Bush W12 8AA
01-734 9533

Shoreditch JC, 57 Kingsland Road, Shoreditch E2 8AQ
01-729 1666

Sidcup JC, 15 Market Parade,
Sidcup High Street, Sidcup, Kent
DA14 6EX
01-300 7711

Southall EO, 68 The Broadway,
Southall, Middlesex UB1 1QD
01-843 2222

Staines EO, Fairfield Avenue,
Staines, Middlesex TW18 4BB
0784 51300

Stepney EO, Settles Street,
Commercial Road E1 1JW
01-247 3242

Stockwell JC, 219-221 Clapham
Road, Stockwell SW9 9BE
01-733 6261

Stratford JC, Boardman House,
66 The Broadway, Stratford
E15 1NQ
01-519 7900

Streatham JC, 103-105
Streatham High Road,
Streatham SW16 1HJ
01-677 1221

Sutton JC, 240 High Street,
Sutton, Surrey SM1 1PA
01-643 0731/2

Swiss Cottage JC, 120 Finchley
Road NW3 5JB
01-794 0941

Swiss Cottage (Camden Town)
JC, 106 St Pancras Way,
Camden Town NW1 9NE
01-485 4181

Tooting JC, 24 Mitcham Road,
Tooting Broadway SW17 9NA
01-767 3414

Tottenham JC, Scotland Green
House, 624 High Road,
Tottenham N17 9TL
01-808 4581

Twickenham JC, 20-24 York
Street, Twickenham, Middlesex
TW1 3LD
01-892 9025

Uxbridge JC, 208-210 High
Street, Uxbridge, Middlesex
0895 56556

Victoria JC, 119-121 Victoria
Street SW1E 6RB
01-828 9321

Waltham Cross JC, 66-67
Bartholomew Court, High Street,
Waltham Cross, Hertfordshire
EN8 7BA
0992 39646

Walthamstow JC, 263-265 Hoe
Street, Walthamstow E17 9PT
01-520 8900/5500

Watney Market JC, 25-27
Watney Market, Stepney E1 2PP
01-790 9033

Wealdstone JC, 31 High Street,
Wealdstone, Middlesex HH3 5BY
01-863 9966

Wembley JC, 528 High Road,
Wembley, Middlesex HA9 7BS
01-903 9491

West Drayton JC, 73 High
Street, Yiewsley, West Drayton,
Middlesex UB7 7QM
0895 440661

West Ealing JC, 156 Broadway,
West Ealing W13 0TP
01-567 3010

West End (Wardour Street) JC,
195-197 Wardour Street W1V 3FA
01-439 4541

Westminster EO, Chadwick
Street, Westminster SW1P 2ES
01-222 8060

West Norwood JC, 19-21
Knights Hill, West Norwood,
London SE27 0HS
01-761 1461

Westway Jobshop, 150 Ladbroke Grove, Westway W10 5NE
01-969 0914

Willesden JC, Harlesden House, 161 High Street, Harlesden NW10 4TL
01-965 6506

Wimbledon JC, 56 Wimbledon Hill Road, Wimbledon SW19 7PJ
01-947 6694

Wood Green JC (Tier 1), 2a Lymington Avenue, Wood Green N22 6JA
01-889 0991/4

Wood Green JC (Tier 2), 54a High Road, Wood Green N22 6BX
01-889 0991/9

Woolwich EO, Box 228, Spray Street, Woolwich SE18 6AS
01-854 2441

Manchester, Greater

Altrincham JC, 18 Old Market Place, Altrincham WA14 4DF
061-941 5950

Atherton EO, St Richards School Annexe, Crab Tree Lane, Atherton, Manchester M29 0AG
0942 892759

Beswick JC, 7–15 Stilton Drive, Beswick, Manchester M11 3RU
061-231 4811

Bolton JC, Elizabeth House, Back Spring Gardens, Bolton BL1 1SS
0204 22371

Bury JC, 29–33 The Rock, Bury BL9 0DE
061-761 2416

Denton JC, 31 Ashton Road, Denton, Manchester M34 3LF
061-320 9252

Didsbury JC, Grove House, 780 Wilmslow Road, Didsbury, Manchester M20 0DR
061-434 7821

Droylsden EO, Greenside Lane, Droylsden, Manchester M35 7AE
061-301 5536

Eccles JC, 136 Church Street, Eccles, Manchester M30 0NN
061-707 1755

Failsworth EO, Wellington Street, Failsworth, Manchester M35 9BR
061-681 2611

Farnworth JC, 122 Market Street, Farnworth, Bolton BL4 9ER
0204 791212

Hazel Grove JC, 204 London Road, Hazel Grove, Stockport SK7 4DF
061-483 9422

Horwich JC, 87–89 Lee Lane, Horwich, Bolton BL6 7BB
0204 66455

Hyde JC, 59 Market Street, Hyde SK14 2AJ
061-368 2664/6

Irlam JC, 610 Liverpool Road, Irlam, Manchester M30 5AA
061 775 2174/3373

Levenshulme JC, Matthews Lane, Manchester M12 4QP
061-224 3281

Manchester EO, 25 Aytoun Street, Manchester M60 7HS
061-236 4433

Manchester JC (Fountain Street), 18–20 Fountain Street, Manchester M2 2AR
061-236 4433

Manchester JC (King Street), 39–43 King Street, Manchester M2 7AT
061-236 4433

Marple JC, Co-op House,
Stockport Road, Marple,
Stockport SK6 6BD
061-427 2142

Middleton JC, 71–75 Long
Street, Middleton, Manchester
M24 3TT
061-643 2214

Moss Side JC, 4–6 Southcombe
Walk, Alexandra Shopping
Centre, Moss Lane East, Moss
Side, Manchester M15 5NW
061-226 8232

Newton Heath JC, Bower Street,
Newton Heath, Manchester
M10 6DR
061-205 2267

Oldham JC, 4–8 St Peter's
Shopping Precinct, Oldham
OL1 1JN
061-652 8411

Openshaw EO, Cornwall Street,
Manchester M11 2WX
061-223 1424

Prestwich JC, 18–20 Longfield
Centre, Prestwich, Manchester
M25 5AY
061-773 9535

Radcliffe EO, 44 Church Street
West, Radcliffe, Manchester
M26 9SQ
061-723 2456

Rochdale JC, 25 Yorkshire
Street, Rochdale OL16 1BW
0706 57421

Royton JC, 5–7 Market Square,
Royton, Oldham OL2 5QD
061-620 2129

Salford EO, Trafford Road,
Salford M5 3AD
061-848 9000

Salford JC, 7–8 Hankinson Way,
Salford M6 5FD
061-848 9000

Stalybridge JC, 46 Grosvenor
Street, Stalybridge SK15 2JN
061-338 2214

Stockport EO, 268 Merseyway,
Stockport SK1 1QR
061-480 0351

Stretford JC, Arndale House,
Chester Road, Stretford,
Manchester M32 9ED
061-865 7031

Swinton JC, 7–11 The Parade,
Swinton, Manchester M27 2BH
061-794 0112

Westhoughton EO, 29–31 Market
Street, Westhoughton, Bolton
BL5 3AG
0942 814771

Wigan JC, 66a Standishgate,
Wigan WN1 1UW
0942 39031

Worsley JC, 10 St Ouen Centre,
Walkden, Worsley, Manchester
M28 5BS
061-790 1511

Wythenshawe JC, Alpha House,
Rowlandsway, Wythenshawe,
Manchester M22 5QR
061-437 0811

Merseyside

Allerton JC, 102 Allerton Road,
Mossley Hill, Liverpool L18 2HH
051-733 8337

Bebington EO, Grove Street,
New Ferry, Bebington L62 5HT
051-644 8888

Belle Vale JC, Units 1 and 2,
Belle Vale Shopping Centre,
Belle Vale, Liverpool L25 2QZ
051-498 4788

Birkenhead JC, 4–6 Milton
Pavement, Grange Precinct,
Birkenhead L41 2YF
051-647 4621

Bootle JC, Stanley Road, Bootle
L20 3PN
051-933 8383

Crosby JC, 117 South Road,
Liverpool L22 0PN
051-920 7007

Ellesmere Port JC, 110–112
Whitby Road, Ellesmere Port,
South Wirral L65 0EL
051-355 5955

Everton JC, 1 The Mall, Breck
Road, Liverpool L5 6SS
051-260 4777

Garston EO, Speke Road,
Garston, Liverpool L19 9JZ
051-494 9222

Hoylake EO, The Priory, Meols
Drive, Hoylake, Wirral L47 4AJ
051-632 3218

Huyton JC, 3 Derby Road,
Huyton, Liverpool L36 9UI
051-480 1777

Kirby JC, Simonswood House,
Newtown Gardens, Town Centre,
Kirby, Liverpool L32 8RW
051-548 5900

Liverpool JC, 18–20 Lord Street,
Liverpool L2 1TA
051-708 8455

Liverpool JC (Industrial, Hotel,
Catering), 20 Williamson Square,
Liverpool L1 1BW
051-708 5675

Neston JC, 12 Brooks Street,
Neston, Wirral L64 9XD
051-336 5771

Newton-le-Willows JC, 9 Market
Street, Newton-le-Willows
WA12 9DS
092 52 4681

Norris Green JC, 23 Broadway,
Norris Green, Liverpool L11 1JD
051-226 9014

Old Swan JC, 650–656 Prescott
Road, Old Swan, Liverpool L13 5YI
051-220 9441

Prescot JC, 69 Eccleston Street,
Prescot L34 5PJ
051-430 9000

St Helens JC, PO Box 76,
15 La Grange Arcade, Shopping
Precinct, St Helens WA10 1BP
0744 54251

Southport JC, Queen Anne
House, 16–20 Eastbank Street,
Southport PR8 1DT
0704 38511

Toxteth JC, 3 Yanwath Street,
Toxteth, Liverpool L8 0XP
051-734 4441

Wallasey JC, 15–17 Greenfield
Way, Wallasey L44 5XX
051-638 0071

Walton Vale JC, 70 Walton Vale,
Liverpool L9 4RQ
051-523 5444

Norfolk

Attleborough EO, London Road,
Attleborough NR19 2BX
0953 452590

Cromer JC, Garden Street,
Cromer NR27 9HN
0263 511561

Dereham EO, High Street,
Dereham NR19 1DX
0362 3315/6

Diss JC, Mere Street, Diss
IP22 3AD
0379 4521

Downham Market JC, 6 High
Street, Downham Market PE38 9JX
0366 388058

Fakenham JC, Government
Offices, Norwich Road,
Fakenham NR21 8HJ
0328 2296

Great Yarmouth JC, 40 Market Place, Great Yarmouth NR30 1LT
0493 58511

Hunstanton JC, 62 Westgate, Hunstanton PE36 5EY
048 53 33472

Kings Lynn JC, 19 Norfolk Street, Kings Lynn PE30 1AN
0553 63361

North Walsham JC, GPO Building, 10 Kings Arms Street, North Walsham NR28 9JT
0692 40296

Norwich JC, 1 Theatre Street, Norwich NR2 1TC
0603 611291

Swaffham JC, The Corn Hall, 7 Market Place, Swaffham PE37 7AG
0760 23553

Thetford JC, Townsend House, Guildhall Street, Thetford IP24 2DT
0842 5536

Wymondham EO, 27 Fairland Street, Wymondham NR18 0AW
0953 603482

Northamptonshire

Corby JC, 33 Queens Square, Corby NN17 1QJ
053 63 67421

Daventry JC, 59 High Street, Daventry N11 4AY
032 72 705013/5

Kettering JC, Dryland Street, Kettering NN16 0AD
0536 512845

Northampton JC, 47 Princes Walk, Grosvenor Centre, Northampton NN1 2EE
0604 21222

Rushden JC, 81 High Street, Rushden, Northampton NN10 0NZ
093 34 50394

Towcester EO, 3–5 Brackley Road, Towcester NN12 7DH
0327 50452

Wellingborough JC, 9–10 Sheep Street, Wellingborough NN8 1DG
0933 222289

Northumberland

Alnwick JC, 1 Clayport, Alnwick NE66 1JJ
0665 602824

Amble EO, 1–3 Bede Street, Amble, Morpeth NE65 0EZ
0665 710800

Ashington JC, South View, Ashington NE63 0RY
0670 813313

Bedlington JC, Longridge House, Front Street West, Bedlington NE22 5TL
0670 823546

Berwick-upon-Tweed JC, 23–33 Woolmarket, Berwick-upon-Tweed TD15 1DL
0289 305088

Blyth JC, Bridge House, Percy Street, Blyth NE24 2BB
067 06 4111

Cramlington JC, 1 Dudley Court, East Square, Cramlington NE23 6QW
0670 714211

Haltwhistle EO (PTO), The Church Hall, Main Street, Haltwhistle NE49 0BE
0498 20287

Hexham JC, 2 St Mary's Wynd, Hexham NE46 1LA
0434 602223

Morpeth JC, 7 Back Riggs,
Morpeth NE61 1PB
0670 57311

Prudhoe EO, Prudhoe House,
South Road, Prudhoe NE42 5NG
0661 33864

Nottinghamshire

Arnold JC, 132 Front Street,
Arnold, Nottingham NG5 7GU
0602 26922

Beeston JC, 25a High Road,
Beeston, Nottingham NG9 2JQ
0602 254287

Bulwell JC, 17–19 Commercial
Road, Bulwell, Nottingham
NG6 8HD
0602 753611

Long Eaton JC, Derby Road,
Long Eaton, Nottingham
NG10 1LX
060 76 732291

Mansfield JC, 39 Stockwell
Gate, Mansfield NG18 1LA
0623 35141

Netherfield JC, 10 Victoria Road,
Netherfield, Nottingham NG4 2HE
0602 870933

Newark JC, 22–23 Market Place,
Newark NG24 1EA
0636 77441

Nottingham JC, Gordon House,
Carrington Street, Nottingham
NG1 7FF
0602 419381

Nottingham JC, 47–51 Maid
Marion Way, Nottingham
NG1 6GE
0602 419381

Nottingham JC, Victoria Centre,
14 Milton Street, Nottingham
NG1 3GL
0602 419381

Retford EO, 32 Bridgegate,
Retford, Nottingham DN22 6AD
0777 704155

Sutton-in-Ashfield JC, 13a
Idlewells Shopping Precinct,
Sutton-in-Ashfield NG17 1BL
0623 512522

Worksop JC, Ryton Street,
Worksop S80 2BJ
0909 476724

Oxfordshire

Abingdon JC, 19 High Street,
Abingdon OX14 5AQ
0235 21548

Banbury JC, 61 Calthorpe Street,
Banbury OX16 8EZ
0295 56401

Bicester EO, Manorsfield Road,
Bicester OX6 7DD
086 92 252751

Didcot JC, 130a The Broadway,
Didcot OX11 7LS
0235 813291

Oxford JC, 28–31 St Ebbes
Street, Oxford OX1 1RR
0865 723241

Wallingford EO, 22 St Mary's
Street, Wallingford OX10 0EW
0491 37365

Wantage JC, 22 Newbury Street,
Wantage OX12 8DA
023 57 65575

Witney JC, 85 High Street,
Witney OX8 6JA
0993 73801

Shropshire

Bridgnorth JC, Carl House,
2 Waterloo Terrace, Bridgnorth
WV16 4BY
074 62 2591

Appendix

Ludlow JC, 8 Castle Street,
Ludlow SY8 1AT
0584 3158/9

Madeley JC, 7 Anstice Square,
Madeley, Telford TF7 5HS
0952 586072

Market Drayton JC, 37–39
Cheshire Street, Market Drayton
TF9 1PH
0630 4311/2

Oakengates JC, New Street,
Oakengates, Telford TF2 6JD
0952 618051

Oswestry JC, 27–29 Willow
Street, Oswestry SY11 1AQ
0691 661531/5

Shrewsbury JC, Princess House,
17–19 The Square, Shrewsbury
SY1 1YA
0743 57321

Telford JC (Tier 1), Mall 1,
Telford Shopping Centre,
Telford TF3 4LG
0952 504299

Wellington JC, 46 New Street,
Wellington, Telford FT1 1NE
0952 47111/2/3

Whitchurch EO, 26 Green End,
Whitchurch SY13 1AA
0948 3059

Somerset

Bridgwater JC, 7 Eastover,
Bridgwater TA6 5AG
0278 56771/4

Burnham-on-Sea JC, 45 High
Street, Burnham-on-Sea TA8 1HP
0278 787878/9

Chard JC, 1st Floor, Buck
House, Holyrood Street, Chard
TA20 2AH
046 06 4611

Frome JC, 9–10 Kingsway Shopping
Precinct, Frome BA11 1BT
0373 64566

Minehead JC, 6 Wellington
Square, Minehead TA24 5NH
0643 5121/2

Street JC, The Cross, Street
BA16 0AP
0458 42019

Taunton JC, Brendon House,
High Street, Taunton TA1 3RL
0823 85123

Wellington JC, 9 High Street,
Wellington TA21 8QT
082 347 4057

Wells JC, 13 High Street, Wells
BA5 2AA
0749 44861

Yeovil JC, 47 Middle Street,
Yeovil BA20 1QL
0935 71111/5

Staffordshire

Biddulph JC, 48 High Street,
Biddulph, Stoke-on-Trent
ST8 6BW
0782 519523/48

Burslem JC, 15 Brickhouse
Street, Burslem ST6 3AY
0782 89931/5

Burton-on-Trent JC, Crown
House, New Street, Burton-on-
Trent DE14 3SN
0283 66351

Cannock JC, 9 Church Street,
Cannock WS11 1EG
054 35 78331

Cheadle JC, 22 High Street,
Cheadle, Stoke-on-Trent ST10 1AF
0538 752166

306

Hanley JC, 32–34 Old Hall Street, Hanley, Stoke-on-Trent ST1 3RW
0782 264471

Kidsgrove JC, The Avenue, Kidsgrove, Stoke-on-Trent ST7 1AH
078 16 71121

Leek JC, 32 Derby Street, Leek ST13 5AJ
0538 382411

Lichfield JC, 6 The Bull Ring, Lichfield
054 32 58519

Longton JC, 54–58 Market Street, Longton ST3 1BV
0782 311421

Newcastle-under-Lyme JC, 83 High Street, Newcastle-under-Lyme ST5 1PY
0782 623861

Rugeley JC, 7 Upper Brook Street, Rugeley WS15 2DP
088 94 6529

Stafford JC, Mill Bank, Stafford ST16 2QU
0785 51341

Stoke EO, Fleming Road, Stoke-on Trent ST4 4AG
0782 48571

Stone JC, 35 High Street, Stone ST15 8AJ
0785 815259/5250

Swadlincote EO, 74 High Street, Swadlincote, Burton-on-Trent DE11 8HP
0283 217933

Tamworth JC, 16–20 Church Street, Tamworth B79 7BX
0827 50656

Uttoxeter EO, Northgate, Church Street, Uttoxeter ST14 8AH
088 93 3734

Suffolk

Beccles JC, 1–5 Hungate Court, Hungate, Beccles NR34 9TR
0502 714922

Bungay EO, 6 St Mary's Street, Bungay NR35 1AX
0986 4123

Brandon EO, 71 High Street, Brandon IP27 0AX
0842 810264

Bury St Edmunds JC, 3 Cornhill, Bury St Edmunds IP33 1BE
0284 64926

Felixstowe JC, 29–31 Hamilton Road, Felixstowe IP11 7AZ
0394 277101

Halesworth EO (PTO), Key Street, Halesworth IP19 8EU
09867 3431

Haverhill JC, 65 High Street, Haverhill CB9 7BB
0440 705356

Ipswich JC, 22 Lloyds Avenue, Ipswich IP1 3HP
0473 217471

Leiston JC, 6 Sizewell Road, Leiston IP16 4AB
0728 831232

Lowestoft JC, The Marina, Lowestoft NR32 1ML
0502 63331

Mildenhall JC, Breckland House, 8 Church Yard, Mildenhall IP28 7EF
0638 716922/713658

Newmarket JC, Wellington Street, Newmarket CB8 0HT
0638 665911

Stowmarket JC, 49 Ipswich Street, Stowmarket IP14 1AH
0449 612292

Sudbury JC, 14 Borehamgate
Precinct, Sudbury CO10 6EG
0787 72281

Woodbridge JC, 59
Thoroughfare, Woodbridge
IP12 1AJ
039 43 5636

Surrey

Camberley JC, 58 Park Street,
Camberley GU15 3NS
0276 62525

Dorking JC, 81 High Street,
Dorking RH4 1AN
0306 883236

Epsom JC, Clayton House, East
Street, Epsom, Surrey KT17 1HW
037 27 26232

Esher EO, 3 High Street, Esher,
Surrey KT10 9RS
0372 63502

Farnham JC, 18 West Street,
Farnham GU9 7DR
0252 721171

Godalming JC, 16 High Street,
Godalming GU7 1EB
048 68 29119

Guildford JC, 2–4 Jefferies
Passage, North Street, Guildford
GU1 4AR
0483 503636

Leatherhead JC, 23–25 Bridge
Street, Leatherhead, Surrey
KT2 8HX
0372 378455/6

Redhill JC, 15 London Road,
Redhill RH1 1BQ
0737 67411

Weybridge EO, 32 Baker Street,
Weybridge, Surrey KT13 8AT
0932 48423/6

Woking JC, 12a Commercial
Way, Woking GU21 1SX
048 62 20802

Sussex, East

Bexhill EO, 41 St Leonards
Road, Bexhill TN40 1HS
0424 211024

Brighton (Pavilion) JC, 13–15
Old Steine, Brighton BN1 1EX
0273 693599

Brighton (Retail and Comm) JC,
51–53 West Street, Brighton
BN1 2RY
0273 693599

Eastbourne JC, 1–3 Langney
Road, Eastbourne BN21 3QF
0323 21399

Hailsham EO, Victoria Road,
Hailsham BN27 2BA
0323 841416

Hastings JC, Arbuthnot House,
Breeds Place, Hastings TN34 3AA
0424 437272

Hove JC, 84 Boundary
Road, Hove BN3 5TG
0273 410266

Lewes EO, 47 Western Road,
Lewes BN7 1RX
079 16 2314

Newhaven JC, 55 High Street,
Newhaven BN9 9PQ
0273 513456

Uckfield EO, River House, Bell
Lane, Uckfield TN22 1AE
0825 67111

Sussex, West

Bognor Regis JC, 19 High Street,
Bognor Regis PO21 1JR
0243 829241

Burgess Hill JC, 25a Church
Road, Burgess Hill RH15 9AD
044 46 45353

Chichester JC, 5 Southgate,
Chichester PO19 2EX
0243 789011

Crawley JC, The Cottage, 107
High Street, Crawley RH10 1DD
0293 546421

East Grinstead JC, Farringdon
House, 140–144 London Road,
East Grinstead RH19 1QU
0342 312988

Gatwick JC, Building 339,
Perimeter Road North, Gatwick
Airport, Gatwick RH6 0NN
0293 546211

Haywards Heath JC, 7–9 South
Road, Haywards Heath RH16 1DS
0444 451525

Horsham JC 2–4 Medwin Walk,
Horsham RH12 1QT
0403 55411

Littlehampton JC, 88 High
Street, Littlehampton BN17 5DX
090 64 21241

Shoreham JC, Norfolk House,
High Street, Shoreham-by-Sea
BN4 5EN
079 17 4585

Worthing JC, 2 South Street,
Worthing BN11 1NF
0903 205100

Tyne and Wear

Blaydon-on-Tyne JC, 36–37 The
Precinct, Wesley Court, Blaydon-
on-Tyne NE21 5AQ
091 4145916

East Boldon JC, South View,
Station Road, East Boldon
NE36 0LD
0783 364831/2

Felling JC, Crowhall Lane,
Felling, Gateshead NE10 9PL
0632 698031

Gateshead JC (Ellison Street),
22 Ellison Street, Gateshead
NE8 1AY
0632 773546/775636

Gateshead EO, Bede House,
Tynegate Precinct, Sunderland
Road, Gateshead NE8 1SF
0632 770222

Houghton-le-Spring EO, Kings
Hall, Durham Road, Houghton-
le-Spring DH4 4DL
0783 841341

Jarrow JC, Ellison Street, Jarrow
NE32 3BX
091 489 1512

Newburn EO, High Street,
Newburn, Newcastle upon Tyne
NE15 8LN
091 267 4107

Newcastle upon Tyne JC, 17–21
Nelson Street, Newcastle upon
Tyne NE1 5AZ
0632 328543

Newcastle upon Tyne JC,
Condercum House, 171 West
Road, Newcastle upon Tyne
NE15 6XE
091 273 8877

North Shields JC, Russell Street,
North Shields NE29 0BQ
0632 582626

Shields Road JC, 6 Flora Street,
Shields Road, Newcastle upon
Tyne NE6 1TB
0632 652501

South Shields JC, Norse House,
22 Ocean Road, South Shields
NE33 2LE
0632 564513/7, 560043

Southwick EO, The Kings Road,
Southwick, Sunderland SR5 2JB
0783 44133

Sunderland JC, 22–24 Walworth
Way, Sunderland SR1 3DR
0783 44133

Wallsend JC, 25–29 High Street
East, Wallsend NE28 8PF
0632 628541

Washington JC, The Galleries,
Washington Centre, Washington
NE38 7SE
091 4165424

West Moor JC, 80 Great Lime
Road, West Moor, Newcastle
upon Tyne NE12 0AL
091 268 3417

Whitley Bay JC, 236 Whitley
Road, Whitley Bay NE26 1PN
091 253 4651

Warwickshire

Atherstone EO (part-time office),
The Arcade, Long Street,
Atherstone PD9 1PS
082 77 2108

Bedworth EO, King Street,
Bedworth, Nuneaton CV12 8HZ
0203 314180

Kenilworth EO (part-time
office), 7 Abbey Court,
Kenilworth
0926 53146

Leamington JC, 69 Warwick
Street, Leamington Spa CV32 4QX
0926 312821

Nuneaton JC, 21–25 Newdegate
Street, Nuneaton CV11 4EJ
0203 387664

Rugby EO, Railway Terrace,
Rugby CV21 3EU
0788 65496

Stratford-upon-Avon JC,
11 Meer Street, Stratford-upon-
Avon CV37 6FH
0789 292024

West Midlands

Aldridge JC, 31 High Street,
Aldridge, Walsall WS9 8LX
0922 57171

Aston EO, 30 Beacon Hill,
Aston, Birmingham B6 6JT
021-327 1955

Bilston JC, 30 Church Street,
Bilston WV14 0AH
0902 49121

Birmingham EO, 281
Corporation Street, Birmingham
B4 7DR
021-359 3051

Birmingham JC (Comm), 76
Corporation Street, Birmingham
B2 4UQ
021-236 7354/7

Brownhills JC, 107 High Street,
Brownhills, Walsall WS8 6EP
0543 370101

Chelmsley Wood JC, 2
Chelmsley Circle, Chelmsley
Wood, Birmingham B37 5TH
021-770 1834

Coventry JC, Bankfield House,
163 New Union Street, Coventry
CV1 2QQ
0203 555133

Cradley Heath EO, Whitehall
Road, Cradley Heath, Warley
B64 5BQ
0384 66468/9

Dudley JC, St Johns House,
High Street, Dudley DY2 8PH
0384 213011

Erdington JC, 196 High Street,
Erdington, Birmingham B23 6TL
021-382 6090

Halesowen JC, 68-70 High
Street, Halesowen B63 3BA
021-550 9941

Handsworth JC, 184-186 Soho
Road, Handsworth, birmingham
B21 9LR
021-551 4311

Kings Heath JC, 21 Alcester
Road South, Kings Heath,
Birmingham B14 7JQ
021-444 8434

Kingswinford JC, 10 Townsend
Place, Kingswinford, Brierley
Hill DY6 9JL
0384 271266/8

National Exhibition Centre JC,
021-780 3514

Northfield JC, 821 Bristol Road
South, Northfield, Birmingham
B31 2PA
021-477 7220

Oldbury EO, Green Street,
Oldbury, Warley B69 4JA
021-552 1626

Sedgley JC, 6 Bull Ring, Sedgley,
Dudley DY3 1RX
090 73 62426

Selly Oak EO, Harborne Lane,
Selly Oak, Birmingham B29 6JP
021-472 3051

Small Heath JC, 337-339
Coventry Road, Small Heath,
Birmingham B10 0XR
021-773 2321

Smethwick JC, 108 High Street,
Smethwick, Warley B66 1AA
021-558 7401/7

Solihull JC, Park House, 74 New
Road, Solihull B91 1BR
021-704 3341

Sparkhill JC, 447 Stratford Road,
Sparkhill, Birmingham B11 4LB
021-773 5351

Stourbridge JC, Remlane House,
Hagley Road, Stourbridge DY8 1NZ
038 43 74801

Sutton Coldfield JC, 92 The
Parade, Sutton Coldfield B72 1PH
021-355 3604

Tipton JC, Owen Street, Tipton
DY4 8HB
021-520 2131/2

Walsall JC, Bayard House,
Lichfield Street, Walsall WS1 1SP
0922 33611/21

Washwood Heath JC, 295
Washwood Heath Road,
Washwood Heath, Birmingham
B8 2XX
021-326 0100

Wednesbury JC, 16 Upper High
Street, Wednesbury WS10 7HQ
021-502 3604

Wednesfield JC, 55 High Street,
Wednesfield, Wolverhampton
WV1 1ST
0902 737116

West Bromwich JC, 155 High
Street, West Bromwich B70 7QX
021-553 7591

Willenhall JC, 16-17 Market
Place, Willenhall WV13 2AD
0902 68993

Wolverhampton JC, 30 Market
Street, Wolverhampton WV1 3AF
0902 772211

Wiltshire

Amesbury JC, The Arcade, Earls
Court Road, Amesbury SP4 7LY
0980 22146

Chippenham JC, 23-24 Market
Place, Chippenham SN15 3HW
0249 652801

Corsham EO, 15 High Street,
Corsham SN13 0EU
0249 712581

Marlborough EO, 29 High
Street, Marlborough SN8 1NT
0672 52056

Devizes JC, Maryport Street,
Devizes SN10 1AH
0380 2467/2235

Melksham EO, Newhall, Market
Place, Melksham SN12 6BR
0225 703361

Salisbury JC, 2 Winchester
Street, Salisbury SP1 1HB
0722 26433

Swindon JC, 1 The Arcade,
Brunel Centre, Swindon SN1 1LL
0793 33601

Trowbridge JC, 46–47 Church
Street, Trowbridge BA14 8DN
022 14 64242/5

Warminster JC, 28 Station Road,
Warminster BA12 9ND
0985 215834/215859

Yorkshire, North

Filey JC, 52a Queen Street, Filey
YO14 9HE
0723 512252

Harrogate JC, 16–18 Beulah
Street, Harrogate HG1 1QW
0423 62621

Malton JC, 43 Wheelgate,
Malton YO17 0HT
0653 3919/4046

Northallerton JC, 141 High
Street, Northallerton DL7 8PF
0609 2523

Pickering JC, 132 Eastgate,
Pickering YO18 7DN
0751 72616

Richmond JC, 13b Finkle Street,
Richmond DL10 4DU
0748 4448

Ripon EO, 18 Water Skelgate,
Ripon HC4 1DF
0765 2176/3895

Scarborough JC, Pavilion
House, Westborough,
Scarborough YO11 1UZ
0723 376271

Selby JC, 11–15 Gowthorpe,
Selby YO8 0BH
0757 702331

Skipton EO, Mount Pleasant,
High Street, Skipton BD23 1LA
0756 2314

Thirsk EO, 17a Kirkgate, Thirsk
YO7 1QB
0845 22248

Whitby EO, 22 Baxtergate,
Whitby YO21 1AZ
0947 600333/4

York JC, 13 Piccadilly, York
YO1 1PF
0904 59251/7

Yorkshire, South

Barnsley JC, 12–16 Midland
Street, Barnsley S70 1SE
0226 243111

Chapeltown JC, Crown Building,
Loundside, Chapeltown,
Sheffield S30 4UP
0742 469241/2

Dinnington JC, 26 Laughton
Road, Dinnington, Sheffield
S31 7PS
0909 567711/2

Doncaster JC, Queensgate,
Doncaster DN1 3LB
0302 21571

Eckington EO, High Street,
Eckington, Sheffield S31 9DP
0246 433481

Firth Park JC, 441 Firth Park
Road, Firth Park, Sheffield
S5 6QY
0742 380376

Goldthorpe JC, 21 Doncaster
Road, Goldthorpe, Rotherham
S63 9HG
0709 894798

Hoyland JC, 2 King Street,
Hoyland, Barnsley S74 9JP
0226 744566/7

Maltby JC, Arndale Precinct,
High Street, Maltby, Rotherham
S66 7LJ
0709 812803

Mexborough EO, Adwick Road,
Mexborough S64 0AD
0709 586101

Rotherham JC, Ship Hill,
Rotherham S60 2HG
0709 73881

Sheffield JC (Ind), Steel City
House, West Street, Sheffield
S1 2GS
0742 752253

Sheffield JC (Comm), 56 Church
Street, Sheffield S1 2GN
0742 752253

Thorne JC, 5-7 King Street,
Thorne, Doncaster DN8 5BD
0405 812496

Wombwell JC, 64 High Street,
Wombwell, Barnsley S73 8BH
0226 754920

Woodhouse JC, Market Street,
Woodhouse, Sheffield S13 7QX
0742 697621

Yorkshire, West

Batley JC, 84 Commercial Street,
Batley WF17 5OS
0924 473411

Bingley JC, 11 Myrtle Walk,
Bingley BD16 1AW
0274 560395

Bradford JC, Provincial House,
Bradford BD1 1TN
0274 392831

Bramley JC, 34 Bramley District
Centre, Town Street, Bramley,
Leeds LS13 2ET
0532 567311

Brighouse JC, Wellington House,
Briggate, Brighouse HD6 1DN
0484 710128/29/30

Castleford JC, 113 Carlton
Street, Castleford WF10 1JQ
0977 510505

Crossgates JC, 37-43 Austhorpe
Road, Crossgates, Leeds LS15 8BA
0532 608626

Dewsbury JC, 8 Corporation
Street, Dewsbury WF13 1PL
0924 460711

Elland JC, 10 Town Hall
Buildings, Elland HX5 0EY
0422 78148

Halifax EO, Portland Place,
Halifax HX1 2JH
0422 55641/7

Hemsworth JC, 21-23 Kirkby
Road, Hemsworth, Pontefract
WF9 4BA
0977 612161

Horsforth EO, 12b Town Street,
Horsforth, Leeds LS18 4RJ
0532 589806

Huddersfield JC, Kirklees
House, Market Street,
Huddersfield HD1 2HT
0484 38231

Hunslet JC, 25–26 Church Street,
Hunslet, Leeds LS10 2AP
0532 704474

Keighley JC, 32–34 Low Street,
Keighley BD21 3QW
0535 65211/3

Knottingley JC, 9 The Arcade,
Hill Top, Knottingley WF11 8EA
0977 85101

Leeds JC (Ind), Fairfax House,
Merrion Street, Leeds LS2 8LH
0532 446181

Leeds JC (Comm), Westminster
House, Bond Street, Leeds LS1 5BE
0532 446181

Morley JC, Milton House,
Queen Street, Morley, Leeds
LS27 9EB
0532 536226

Normanton JC, 49–51 High
Street, Normanton WF6 2BY
0924 893638

Otley JC, 12 Kirkgate, Otley
LS21 3HJ
0943 462702

Pontefract JC, 1–3 Horsefair,
Pontefract WF8 1PE
0977 795361

Pudsey JC, Park House, Park
Square, Pudsey LS28 7RG
0532 567033/4

Rothwell JC, 80 Commercial
Street, Rothwell LS26 0QE
0532 821421

Seacroft JC, Crown House, 310
North Parkway, Seacroft Town
Centre, Leeds LE14 6PW
0532 735191/3

Shipley EO, Wainman Street,
Shipley BD17 7DN
0274 582155

South Elmsall JC, 66 Barnsley
Road, South Elmsall, Pontefract
WF9 2RG
0977 45561

Sowerby Bridge JC, 3 Regent
Parade, Wharfe Street, Sowerby
Bridge HX6 2EG
0422 833332

Spen Valley EO, 411 Bradford
Road, Liversedge WF15 6DD
0924 406816

Wakefield JC, 24 Wood Street,
Wakefield WF1 2ED
0924 371901

Wetherby JC, 10 North Street,
Wetherby LS22 4NN
0937 64536/7

Yeadon JC, 55–57 High Street,
Yeadon LS19 7SP
0532 506665

SCOTLAND

Borders

Berwick JC, 23 Woolmarket,
Berwick-upon-Tweed TD15 1DH
0289 305088

Eyemouth JC, Upper Houndlaw,
Eyemouth, Berwickshire TD14 5BS
0390 50070

Galashiels JC, 95–97 Channel
Street, Galashiels, Selkirkshire
TD1 1BN
0896 55351

Hawick JC, Teviot Crescent,
Hawick, Roxburghshire TD9 9HR
0450 72363

Kelso JC, 2 Crosskeys Arcade,
The Square, Kelso,
Roxburghshire TD5 7HL
0573 23781

Peebles JC, 35 Northgate,
Peebles EH45 9BN
0721 20194

Central

Alloa JC, 7 Drysdale Street,
Alloa, Clackmannanshire FK10 1JL
0259 215123

Denny JC, 133–137 Church
Walk, Denny, Stirlingshire
FK6 6DE
0324 823344/825260

Falkirk JC, 8–14 High Street,
Falkirk, Stirlingshire FK1 1EY
0324 36141

Grangemouth JC, 15 La Porte
Precinct, Grangemouth,
Stirlingshire FK3 8AZ
0324 471757

Stirling JC, 9 Barnton Street,
Stirling FK8 1HF
0786 70307

Dumfries and Galloway

Annan JC, High Street, Annan
DG12 6AD
046 12 2563/2511

Castle Douglas EO, Carlingwalk
Street, Castle Douglas,
Kirkcudbrightshire DG7 1DP
0556 2308

Dumfries EO, 139 Irish Street,
Dumfries DG1 2NU
0387 55161

Lockerbie JC, 136 High Street,
Lockerbie DG11 2BX
057 62 3412/3

Newton Stewart JC, 22 Victoria
Street, Newton Stewart,
Wigtownshire DG8 6BU
0671 2050

Sanquhar EO, Queensberry
Square, Sanquhar DG4 6BY
065 92 437

Stranraer JC, 7 Charlotte Street,
Stranraer, Wigtownshire DG9 7EQ
0776 3524

Fife

Cowdenbeath JC, 246 High
Street, Cowdenbeath KY4 9MP
0383 512685

Cupar JC, 73 Bonnygate, Cupar
KY15 4DH
0334 54061

Dunfermline JC, 7 New Row,
Dunfermline KY12 7NP
0383 734056

Glenrothes JC, 3 Postgate,
Glenrothes KY7 5LL
0592 752165

Kirkcaldy JC, 268 High Street,
Kirkcaldy KY1 1JR
0592 268581

Leven JC, 10 Shorehead, Leven
KY8 4NR
0333 26547

St Andrews JC, 187 South Street,
St Andrews KY16 9EE
0334 75953

Grampian

Aberdeen JC, St Martin's House,
181 Union Street, Aberdeen
AB9 1BH
0224 588931

Banff JC, 23–25 Castle Street,
Banff AB4 1DG
026 12 5056

Buckie JC, Shanks Lane, Buckie,
Banffshire AB5 1AF
0542 31796

Elgin JC, 48 South Street, Elgin,
Morayshire IV30 1JX
0343 2671

Forres EO, Tytler Street, Forres,
Morayshire IV36 0EL
0309 72768

Fraserburgh EO, 49 Saltoun
Place, Fraserburgh, Aberdeenshire
AB4 5RZ
0346 23197

Peterhead JC, 4 Marischal
Street, Peterhead AB4 6MU
0779 78585

Highland

Dingwall JC, 3 High Street,
Dingwall, Ross-shire IV15 9HL
0349 64666

Fort William JC, 97 High Street,
Fort William, Inverness-shire
PH33 6DG
0397 4233

Invergordon JC, 102 High Street,
Invergordon, Ross-shire IV18 0DL
0349 852727

Inverness JC, Metropolitan
House, 31–33 High Street,
Inverness IV1 1JD
0463 239171

Nairn JC, 79a High Street, Nairn
IV12 4BW
0667 53882

Thurso JC, 17 Rotterdam Street,
Thurso, Caithness KW14 7BN
0847 64699

Wick JC, Government Buildings,
Girnigoe Street, Wick KW1 4HJ
0955 4347/8

Lothian

Bathgate JC, 17 George Place,
Bathgate, West Lothian EH48 1QP
0506 631300

Bo'ness JC, North Street,
Bo'ness, West Lothian EH15
0506 823311/2

Broxburn JC, East Main Street,
Broxburn, West Lothian EH52 5EE
0506 856771

Dalkeith JC, 20 High Street,
Dalkeith, Midlothian EH22 1LF
031-663 9801

Edinburgh JC (Leith), 3 Leith
Walk, Leith Edinburgh EH6 8TD
031-553 3311

Edinburgh JC (Portobello),
74 Portobello High Street,
Edinburgh EH15 1AN
031-669 7232

Edinburgh JC (Shandwick
Place), 25a Shandwick Place,
Edinburgh EH2 4RG
031-228 1451

Edinburgh JC (South St Andrew
Street), 11–13 South St Andrew
Street, Edinburgh EH2 2BT
031-556 9211

Edinburgh JC (Wester Hailes),
4 Wester Hailes Shopping
Precinct, Edinburgh EH14 2SP
031-442 1092

Haddington JC, 22 Hardgate,
Haddington, East Lothian
EH41 3JR
062 082 4921

Loanhead JC, Polton Road,
Loanhead, Midlothian EH20 9BX
031-440 0300

Livingston JC, Unit 16b,
Regional Centre, Almondvale
South, Livingston, West Lothian
EH54 6NQ
0506 31913

Musselburgh JC, 159–161 High
Street, Musselburgh, Midlothian
EH21 7EH
031-665 8101

Penicuik JC, 14a John Street,
Penicuik, Midlothian EH26 8AB
0968 75102

Orkney Islands

Kirkwall EO, Bridge Street,
Kirkwall, Orkney KW15 1HR
0856 5113

Shetland Islands

Lerwick JC, Charlotte House,
Commercial Road, Lerwick,
Shetland ZE1 0LT
0595 4343

Strathclyde

Airdrie JC, 1 Graham Street,
Airdrie, Lanarkshire ML6 6AJ
023 64 56264

Alexandria JC, 86–88 Main
Street, Alexandria,
Dumbartonshire G83 0PX
0389 59511/3

Ayr JC, 8 Arthur Street,
Ayr KA7 1NH
0292 261127/268721

Barrhead JC, 20 Paisley Road,
Barrhead, Glasgow G78 1NF
041-881 1015

Bellshill JC, 168–170 Main
Street, Bellshill ML4 1AP
0698 746028

Blantyre EO, Boswell Drive,
Blantyre, Glasgow G72 0BJ
0698 823281/2

Cambuslang JC, 23 Main Street,
Cambuslang, Glasgow G72 7HL
041-641 7788

Campbeltown JC, New Quay
Street, Campbeltown, Argyll
PA28 6BA
0586 52233/54314

Carluke JC, 23 Hamilton Street,
Carluke, Lanarkshire ML8 4HG
0555 71970

Clydebank JC, 90 Sylvania Way,
Clydebank, Dumbartonshire
G81 2TJ
041-941 1441

Coatbridge JC, 106 Main Street,
Coatbridge, Lanarkshire ML5 3BT
0236 33461

Cumbernauld JC, 50 Teviot
Walk, Cumbernauld, Glasgow
G67 1NH
023 67 25054

Cumnock JC, Unit 13, Glaisnock
Shopping Centre, Cumnock,
Ayrshire KA18 1EN
0290 22240

Dumbarton JC, 2a High Street
Dumbarton G82 1LD
0389 67721

Dunoon EO, 31 Thom-A-Mhois
Road, Dunoon, Argyll PA23 7HP
0369 4252

Easterhouse JC, 40 Township
Centre, Easterhouse, Glasgow
G34 9DX
041-771 8407

East Kilbride JC, 51 The Plaza,
Town Centre, East Kilbride,
Glasgow G74 1LW
035 52 46711

Glasgow Central JC, 50–58 Jamaica Street, Glasgow G1 4HY
041-204 1971

Glasgow City JC (Hotel and Catering), 87–97 Bath Street, Glasgow G2 2EB
041-332 9452

Glasgow Trongate JC, 21 Trongate, Glasgow G1 5EZ
041-552 6066

Glasgow West JC, 4 Merkland Court, Glasgow G11 6BY
041-357 2727

Girvan JC, 75 Dalrymple Street, Girvan, Ayrshire KA26 9BS
0465 4241/4266

Govan Cross JC, 35 McKechnie Street, Govan, Glasgow G51 3AD
041-440 2357

Greenock JC, 101 Dalrymple Street, Greenock, Renfrewshire PA15 1QJ
0475 29411

Greenock JC (Tier 1), 11 Clyde Square, Greenock, Renfrewshire PA15 1NB
0475 29411

Hamilton JC, Brandon Street, Hamilton, Lanarkshire ML3 6BP
0698 283399

Helensburgh JC, 52 West Clyde Street, Helensburgh, Dumbartonshire G84 8BU
0436 71333/4

Hillington JC, Queen Elizabeth Avenue, Hillington, Glasgow G52 4TJ
041-882 9061

Irvine JC, 26 Bridegate, Ayrshire KA12 8BJ
0294 74025

Johnstone JC, 33–35 Houston Court, Johnstone, Renfrewshire PA5 8DJ
0505 28112

Kilbirnie JC, 87 Main Street, Kilbirnie, Ayrshire KA25 7AA
0505 685416

Kilmarnock JC, 18 Burns Precinct, Kilmarnock, Ayrshire KA1 1LT
0563 33231

Kilsyth EO, 2a Station Road, Kilsyth, Glasgow G65 0AB
0236 822255

Kilwinning JC, 3 Almswall Road, Kilwinning, Ayrshire KA13 6BL
0294 57531/2

Kirkintilloch JC, 11 Alexandra Street, Kirkintilloch, Glasgow G66 1PA
041-776 2101

Lanark JC, Athol House, 55–57 Bannantyne Street, Lanark ML11 9HA
0555 61321

Largs JC, 126 Main Street, Largs, Ayrshire KA30 8JY
0475 673106/674939

Larkhall JC, 27 Union Street, Larkhall, Lanarkshire ML9 1HY
0698 885024

Linwood JC, Linwood Shopping Centre, Paisley PA1 2TL
0505 31638

Maryhill JC, 1480 Maryhill Road, Maryhill, Glasgow G21 9DJ
041-945 0114

Motherwell JC, 95–97 Brandon Parade South, Motherwell, Lanarkshire ML1 1RR
0698 53421/8

Oban JC, 21–23 Argyll Square,
Oban, Argyll PA34 4AT
0631 64116

Paisley JC, 53 Central Way,
Paisley, Renfrewshire PA1 1DT
041-887 7801

Parkhead JC, 29 Westmuir
Street, Parkhead, Glasgow G31 5ER
041-554 8881

Port Glasgow JC, 40–42 Princes
Street, Port Glasgow,
Renfrewshire PA14 5JQ
0475 44116

Renfrew JC, 5 High Street,
Renfrew PA4 8QL
041-886 6771

Rothesay JC, 25 Victoria Street,
Rothesay, Bute PA20 0AJ
0700 4539/4562

Rutherglen JC, 35 Mitchell
Arcade, Rutherglen, Glasgow
G73 2SW
041-643 0156

Saltcoats JC, 13 Dockhead
Street, Saltcoats, Ayrshire KA21 5EF
0294 69131

Shawlands JC, 118–122
Kilmarnock Road, Glasgow
G41 3NN
041-649 9211

Shotts EO, 7 Windsor Street,
Shotts, Lanarkshire ML7 4DW
0501 20069

Springburn JC, 494 Springburn
Road, Springburn, Glasgow
G42 3NF
041-558 2881

Troon JC, 91 Templehill, Troon,
Ayrshire KA10 6BQ
0292 316992

Uddingston JC, 103 Main Street,
Uddingston, Glasgow G71 7BW
0698 817226

Wishaw JC, 41 Main Street,
Wishaw, Lanarkshire ML2 7EP
0698 355911

Tayside

Arbroath EO, Millgate Loan,
Arbroath, Angus DD11 1PP
0241 72061

Blairgowrie JC, 32 Allan Street,
Blairgowrie, Perthshire PH10 6AD
0250 4488

Crieff EO (PTO), 71
Commissioner Street, Crieff,
Perthshire PH7 4DD
0764 2646

Dundee JC, City House,
16 Overgate, Dundee, Angus
DD1 1UP
0382 23061

Forfar JC, Castle Street, Forfar,
Angus DD8 3HY
0307 63189

Montrose JC, 77–79 Murray
Street, Montrose, Angus DD10 8JZ
0674 74022

Perth JC, 65–69 South Street,
Perth PH2 8PW
0738 33444

Western Isles

Stornoway JC, 12–15 Francis
Street, Stornoway, Isle of Lewis
PA87 2NA
0851 3086

Isle of Skye

Portree EO, Bridge Road,
Portree, Isle of Skye IV51 9ER
0478 2946

Appendix

WALES

Clwyd

Buckley JC, Town Hall, Old
Road, Buckley CH7 2JH
0244 548888

Cefn Mawr JC, Crane Street,
Cefn Mawr, Wrexham LL14 3AB
0978 821616

Colwyn Bay JC, 45a Conway
Road, Colwyn Bay LL29 7AU
0492 31922

Denbigh JC, 22 Vales Street,
Denbigh LL16 3BQ
074 571 3344

Flint JC, Unit 1, Church Street,
Flint CH6 5AE
035 26 5417/61163

Holywell JC, 1 Tower Gardens,
Holywell CH8 7TA
0352 712917

Llangollen JC, 32 Castle Street,
Llangollen LL20 8PQ
0978 860015

Mold JC, Unit 16, Daniel Owen
Centre, Mold CH7 1BZ
0352 56506

Prestatyn EO (PTO), 7 Nant
Hall Road, Prestatyn LL19 9LR
074 56 2816

Rhyl JC, 17–21 High Street, Rhyl
LL18 1EN
0745 31331

Ruthin EO (PTO), 46 Clwyd
Street, Ruthin LL15 H1P
082 42 2740

Shotton JC, 85–87 Chester Road
West, Shotton, Deeside CH5 1EE
0244 817376

Wrexham JC, 2 King Street,
Wrexham LL11 1NS
0978 356001

Dyfed

Aberystwyth JC, Great Darkgate
Street, Aberystwyth SW23 1DE
0970 4911

Ammanford JC, College Street,
Ammanford SA18 3AB
0269 3941

Carmarthen JC, 13a King Street,
Carmarthen SA31 1DH
0267 231661

Cardigan JC, 53 Pendre,
Cardigan SA43 1JR
0239 614401/614403

Fishguard JC, Crown Buildings,
Brodog Lane, Fishguard SA65 9NT
0348 872269

Garnant JC, 26 Dynevor Road,
Garnant, Ammanford SA18 1NP
0269 823535

Haverfordwest JC (Tier 1),
8 Victoria Place, Haverfordwest
SA61 2LB
0437 5751

Haverfordwest JC (Tier 2), 10
High Street, Haverfordwest
SA61 2DW
0437 5751/4

Kidwelly JC, Bridge Street,
Kidwelly SA17 4UU
0554 890231

Lampeter JC, Government
Buildings, Pontfaen Road,
Lampeter SA48 7BN
0570 422232

Llandeilo EO, 1 King Street,
Llandeilo SA19 6AD
0558 823484

Llandovery JC, Market Hall,
Llandovery SA20 0AA
0550 20415

320

Llandyssul JC, Bizerta House, Wind Street, Llandyssul SA44 4BH
055 932 3291

Llanelli JC, 1–9 Market Arcade, Llanelli SA15 1QE
055 42 56551

Milford Haven JC, 40 Charles Street, Milford Haven SA73 2AF
064 62 3086

Pembroke JC, 91 Queen Street, Pembroke Dock SA72 6JE
0646 684181

Tenby EO, Glendover House, Civic Centre, The Norton, Tenby SA70 8AN
0834 2387/3696

Tumble EO, Crown Buildings, Bethesda Road, Tumble SA14 6HY
0269 841553

Glamorgan, Mid

Aberdare JC, 4 Victoria Square, Aberdare CF44 7LA
0685 872541

Bargoed JC, 30a High Street, Bargoed CF8 8XX
0443 833003

Bridgend JC, 12–14 Adare Street, Bridgend CF31 1HN
0656 61241

Bridgend Site Office, Unit 4, Bridgend Industrial Estate, Bridgend CF31 3SA
0656 57497

Caerphilly JC, The Twyn, Caerphilly CF8 1JL
0222 868821

Ferndale JC, 69 High Street, Ferndale, Rhondda CF43 4RR
0443 731631

Llantrisant JC, 13–15 Ely Valley Road, Talbot Green, Pontyclun CF7 9YE
0443 224513

Maesteg JC, 29 Commercial Street, Maesteg, Bridgend CF34 9DU
0656 732286

Merthyr Tydfil JC, Glebeland Street, Merthyr Tydfil CF47 8JF
0685 71561/5451

Mountain Ash JC, New County Road, Mountain Ash CF45 4HU
0443 473599

Pontlottyn JC, Merchant Street, Pontlottyn, Bargoed CF8 9UF
0685 840901

Pontypridd JC, Oldway House, Broadway, Pontypridd CF37 1QT
0443 405161

Porth JC, 33–34 Hannah Street, Porth, Tonypandy, Rhondda CF39 9DW
0443 684713

Porthcawl EO, 5 Mary Street, Porthcawl CF36 3YE
065 671 3522

Pyle JC, Ffald Road, Shopping Centre, Pyle CF33 6PC
0656 742036

Tonypandy JC, 3 Dunraven Street, Tonypandy, Rhondda CF40 1QJ
0443 437211

Tonyrefail JC, 24 Mill Street, Tonyrefail, Porth CF39 8AA
0443 670249

Treforest JC, Treforest Industrial Estate, Pontypridd CF37 5UR
044 385 2168

Treharris EO, (PTO), 10 Perrot Street, Treharris CF46 5ES
0443 410123

Treorchy EO, Oldway House, Bute Street, Treorchy, Rhondda CF42 6TE
0443 775101

Ystrad Mynach JC, 22 Penallta Road, Ystrad Mynach, Hengoed CF8 7AP
0443 813789

Glamorgan, South

Barry JC, 100 Holton Road, Barry CF6 6TJ
0446 733131

Cardiff JC (Comm), Pearl Assurance Building, The Friary, Cardiff CF1 4AA
0222 395041

Cardiff JC (Ind), Golate House, 98 St Mary Street, Cardiff CF1 1LS
0222 399931

Llantwit Major JC, Hayes Rooms, Town Hall Square, Llantwit Major CF6 9SD
044 65 3451

Penarth JC, 1 Stanwell Road, Penarth CF6 2YZ
0222 701112

Glamorgan, West

Cymmer JC (PTO), The Institute, Old Colliery Buildings, Cymmer, Port Talbot SA13 3HS
0639 850937

Glyn Neath JC, 61 High Street, Glyn Neath SA11 5EH
0639 720913

Gorseinon JC, 7 Alexandra Road, Gorseinon, Swansea SA4 2NS
0792 895544

Morriston JC, 15–17 Woodfield Street, Morriston, Swansea SA6 8BY
0792 781351

Neath EO, 28 Queen Street, Neath SA11 1DL
0639 3567

Pontardawe JC, 71 Herbert Street, Pontardawe SA8 4EF
0792 862872

Port Talbot JC (Tier 1), Unit 30d, Aberafon Centre, Port Talbot SA13 1SB
0639 881854

Port Talbot JC (Tier 2), 1st Floor Office Block, Aberafon Centre, Port Talbot SA13 1SB
0639 881854

Resolven JC, Resolven House, 25 Commercial Street, Resolven, Neath SA11 4HB
0639 710471

Swansea JC (Tier 1), 27–28 Castle Street, Swansea SA1 1HY
0792 41451

Swansea JC (Tier 2), Grove House, 2–3 Grove Place, Swansea SA1 5DH
0792 41451

Ystradgynlais EO, Wind Road, Ystradgynlais, Swansea SA9 1AB
0639 843122

Gwent

Abergavenny JC, Newbridge House, Tudor Street, Abergavenny NP7 5EJ
0873 4511/7

Abertillery JC, 11 High Street, Abertillery NP3 1XD
0495 212251

Blackwood JC, 81a High Street, Blackwood NP2 1YX
0495 226830

Blaenavon JC, 69 High Street, Blaenavon NP4 9XN
0495 790246

Brynmawr JC, 23 Beaufort Street, Brynmawr NP3 4XX
0495 311605

Chepstow JC, Station Road, Chepstow NP6 5YZ
029 12 2381

Cwmbran JC, 24 The Parade, Cwmbran NP4 1PT
063 33 5174

Ebbw Vale JC, 21–22 Market Street, Ebbw Vale NP3 6XR
0495 302457

Monmouth EO, New Market Hall, Priory Street, Monmouth NP5 3XA
0600 3541

Newbridge EO, Ashfield Road, Newbridge, Newport NP1 4YD
0494 243791

Newport JC, John Frost Square, Newport NP1 1XH
0633 53571

Pontypool JC, 134 Osborne Road, Pontypool NP4 6LT
049 55 56891

Risca JC, 66–67 Tredegar Street, Risca, Newport NP1 6YE
0633 614017

Tredegar JC, 24 Gwent Shopping Centre, Tredegar NP2 3YE
049 525 5219

Gwynedd

Amlwch JC, 9 Market Street, Amlwch LL68 9LB
0407 831211

Bangor JC, 339 High Street Bangor LL57 1YA
0248 352166

Barmouth JC, Post Office Building, King Edward Street, Barmouth LL42 1PB
0341 280486

Beaumaris JC, Masonic Chambers, Margaret Street, Beaumaris LL58 8DW
0248 810363

Bethesda JC, Post Office Buildings, Ogwen Terrace, Bethesda, Bangor LL57 3AY
0248 600345

Blaenau Ffestiniog JC, 46 High Street, Blaenau Ffestiniog LL41 3AA
0766 830438

Caernarvon JC, 29 Bangor Street, Caernarvon LL55 1AR
0286 3351

Conwy JC, 13 High Street, Conwy LL32 8DE
049 263 2021

Dolgellau EO (PTO), Government Building, Aran Street, Dolgellau LL40 1BP
0341 422217

Holyhead JC (Tier 2), 1 Stanley Terrace, Holyhead LL65 1HG
0407 2362

Llandudno JC, Abbevale, 24 Trinity Square, Llandudno LL30 2RE
0492 77295

Llangefni EO, Unit A, Arcadia
Buildings, Stryd y Bont,
Llangefni LL77 7PN
0248 823321

Llanrwst JC, Bradford House,
6 Denbigh Street, Llanrwst
LL26 0LL
0492 640409

Porthmadog JC, Thedford
House, Porthmadog LL49 9HA
0766 3404

Pwllheli JC, 12 Penlan Street,
Pwllheli LL53 3DG
0758 612261

Powys

Brecon JC, 2 The Struet, Brecon
LD3 7LH
0874 4425/6

Llandrindod Wells JC, Stratford
House, Station Crescent,
Llandrindod Wells LD1 5DD
0597 2819

Machynlleth JC, Liverpool
House, 17 Maengwyn Street,
Machynlleth SY20 8EW
0654 2696

Newtown JC, Ladywell House,
Park Street, Newtown SY16 1QR
0686 25800

Welshpool JC, Mansion House,
Severn Street, Welshpool SY21 7AD
0938 2988

Abbreviations

MSC Abbreviations

AC	Accredited Centre
AMB	Area Manpower Board
AT	Adult Training
ATS	Adult Training Strategy
BPRO	Blind Persons' Resettlement Officer
BPTO	Blind Person Training Officer
CEP	Community Enterprise Programme (now obsolete)
CI	Community Industry
COIC	Careers and Occupational Information Centre
CP	Community Programme
CPA	Community Programme Agents
DAS	Disablement Advisory Service
DISC	Drop-in Skills Centre
DRO	Disablement Resettlement Officer
DMS	Department of Manpower Services
ED	Employment Division
ERC	Employment Rehabilitation Centre
ESL	English as a Second Language
ETS	Employment Transfer Scheme
FFF	Free Forward Fares
ILTU	Industrial Language Training Unit
ITEC	Information Technology Centre
ITB	Industrial Training Board
ITO	Industrial Training Organisation
JIS	Job Introduction Scheme
JRS	Job Rehearsal Scheme
JSS	Job Search Scheme
LCP	Local Collaborative Project
MAP	Micro-Processor Application Project
MARIS	Materials and Resources Information Service
MATU	Merseyside Adult Training Unit
MEP	Microelectronic Education Programme
MEP	Management Extension Programme
MIPD	Manpower Intelligence and Planning Division
MSC	Manpower Services Commission
NATVACS	National Vacancy Circulation System
NEP	New Enterprise Programme
NILTC	National Industrial Language Training Centre

NTACs	New Technology Access Centres
NTI	New Training Initiative
OT	Occupational Training
OTF	Occupational Training Families
OTP	Open Tech Programme
OTTSU	Open Tech Training and Support Unit
OTU	Open Tech Unit
PER	Professional and Executive Register
PRT	Programme Review Team
PTF	Practical Training Facilities
RDO	Regional Development Officer
RTS	Residential Training Centres
SBC	Small Business Courses
SCOTTSU	Scottish Open Tech Training and Support Unit
SEC	Self Employment Courses
SEPACS	Sheltered Employment Procurement and Consultancy Group
SIG	Sheltered Industrial Group
ST	Sectors Training
STA	Skillcentre Training Agency
STC	Staff Training Co-ordinator
TCR	Trainee Centred Reviewing
TD	Training Division
TIF	Training Information Framework
TOPS	Training Opportunities Scheme
TSH	Transfer Scheme Handbook
TVEI	Technical Vocational and Education Initiative
TWI	Training Within Industry
YOP	Youth Opportunities Programme (now obsolete)
YP	Young People
YTB	Youth Training Board
YTN	*Youth Training News*
YTS	Youth Training Scheme
YWS	Young Workers Scheme
UVP	Unified Vocational Programme (now obsolete)
VACS	Vacancy Circulation System
VPP	Voluntary Projects Programme
WEEP	Work Experience on Employers' Premises (now obsolete)
WOC	Wider Opportunities Course
WOW	Wider Opportunities for Women

Selected Non-MSC Abbreviations

CET	Council for Educational Technology
CPVE	Certificate of Pre-Vocational Education
DL	Distance Learning
DES	Department of Education and Science

DTI	Department of Trade and Industry
ESF	European Social Fund
FEU	Further Education Unit
LEA	Local Education Authority
NAFE	Non-Advanced Further Education
NEC	National Extension College
OL	Open Learning
PICKUP	Professional Industrial and Commercial Updating

Index